AN ANCIENT W

AN ANCIENT WORLD IN CHAOS

Part of the 'God King Scenario' Series

by
Gary Gilligan

www.gks.uk.com

Copyright © 2007 Gary Gilligan

The moral right of the author has been asserted.

Apart from any fair dealing for the purposes of research or private study, or criticism or review, as permitted under the Copyright, Designs and Patents Act 1988, this publication may only be reproduced, stored or transmitted, in any form or by any means, with the prior permission in writing of the publishers, or in the case of reprographic reproduction in accordance with the terms of licences issued by the Copyright Licensing Agency. Enquiries concerning reproduction outside those terms should be sent to the publishers.

Matador
9 De Montfort Mews
Leicester LE1 7FW, UK
Tel: (+44) 116 255 9311 / 9312
Email: books@troubador.co.uk
Web: www.troubador.co.uk/matador

ISBN 978-19065100008

Cover design and illustrations by Gary Gilliigan
Pyramids photo © Photos.com

Printed in the UK by TJ International Ltd, Padstow, Cornwall

Matador is an imprint of Troubador Publishing Ltd

CONTENTS

List of Illustrations	ix
Acknowledgements	xi
Foreword	xiii
Introduction	1
Physical and Mythical Gods as Part of Our World	5
Human Relations with Devine Entities	13
Cosmic Chaos	27
In Search of Chaos	47
Ancient History is Cosmic Chaos	59
The Testimony of Ancient Egypt Carved in Stone	69
A Twilight World	81
The Solar System Besieged by Space Debris	95
Earth's Ring of Debris	115
Hathor and Isis	133
Children of the Sun	153
Who Was King?	175
Planets Ruled as God Kings	191
Following the Doctrine of Heaven	205
Lack of Archaeological Evidence for Battles	219
Identifying the Monarchy	233
The New Kingdom	253
Understanding the Will of the Gods	271
The Two Egyptian Lands of Heaven and Earth	291
The Real Firmament Above	311
The Unification of Heaven and Earth	329
Our Ancient Forebears are with us	349
The Heavens Dictate and Humans Follow	371
Bibliography	389
Index	391

LIST OF ILLUSTRATIONS

Immanuel Velikovsky	28
Red Disks Representing Re	84
The Aten	88
Hathor	123
Hieroglyph for Hathor	129
Hatshepsut Suckling Hathor	135
Isis	141
Isis Suckling Horus	147
Symbol for Son of Re	153
Horus	183
Pharaoh Smiting the Enemy	210
The Cartouche	235
Hieroglyph for the Two Lands	304
Djed Pillar	315
The Crowns of Upper & Lower Egypt	336
Sema-tawef Motifs	339
Osiris	341
Hieroglyph for Osiris	349
Anubis	353
The Ka	360
The Ba	365
The Akh Stars	368
The World as Viewed by Ancient Egyptians	370

ACKNOWLEDGEMENTS

Immanuel Velikovsky, for sowing the seeds of Catatrophism and inspiring me to write this book.

Theresa Saliba, for her thoroughly professional editing skills and sound advice.

My son Stefan, for assisting me with the cover design.

FOREWORD

By Theresa Saliba

When I first heard about planets in chaos and Gary Gilligan's method of using ancient history to answer ancient mysteries, I assumed it was just another wacky assumption based on little green men from outer space. How wrong I was! Gilligan's theory, and indeed this book, is well-researched and extremely well-written. It certainly deserves to be studied seriously and acknowledged by academia worldwide.

Most people are familiar with the monsters, dragons, demons, gods and goddesses that 'ruled' the ancient world, and perhaps we have made the same mistake of assuming they were fictitious creatures _ mythical gods created as part of ancient folklore. We may suppose they were invented to excite and control the populace by providing answers to the mysteries of the universe, the meaning of life etc.

However, what if these creatures were inspired by a real world dominated by cosmic chaos and authentic god-king planets which visited Earth repeatedly for an incredible 3,000 years? According to 'An Ancient World in Chaos', this is exactly what occurred over the past millennia. Mars and Venus visited Earth numerous times to dominate the heavens for thousands of years before being joined by Mercury and the Moon. Gilligan's theory also explains that cosmic chaos resulted in a diminished sun. This is such a revelation and explains so many enigmas that I can't believe I didn't think of it myself! It ties in exactly with ancient history and elucidates numerous conundrums that other scholars of Egyptology have completely failed to grasp.

Yet you may be wondering where it is written that cosmic chaos actually occurred throughout history? Where are the epic tales of god kings visiting Earth or the heroic fables of explosive battles among the planets? The key lies with one of the most fascinating and awe inspiring civilisations of antiquity _ the ancient Egyptians and their 'sacred' hieroglyphs.

It is ironic that, with the wealth of information available to us regarding this culture, we understand little about the world of the ancient Egyptians. Yet it is essential that we fully understand this fascinating world if we are to truly make sense of our ancient forebears and their myriad of deities. And that is exactly what this book does. It is a work that is both fascinating and intriguing and will appeal to all who are interested in Egyptology, astronomy, science, history, ancient mythology, archaeology, physics, anthropology or simply human nature.

In this first book in the series, 'An Ancient World in Chaos', we trace the period from the birth of civilization to the birth of Christ which is the legacy of cosmic chaos. We are also introduced to incalculable amounts of debris created by planetary chaos and the way in which this debris was deified by ancient Egyptians.

Gilligan is frank in his admiration for the Egyptian civilisation, yet he is always totally loyal to the actual facts and refuses to overlook (or cover up!) inconveniences which don't fit in with his proposals, something which cannot always be said of other experts.

As the series unfolds, we will uncover the mysteries of over 3,000 years of ancient history. But please note _ this is NOT a book based on mythology and it is important to make this point clear from the outset. The series is based firmly on facts as provided by ancient historical documents and artefacts. These stories were faithfully recorded via ancient Egyptian hieroglyphs and explain the very origins of this people.

Gary Gilligan's series celebrates the spirit of a unique land and his great anthology must be read by everyone interested in the great tradition of Egyptian history and literature. It evokes a portrait of a land complete with the associated beauties and horrors that formed the lives of its people, from common folk to monarchy. It reflects the feel and atmosphere of the age in which these tales of mythology and ancient lore were first told and provides a vivid portrait of a once great land.

This is the first book in the 'God King Scenario' series.

INTRODUCTION

If you were asked to name something typically associated with ancient Egypt, you would probably mention the pyramids, mummified bodies, intricate hieroglyphics, the myriad of gods and goddesses or the vast stone monuments. But have you ever wondered what motivated the Egyptians to engineer such incredible monuments? What was it about this ancient population that inspired them to create such magnificent works of art?

'An Ancient World in Chaos' is the first book in the 'God King Scenario' series. It will outline what encouraged the ancient Egyptians to create such a vast array of mythical deities. It will also explain what moved them to look to the heavens for guidance. And more importantly, it will reveal how cosmic chaos is staring us in the face via ancient history. Welcome to the most outrageous theory you will ever hear.

Ancient Egypt – a bizarre world!

Ancient Egypt was an awesome period in human history. Springing to life on the banks of the Nile, Egypt was one of the world's first great civilisations and still invokes fascination. Spanning over three millennia, it was certainly the most long lived of world powers. Any mention of Egypt immediately conjures up images of the pyramids, the great Sphinx at Giza, the enormous temples and fabulous treasures such as those found buried with the legendary boy-king, Tutankhamun.

For thousands of years the ancient Egyptians carved their lives onto stone on a scale that no other civilization had ever done, or ever would. The resources of the whole nation were invested in massive monuments and incredible structures. Almost everything we know about the ancient Egyptians comes from these glorious works of art.

Egypt was once ruled by pharaohs. Worshipped as 'gods on Earth,' they were the pinnacles of Egyptian religion. The nation regarded them as receptacles of the supernatural and the divine; intermediaries between the mortal world and the world of the gods. They held the power of life and death in their hands and their symbols of office, the crook and the flail, were indicative of this. The legacy of these gods can be seen adorning almost every temple and tomb throughout pharonic Egypt. The pharaohs' battles, coronations, state visits and interactions with the gods were immortalized within glorious images and 'sacred' writings or hieroglyphs.

Modern students of mythology and ancient history point to a time when humanity looked for supernatural guidance from a myriad of gods. The ancient Egyptians were no exception and the backbone of Egyptian life was 'divine order' and the worship of the gods. Male, female and anthropomorphic deities presided over particular aspects of Egyptian life and played a significant role in shaping the nation, and in a wider sense in shaping modern mankind.

The Egyptian belief in polytheism, or faith in many gods, held strong until their demise sometime in the third century BC. Many of these gods dwelt invisibly in the mortal world and acted through sacred sites, animals and the divine royal family. In the quest for immortality, the spirits of the deceased, if remembered and honored, could aid and guide the living from their position in the 'next world.' These deities were beautiful to behold, luminous beings that walked the Earth as they guided the human race to paradise. They were more powerful than humans, yet they displayed humanlike qualities: they showed anger and despair, fought with one another, had offspring, and fell in love; they lived lives which mirrored their worshippers.

Despite the wealth of information available to us, we understand little about the bizarre world of the ancient Egyptians. The backbone of their culture, their gods and beliefs and the numerous stories associated with them, are completely alien to us. Although their gods dictated and shaped every aspect of their lives, mystery surrounds their origins. It is commonly believed that the modern preference for a single deity is more advanced than the pagan beliefs of our ancestors. Yet this mindset fails to understand why the Egyptians invented and worshipped such a colorful array of gods. It is important to examine how and why this polytheistic culture evolved and what motivated such beliefs if we are to truly understand the enigma that is ancient Egypt.

Why is this world so alien to us?

There is a universally accepted explanation for the evolution of this complex world. According to modern Egyptologists, the ancient Egyptians were attempting to explain the workings of the cosmos. By creating a myriad of gods and a whole host of enigmatic stories and strange beliefs, they were striving to find a purpose for the cosmos and their place in it. Egyptologists believe that this is the only plausible theory, but are things really that simple or straightforward? If this is the only logical explanation, why is it so alien to us, and why do we struggle to understand even the most fundamental aspects of it?

The Sun rises and sets in a regular cycle which brings day and night; this perennial cycle is so predictable we barely give it a second thought. The seasons and the number of days in a year are equally predictable and easily measured even without a modern timepiece. The same can be said of the phases of the Moon as it orbits the Earth in a regular and orderly fashion. Even the planets and stars which reside in the heavens have their own cycles that can be predicted and monitored. It all seems so simple, particularly when we consider that Egypt has one of the sunniest and driest climates in the world.

Does modern Egypt accurately reflect ancient Egypt? Were ancient Egyptians describing the same world with their sky gods, enigmatic beliefs and incredible stories? If so, why is it so difficult to identify with their world?

Could there be an alternative explanation to the current theory? I believe there is. However, before I offer a radical new interpretation, it is necessary to investigate some of the bizarre aspects of ancient Egypt and call into question the orthodox view. By doing so, I hope to prove there is something drastically wrong with the conventional understanding.

PHYSICAL AND MYTHICAL GODS AS PART OF OUR WORLD

Does the invention of hundreds of mythical gods explain the natural world?

From our modern day perspective, there were two types of gods in ancient Egypt. Firstly, there were those attributed to physical objects and natural phenomena such as the Earth, Sun, Moon and the elements (air, fire, water, etc). There were also those that could not be placed in the physical world – in other words 'made-up' gods or gods of a fictitious nature. To simplify things, they will be separated into two categories – 'real gods' and 'mythical gods'.

Real gods

An extremely important 'real' god with a physical association was the solar deity Re (or Ra). Re was one of the original creator gods and was typically represented as a hawk-headed human wearing a sun-disk headdress. There were many enigmatic beliefs attributed to this god and epithets included 'Praise Re when he riseth at the beginning of each day' and 'Re is the great light who shineth in the heavens'. Re's most common symbol was a solar disk which is clear evidence that Re was the Sun. In effect, the Egyptians were providing the Sun with an identity by deifying it in the form of Re. When we consider the life-supporting properties of the Sun and the fact that it is the most prominent orb in the heavens, this is understandable.

Another example of a 'real god' embodied in a physical object was the lunar god Thoth. There were numerous enigmatic myths surrounding this god and epithets included 'One who made calculations concerning the heavens, the stars and the Earth' and 'The reckoner of times and of seasons'. It is therefore clear that the Egyptians deified the Moon as the god Thoth.

There were also many lesser 'real' gods. Geb was the god of the Earth and his sister-wife Nut was the goddess of the sky. Moisture and air were embodied by the gods Tefnut and Shu. Heryshef was the Ruler of the Riverbanks and Hapi was the personification of the Nile. Hapi was in charge of the waters that flowed during the floods, although the Egyptians had no idea how or why the Nile flooded each year. They believed that the gods Khnemu, Anqet, and Satet (Goddess of the Inundation) were the guardians of the source of the Nile and their duty was to make sure the right amount of silt was released during the yearly inundation. Baal was a rider of clouds, most active during storms and considered to be a 'lord of heaven and Earth,' even controlling Earth's fertility. He was the god of thunderstorms, the most vigorous and aggressive of the gods and the one on whom mortals most depended. Other 'real' gods included:

Kek and Kauket – Deities of darkness, obscurity and night
Nun and Naunet – Deities of chaos and water
Mafdet – Goddess of scorpions and snakes
Min – God of fertility
Nefertem – Lord of the Sunrise

Deifying the Sun and Moon was understandable for a primitive people because they were the two largest orbs in the heavens. It was also logical to deify other natural phenomena such as air and moisture. Ancient cultures understood little about the workings of the cosmos and the ancient Egyptians were merely identifying with the physical things around them. They attributed natural phenomena to the workings of the gods as a means of explaining the physical world. But what of the hundreds of mythical gods that cannot be placed in the physical world? How did they originate and what prompted their creation?

A few mythical gods

A prime example of a mythical god which was not attributed to a physical object or natural phenomenon was Amun (also spelt Amen or Amon). Amun, whose name means 'the hidden one', was a creator-god who rose to prominence in the New Kingdom. He was the chief deity of ancient Egypt and his popularity eclipsed that of other deities including Re. He is depicted as a human wearing a flat top crown with two long plumes. As the king of the gods, his image is found on numerous temple walls throughout Egypt. He was revered so highly that the largest religious structure in the world, the temple of Karnak, was dedicated to him. Amun was closely associated with the pharaohs and it was he who dictated the throne of Egypt. Great pharaohs such as Ramesses the Great, Tuthmosis III (the Napoleon of ancient Egypt) and many others ruled under the authority of Amun and were depicted in a variety of scenes with him. Examples included Amun receiving offerings from the pharaohs, Amun taking part in the coronation of the king, Amun handing the *khepesh* sword to the pharaohs (symbol of invincibility), and Amun handing a palm frond, the symbol of long rule, to kings such as Ramesses II.

Despite Amun's omnipresence, we cannot place him in the natural world. There is nothing that we can point to, or feel or sense which is connected with this god. Even if we consider the invisible elements such as light, air or wind, nothing can conclusively be attributed to Amun. He was 'mysterious of form' and 'one whose true identity and appearance could never be known' just as his epithets imply. There has been much speculation regarding Amun's origins. However, there is little agreement on the matter and any physical identification is pure speculation.

Egyptologists understand Amun's role in pharonic times as 'king of the gods' under whose authority the pharaohs ruled, but they are completely mystified as to his origins. We do not know how or why a fictitious deity 'whose true form could never be known' rose to such a powerful position.

There are many enigmas surrounding Amun. For example, Amun's epithets refer to him as 'mysterious of form', yet his images, that of a human figure wearing a double-plumed crown, were everywhere. He was clearly seen interacting with the monarchy in numerous reliefs throughout Egypt. Pharaohs including Ramesses the Great and Tuthmosis III were pictured alongside Amun in a variety of scenes. How do we explain this contradiction? How was it possible to be mysterious of form whilst taking on a clear and easily recognizable human form?

Amun was later combined with the Sun-god Re and was referred to as 'Amun-Re'. Yet how could a god who was known as 'the one whose true form could never be known' be associated with a god who took on the most distinctive and easily recognisable form known to man – the Sun? The golden orb that rises and sets on a daily basis is not 'mysterious of form' so how do we explain this syncretism?

Another puzzling aspect of Amun and Re concerned their images. The human form of Amun was never combined with the hawk-headed figure of Re. It seems that the composite god existed in name only. Both Amun and Re maintained their pictorial independence despite references to the combined god Amun-Re. When we find references to Amun-Re complete with images, it is the human form of Amun that is shown, not the hawk-headed figure of the Sun god Re. It is perplexing that a god who was embodied in a real physical object was combined with a completely mythical god.

One of the most easily recognizable of Egyptian goddesses was Hathor, whose name means 'house of the king'. She was a bovine goddess who was referred to as both the mother and daughter of Re. Her influence was vast and she existed for the entire history of ancient Egyptian culture as a powerful and influential deity. In early Egyptian mythology she was the mother of the sky god Horus, but she was later replaced by Isis who played a similar maternal role. In fact, in the New Kingdom, Isis superseded Hathor as the goddess who encapsulated the virtues of the archetypical Egyptian wife and mother. Both Hathor and Isis featured prominently in the births and deaths of the Egyptian royal family. Both goddesses exerted a powerful influence over Egyptian civilisation, and yet their origin and the reasons behind their invention remain a complete mystery.

Another example of a fictitious deity was Osiris, the god of the afterlife. Osiris was a primary deity. In power, he was second only to his father, Re, and was the leader of the gods on Earth. He was the husband of Isis and the father of Horus (and a number of other gods according to some stories). Osiris is usually depicted as a mummy whose hands projected through the wrappings to hold the royal insignia of crook and flail. He wore the tall white crown of Upper Egypt flanked by two tall plumes, otherwise known as the *atef* crown.

As resurrectionists, the Egyptians believed that when they died they would be reborn as stars in the 'kingdom of Osiris' also known as 'the field of reeds'. The monarchy was typically portrayed in the mummified form of Osiris because it was vital for a monarch to be strongly associated with this god. This ensured that, at the time of their death, they would be called by their own name + Osiris, for example 'Tutankhamun Osiris' or 'Ramesses Osiris'. This practice also applied to commoners, the ordinary rank and file Egyptians. They too appended Osiris onto their own name as it was believed that adding this name guaranteed a resurrection into the next world. Like Hathor and Isis, Osiris was an invisible, fictitious god strongly associated with Egyptian religion.

There are a number of other mythical deities who are worthy of a brief mention: Seth, the god of evil and chaos and brother to Osiris; Horus, the hawk-headed god who was the son of Osiris – it was believed that all pharaohs were the god Horus on Earth; Anubis, the jackal-headed god who was the son of Osiris and the god of mummification and care of the deceased; Nephthys, the patron god of the dead, funerals, the house, and women and who was a companion of Isis. It is evident that the Egyptian world consisted of hundreds of mythical entities and their legacy is apparent today in the numerous temples and shrines that were built in their honour.

Having examined a small selection of Egyptian gods, the question remains: How did the invention of numerous 'made-up' gods who were not attributable to physical phenomena explain the workings of the cosmos? Why were fictitious gods generally the dominant force in Egyptian religion, and by extension Egyptian life? Surely the invention of a pantheon of mythical gods alongside 'real-gods' complicated a relatively simple world.

The only thing that separates us from our ancient forebears is time and technology. Is this sufficient to create such a diverse, contrasting and incomprehensible world? If we stripped ourselves of modern beliefs and knowledge, would we emulate the Egyptians and create our own enigmatic world? If not, why not? What is the difference between their world and ours?

Depicting the Sun and Moon as the gods Re and Thoth seems reasonable. After all, they are the two largest celestial bodies in the heavens. However, consider the task of educating the population of Egypt and explaining the existence of 'real' gods as well as thousands of imaginary gods, many of whom were either equal to or higher in status than the Sun and Moon. Imagine the difficulty of explaining who they were and the integrated and complicated roles they played.

The matter was further complicated by mythical gods such as Amun, Osiris, Hathor and Isis – there was nothing to associate them with, no point of reference or physical object to illustrate their form. How and why were these gods perpetuated for an incredible 3,000 years?

It would be easier to understand the Egyptian world if we could split it into two worlds: a divine world and a mortal world. The divine world would be inhabited by mythical gods and the physical world by physical gods who played a real part in explaining the workings of the universe. Unfortunately the situation was far more complicated than that. Egyptian mythical gods not only inhabited the same world as 'real' gods, but they also interacted with them. Mythology even depicts deities such as Hathor and Isis interacting with the solar deity Re. How can such beliefs explain the workings of the cosmos?

HUMAN RELATIONS WITH DIVINE ENTITIES

Bizarre relations with our mythical gods

How did the belief that pharaohs were directly related to real and mythical gods explain the workings of the cosmos?

All pharaohs had the title 'son of Re' (*sa-re*) as they were considered offspring of the Sun. Queens were referred to as the 'daughters of Re' or daughters of the Sun. Until the 'birth' of Amun, the Sun was regarded as master of the universe. As a visible, physical object, it was easy to identify Re with the Sun. It also seemed sensible to placate the original creator god by promoting the belief that all pharaohs were children of the Sun. After all, were not the Egyptians merely associating themselves with the ultimate creative life force on Earth?

Once again, things were not that simple. Not only did the monarchy consider themselves offspring of Re, but they also considered themselves offspring of a number of mythical gods. Many monarchs referred to themselves as sons or daughters of gods such as Amun, Hathor and Isis. Examples include Tutankhamun's Restoration Stele, which referred to him as 'the good god (Tutankhamun), son of Amun'. The pharaoh Amenhotep considered himself son of Amun. Hatshepsut (the queen who would be king) recorded that she had built her mortuary temple as a 'garden for my father Amun'. She also erected giant obelisks in honor of her father.

Although not a distinct reference to parentage, many pharaohs also had the title 'Beloved of Amun'. Famous examples included Ramesses the Great and Tuthmosis III. Hathor, the goddess of fertility, women, and childbirth was referred to as the divine mother of the king, and one of the titles given to the kings was 'son of Hathor'. Her role as royal mother can be gleaned from a statue (currently in the Egyptian Museum in Cairo) which depicted Hathor in the form of a cow suckling the pharaoh Amenhotep II.

Isis was the sister-wife of Osiris and mother to Horus. As such she was the symbolic mother of the pharaoh, who himself was regarded as the human manifestation of the god Horus. This divine relationship regularly described the king as the son of the goddess Isis.

The practice of attributing one's parentage to a 'real' god such as Re, as well as to 'made-up' divinities such as Amun, Hathor and Isis, appears confusing. For example, what of the monarchy's mortal parents who barely played a part in this divine game of happy families? For the pharaohs, it appears their physical parents played a secondary role. If we add this collection of parents together, certain pharaohs had three fathers and in many cases three mothers.

An example of this concept of multi-parenting was Ramesses the Great. His mortal father was the pharaoh Seti I and his mother was Tuya. Yet he also considered the solar god Re and the 'hidden' god Amun as his fathers and the goddesses Hathor and Isis as his mothers. It is interesting to note that, as the kings were regarded as Horus on Earth, Isis would also be linked to Ramesses as a symbolic mother.

From a modern perspective this was a bizarre and confusing practice. It was not merely a case of having one set of mortal parents and one set of divine parents. Scholars therefore struggle to comprehend the physical lineal ancestry of the pharaohs as well as the belief that the monarchy considered themselves offspring of 'mythical' gods and goddesses.

Consider Tutankhamun – his parents were a complete enigma. His mother is thought to have been Kia, while his father is believed to have been the 'heretic' pharaoh Akhenaten. However, this is pure speculation as we do not know who Tutankhamun's parents were. How does this complicated situation explain our simple world? How can this myriad of gods and goddesses attain such physical presence and direct involvement with mortals and yet have a fictitious origin?

It was believed that the lineage of kings would come to an end if the queens did not directly copulate with the mythical god Amun. It was also believed that the universe would fall into chaos if the very same queens did not directly interact with Amun. How does this explain the real world?

The pharaohs, as 'beloved of Amun', were obviously close to Amun. However, in the New Kingdom the queens (the king's great wives) had an even closer relationship with this 'great god'. They were known as 'god's wife of Amun' and 'hand of the God' and interacted directly with Amun. It was understood that the kings were conceived from the union of Amun and the queen. It was believed that without the intercession of these 'god's wives' the very universe would fall apart. In certain sections of Amun's temple at

Karnak, there are numerous reliefs highlighting the intimate relationship that existed between queen and god. They typically depicted Amun and the queen standing side by side with the queen's arms around the god; Egyptologists have labeled such scenes as a 'god's wife embrace'.

We may wonder how it was possible for the queens to have such a close and intimate relationship with an invisible god. The queen was both wife to the pharaoh and spouse to the 'hidden' god Amun, not to mention 'daughter of the Sun'. How could such a union produce the next god-king? How were sexual relations between gods and mere mortals possible?

If we consider the absence of scientific knowledge in ancient times, it is entirely plausible for Egyptians to have had a belief in the Sun as father to all and to have considered themselves children of the Sun god. However, marriage to an imaginary god such as Amun seems totally alien to us. Yet for pharaohs to be conceived from this 'divine marriage', the queens were required to mate with an imaginary god.

The 'god's wives' of Amun were also responsible for the safe keeping of the universe and they prevented it from descending into chaos. The Egyptians believed that the universe would be doomed and the cosmos would fall apart if the queens didn't have sexual relations with a god whose true form could never be known. How was this belief perpetuated and where is the evidence for this cosmic chaos? Were there occasions when the queens were not 'accommodating', and did this lead to periods of turmoil on earth?

Mortals equal in status to imaginary gods

How did the practice of considering oneself divine and equal to the gods explain the working of the cosmos?

The Egyptian monarchy risked the wrath of the gods by proclaiming themselves equal in status. Pharaohs were worshiped as living 'gods on Earth' and acted as intermediaries between the mortal and the divine. As such they were receptacles of supernatural power and coequal to gods such as Amun, Osiris, Hathor, Isis, and Horus.

The divine status of the monarchy was clearly evident in Egyptian artwork. The royal family was depicted as equal in size to the gods whereas ordinary people, or commoners, were portrayed as smaller. In Egyptian reliefs, paintings and statues, whenever gods and monarchs were shown together they were the same size; equal in stature and equal in status as gods incarnate. A example can be found in the Great Temple of Ramesses II at Abu Simbel. In the innermost part of the temple are four large, seated statues of Ptah, Amun, Ramesses II and Re-Horakhty. Of significant importance is Ramesses who was sculptured exactly the same size as the gods. The divine status of the monarchy was unmistakable in such a representation, but how or why mortal kings came to be exalted to such a lofty position is a mystery.

Why were humans regarded as gods and equal to mythical deities such as Amun, Osiris, Hathor and Ptah? How could mortals be receptacles of supernatural powers? Does this bizarre world reflect our world, and if so, how does this explain the cosmos?

We have established that Egyptian society comprised an ideology whereby hundreds of mythical gods and a host of real gods inhabited the same world. It was a world where real gods interacted with mythical gods, and where all deities had very intimate and close relations with humans. Egyptian pharaohs were considered to be gods amongst gods, and their entire civilization rested on the successful sexual union of mortal and divine beings.

Divine order

How and why were mortals responsible for divine order? Where did the belief that the universe would fall into chaos without a king at the helm originate?

'The function of the king as representative of the gods was to preserve and restore the original harmony of the universe.'

(Nicholson, 2002, p 153)

It was the role of the pharaoh, as the incarnation of the 'good and just' god Horus, to maintain a balance between order and chaos (*ma'at*). If he failed, the cosmos would fall into chaos and the waters of Nun would swallow up the world. A statue of Ramesses III in the Cairo Museum provides a perfect example of a pharaoh symbolically maintaining 'divine order'. Ramesses stands between the good god Horus and the evil god Seth. This stance, where the pharaoh was of equal size to both gods, clearly reveals his role as mediator between good and evil, order and chaos.

What is this chaos that the Egyptians referred to? Could it be the same chaos that would befall mankind if the queens (god's wives) didn't mate with the all powerful hidden god Amun? It was believed that the king had the power to prevent such chaos, but how could a mortal have the power to maintain 'divine order' and prevent chaos in the universe?

Modern Egypt has a stable environment and one of the sunniest and driest climates in the world. It is therefore logical to assume that the Egyptian reference to 'order' or *ma'at* points to the same calm, peaceful world that exists today. It also seems reasonable to suppose that ancient Egyptians experienced chaos in some form or another. After all, the threat of chaos influenced their daily lives and they looked to their pharaoh to safeguard the nation. If we can establish the exact nature of this chaos, it should be possible to discover how this bizarre belief evolved and why the Egyptians assumed their pharaohs were endowed with such prodigious powers.

Before we consider the origin of such beliefs, we need to examine the possible causes of Egyptian chaos. As a starting point, we could examine the adverse periodic weather conditions in Egypt such as sandstorms, or the less frequent flash floods which occur in certain parts of Egypt every few years, or even very rare phenomena such as earthquakes. Could such forces of nature have been responsible for the daily conflict between order and chaos?

Although this sounds entirely plausible, the answer is no. It is true that sandstorms occurred regularly and flash floods occasionally saturated the land of Egypt. However, such natural phenomena could not have been regarded as precursors to the end of the world. The Egyptians had only to experience a few sandstorms and flash floods to realise that their world was not coming to an end. Clearly the modern day population of Egypt do not consider such natural occurrences as harbingers of doom.

Could earthquakes have been responsible for the daily threat of chaos which gripped the Egyptian nation? They undoubtedly caused death and destruction on a much grander scale than floods or sandstorms. However, once the Egyptians had experienced one or two earthquakes, they would have realised that the angry 'Earth god' was not going to destroy the earth. We must also remember that the threat of chaos was a cosmic myth and the participants were sky gods, so we need to look elsewhere for an answer.

If we consider the cause from a cosmic angle, it would seem logical to explore global dark ages as possible architects of chaos. These were periods when the skies blackened and blotted out the Sun, and when crops failed leading to starvation, death and disease. There were at least three dark ages in ancient times at 3100 BC, 2200 BC and 1200 BC. These global catastrophes lasted from 100 to 200 years and their causes were unknown. Egyptologists have labelled these periods Intermediate Periods, times when little or no archaeological evidence of activity exists. They were periods when Egyptian civilisation totally collapsed and fell into turmoil – quite literally dark ages – the exact opposite to the order (*ma'at*) that exits today. Could this be the chaos the Egyptians were referring to?

The time span between dark ages was approximately 1,000 years and the average life span of an Egyptian was thirty years. Therefore there were thirty-three generations between dark ages. As Egyptian civilisation emerged from each dark age, the threat of a global catastrophe was indelibly stamped on the minds of the people and they would have lived in constant fear of evil returning. However, after one or two generations of order and calm, it would have been apparent that Seth, the antagonist of anarchy, was no longer a daily threat. The Egyptians would have concluded that Seth was banished forever as memories of chaos faded, demoted to the realms of mythology.

If the Egyptians were referring to global catastrophes as the instigators of chaos, it would be sensible to consider whether or not we are living in fear of impending chaos. After all, Earth suffered a global dark age in the 6th century AD, the cause of which is unknown. Does this major global disturbance over 1400 years ago still govern our lives? Do we live in constant fear of the cause of this catastrophe returning? Of course not, and it is absurd to suggest such a thing.

It is apparent that global dark ages were not the source of Egyptian chaos. With thousands of years between them, dark ages were not frequent enough and did not occur on a daily basis, which is a crucial point. We know that the Egyptians regarded chaos as a daily threat and this belief was perpetuated for 3,000 years. In fact, they believed there was such a fine line between order and chaos that the universe could fall into chaos at any time. Without a plausible explanation for Egyptian chaos, scholars are at a loss to explain the related belief that pharaohs had the power to prevent a global catastrophe. After all, how can they possibly explain the power of Egyptian kings to prevent global chaos if they cannot identify the nature of this chaos?

If it were possible to prove that global disturbances, flash floods, earthquakes or some other phenomena were responsible for chaos, would this explain how or why mortal beings had the power to prevent it? Was the supernatural power of the pharaohs ever tested? With the advent of impending chaos, did the pharaohs simply raise their hands and order it to stop in the style of King Canute? Our rational minds realise that humans, even in the form of god-kings, would have had absolutely no power over natural phenomena, and anyone making such a false claim would have been exposed as a fraud.

Celestial origin

Given the close interaction between ancient Egyptians and mythical gods, many scholars endeavour to give physical presence to these gods. They reason that such gods loom too large and too prominent to be of mythical origin and must have been inspired by something in the natural world. For example, just as Re was a real god who played a crucial part in Egyptian life, there must have been something physical with which to associate the other primary deities. If we can establish what these physical features were, it may bring us closer to understanding the enigmatic world of the Egyptians.

Attempting to give physical identification to mythological gods is a complex task. There are numerous circular proposals but no definitive answers and this has resulted in little agreement. The crux of the problem is that major gods such as Amun, Osiris, Hathor, Isis, Ptah, Seth, and Horus were 'sky' gods. Apart from the Sun, the Moon and the backdrop of stars, there is very little to identify them with. Obviously there are planets in our solar system, but from the perspective of the Earth they al look like stars that move through the sky.

The largest astral bodies which are visible from the Earth are the Sun and Moon. Egyptologists have therefore attempted to 'double up' by identifying many gods and goddesses with the same celestial body. For example, they identify the mother goddesses Hathor and Isis with the Sun because they are often depicted with a head-dress consisting of a solar disk between a set of cow's horns. Egyptologists have assigned most deities to the Sun because it is the only way they can make sense of this bizarre world. However, some have suggested that Osiris (the god of the afterlife), Hathor and Isis may have been embodied in the Moon. There is also a suggestion that the Dog Star, Sirius (constellation Orion) was associated with Isis.

Egyptologists have continued to put forward erroneous proposals regarding Egyptian deities. For example, scholars reason that, as Jupiter is the largest planet in the solar system, and as Amun was the 'king of the gods', Amun must therefore be Jupiter. However this theory demonstrates an incredibly poor understanding of ancient civilizations. Viewed from the Earth, the planet Jupiter (and any other visible planet) looks like a bright star. Are we therefore to assume the Egyptians were privy to information about the solar system which astronomers have only discovered in the last few decades? How else would they know that Jupiter is a planet of such gigantic proportions? What of epithets which refer to Amun as 'the hidden one' or 'the one whose true form could never be known'? If Amun was Jupiter, we could reason that his true form was known because he was a bright star.

This is not the only inconsistency regarding Jupiter. For example, why was a speck of light so deeply involved with events on Earth, and how could it dictate kingship? How could the 'god's wife of Amun' have sexual encounters with a speck in the night sky? Have scholars attempted to pair up any other planets from the solar system?

At its brightest, Saturn outshines all visible stars except Sirius and Canopus. As it shines as brightly as Jupiter, what god was chosen to represent Saturn? What of Mercury, which can only be seen in the morning or evening twilight because of its close proximity to the Sun? If ancient cultures had deified Mercury, we would expect to find references to a god who was rarely seen, and then only at dawn or dusk.

Venus is the brightest planet and at certain times of the year it is clearly visible in the morning and evening. Where are the ancient references to these planetary traits? Why did ancient cultures refer to this star as female? What is the difference between Venus and the bright star Jupiter?

What of Mars? Its movements bring it close to Earth approximately every seventeen years and it is possible to pick out its distinctive reddish hue with the naked eye. The colour of the gods was of paramount importance to ancient cultures, and what other body reveals such a distinctive colour trait? We would therefore expect to find at least one red Mars god amongst the numerous ancient civilisations.

It is not possible to conclusively associate any of the planets with their respective deities for any ancient culture prior to 300 BC. We can identify gods such as the solar deity Re and the lunar god Thoth, but we cannot determine which gods represented the brightest planetary stars such as Saturn, Jupiter and Venus. Any identification is pure speculation because there are too many gods to share amongst a handful of planets.

Is the world we live in the same as the world of our ancient ancestors? If the planets have not altered their paths across the heavens for millions of years, why is it so difficult to understand the concept of sky gods paired with planetary bodies? Common sense dictates that there should be a common thread running through all ancient cultures linking certain gods to their respective planets. It is also logical to assume that this thread should be easily recognizable to us today. However, this is not the case.

In summation of a bizarre world

We have demonstrated that the ancient Egyptians lived in a bizarre world dominated by hundreds of fictitious gods, extraordinary stories and enigmatic beliefs. We find it difficult to associate with this world because it is totally alien to us, yet it was entirely normal to the Egyptians. Their gods, myths and stories were clearly understood by the entire population.

Research reveals that all ancient cultures lived in similar environments dominated by mythical gods and strange beliefs. A prime example of an ancient culture is the Sumerians who emerged between the Tigris and Euphrates rivers (modern day Iraq) around the same time as the ancient Egyptians (approx. 3200 BC). The Sumerian pantheon of gods controlled every aspect of Sumerian life.

They included mythical deities such as the creator god Anu, his sons Enlil and Enki who were mythical sky gods, and Ishtar who was the 'lady of Heaven' and the most important female deity.

Sumerian culture consisted of thousands of mythical gods who were not represented by anything in the corporeal world. However, while nothing physical could illustrate their form, they were created in a quest to explain the natural world. Many ancient cultures and religions had much in common with early Egyptian civilization. However, the wealth of information available concerning ancient Egypt makes it an ideal subject to study.

Are scholars correct in their assumption that the ancient Egyptians, and by extension all ancient cultures, created thousands of imaginary gods to explain the workings of the cosmos? Were the enigmatic myths and legends associated with these gods created with the sole purpose of explaining our world? If so, why does this world seem so strange and unfamiliar? If we could strip ourselves of modern knowledge and technology, would we view the world in the same way as our ancient ancestors?

I believe there is an alternative theory which explains the development of the Egyptian civilization which spanned over 3,000 years. Scholars have therefore overlooked a relatively simple explanation for this world of mythical gods.

COSMIC CHAOS

Planetary Chaos according to catastrophists

It may sound incredible, but there is an alternative theory to explain the origins of ancient Egyptian beliefs which does not deviate from the orthodox view. The ancient Egyptians were attempting to explain the workings of the cosmos.

The Egyptians created a host of deities to explain the world and their place in it, but this was not the same world that exists today. It was a world dominated by incredible events in the heavens, where a fine line existed between order and cosmic chaos. This alternative theory has been put forward by a group of people called 'catastrophists'. A catastrophist is somebody who believes that the solar system has undergone a radical upheaval in the history of man, and so exists as a smoking gun of recent cosmic chaos.

As most readers will be unfamiliar with planetary chaos, I will explain the concept of catastrophe in simple terms. First we will examine a great man who brought catastrophism to the forefront of cosmic science.

In the 1950s, Immanuel Velikovsky, a Russian physiologist, wrote a book called '*Worlds in Collision*'. In this extraordinary book, Velikovsky proposed that many myths and traditions of ancient peoples and cultures were based on actual events. These events were worldwide global catastrophes of a celestial origin, and they had a profound effect on the lives, beliefs and writings of early mankind.

Immanuel Velikovsky 1895-1979 (Photograph reproduced courtesy of Randall Hagadorn, Photographer)

'Worlds in Collision' is a book of 'wars' in the cosmos which took place in historical times. This historical-cosmological work is based on evidence from a number of sources including 'the historical texts of many nations, classical literature, epics of the northern races, sacred books of the peoples of the Orient and Occident, traditions and folklore of primitive peoples, old astronomical inscriptions and charts, archaeological finds, and geological and paleontological material' (*'Worlds In Collision'* Preface). In 1956, Velikovsky produced a follow-up entitled *'Earth in Upheaval'* to present conclusive geological evidence of terrestrial catastrophism.

When *'Worlds in Collision'* was first published, it caused great controversy. It was denounced by leading scientists, particularly cosmologists, and some even tried to prevent the book from being stocked in bookstores and libraries. After reaching number one in the best-seller chart, a number of academic institutions actually banned it and this created an unprecedented scientific debacle that became known as 'The Velikovsky Affair'. Velikovsky's detractors thought they were protecting the public from erroneous ideas and fiction masquerading as fact, but they only succeeded in making Velikovsky a martyr in the eyes of his followers.

According to Velikovsky, during the second millennium BC, a large comet-like object (which later became the planet Venus) was ejected from Jupiter. Around 1450 BC the comet approached Earth which caused our planet to pass through the comet's tail. As it did so, it received a fall of red meteorite dust which turned rivers and seas blood red. Ash-like dust, burning meteorites and petroleum rained down upon terror-stricken nations and fires raged everywhere. As Earth plunged more deeply into the tail and approached the comet's head, a pall of darkness occurred that lasted for days. The Earth's rotation slowed down which caused Earthquakes around the globe. Hurricane-force winds swept across the terrain, and huge tidal waves deposited vast amounts of water on some areas, leaving some former sea beds (such as the Red Sea) uncovered for a time.

When the Earth emerged from the tail, the comet Venus looked like a pillar of smoke during the day and a pillar of fire at night. Violent electrical discharges flashed between the Earth and the comet and between the comet's head and its own tail, creating the appearance of a great battle raging in the sky. The disturbance to Earth's rotation generated so much heat that rocks melted, lava flowed from new as well as old volcanoes, new mountain ranges appeared and the seas boiled. The intense heat caused frogs, flies, and other vermin to propagate at a feverish rate.

It is possible that vermin, which hatched from eggs and larvae carried in the trailing atmosphere of the comet, may have infested the Earth. Clouds of water vapour and dust covered the Earth for many years. Within these clouds, chemical reactions between the carbon and hydrogen from the tail of the comet produced carbohydrates that rained down as 'heavenly food'. Could this have been the heavenly manna or ambrosia?

Gradually the comet Venus receded, but fifty-two years later its erratic orbit brought it very close to Earth. On this occasion the Earth's rotation gradually slowed and stopped for a short time, enabling Joshua and the Israelites to defeat their enemies while the Sun appeared to stand still. Once more, meteorites rained from the sky, earthquakes split the surface of the ground, volcanoes erupted, and tidal waves overwhelmed portions of the Earth. By the time this crisis passed, people had accepted the comet as part of the solar system and began worshipping it as a divinity (Venus, Ishtar, etc), carefully observing its movements.

For six hundred years between 1400 and 800 BC, the solar system was spared from further cataclysms. In the eighth century BC, Venus collided with Mars and knocked the red planet from its long-established orbit. Mars approached Earth a number of times (776, 747, 717 or 702, and 687 BC) which created further catastrophes that supposedly destroyed Mycenaean citadels in Greece and the Assyrian army that besieged Jerusalem. As a result of these contacts, both Mars and Earth settled into their present orbits. The Earth's year – the time it takes to make one revolution around the Sun – was lengthened from 360 days to approximately 365 _ days. Meanwhile, the elliptical orbit of Venus was modified to its present nearly-circular pattern by its collision with Mars. The solar system had at last attained the stable arrangement observable today.

As cosmic catastrophes ended, a collective amnesia gradually developed to protect mankind from traumatic memories of these events. References to the upheavals in myths, legends, folklore and the Bible were veiled by poetic language and explained as miracles or magic. The world chose to forget how close it had come to annihilation. This, in brief, is the essence of Velikovsky's claim.

We can summarise Velikovsky's research as follows:

- Planets that now move on stable orbits several millions of miles away from Earth have not always moved on these paths.

- The solar system has been unstable within human memory i.e. within the last few thousands years.

- Errant planets menaced the Earth on several occasions in recent history and man recorded these spectacular celestial events.

- The primary powers in ancient myths and legends were planets and hence we cannot understand these myths by reference to the way things are today.

- The planet Venus is a recent addition to the solar system; it was expelled from the planet Jupiter.

- Venus, due to its recent birth, once possessed a comet-like tail and its orbit brought it into confrontation with the Earth several times.

- The planet Mars, the god-of-war of the ancient world, participated directly in Earth-changing catastrophes and appeared to battle other celestial bodies in the sky.

- Ancient cultures gave different names to rogue planets, sometimes swapping or rotating them around several times. Some cultures used the same or equivalent names, but applied them to different planets.

- There were many 'sex changes' of planets i.e. god-to-goddess and vice versa.

To date, Velikovsky remains relatively obscure. Yet, it is possible that he was correct regarding planetary chaos in the history of man. Venus may be a new planet which was ejected from Jupiter, and in the past Venus and Mars may have 'visited' Earth many times. Perhaps there is a direct correlation between the religion, enigmatic beliefs and myths of ancient cultures and planetary chaos. Cosmic chaos may yet provide an explanation for the bizarre world of the ancient Egyptians. Ancient gods may once have had a physical presence which has since disappeared because planetary chaos has subsided and they are no longer visible.

If Velikovsky was correct, planetary chaos produced an incalculable amount of space debris including asteroids, comets, dust and gasses. Where did this debris go? It orbited around the very planets that produced it – Mars and Venus. These planets were a hive of activity as swarms of rocky bodies orbited them.

Debris collided and rocks catastrophically crashed into planets which created further dust and debris. Anything that escaped the gravitational pull of Mars and Venus swarmed into the sky and armies of asteroids charged across the heavens in colossal cosmic battles. Passive Moon-sized bodies were shrouded in clouds of dust as they kept watch from a distance. Pairs of asteroids orbited one another in a cosmic dance much like Pluto and Charon do today. Intense cosmic chaos blotted out the Sun as meteorites crashed into Earth and set in motion a sequence of events which led to starvation, death and destruction. Electrical discharges between planetary bodies lit up the sky in a spectacular firework display. Planetary chaos was a magnificent melee which spanned thousands of years.

To explain such a chaotic universe, it would have been necessary for ancient cultures to create a world inhabited by a confusing array of gods with humanlike qualities. These gods would have shown anger and despair, fought with one another, fallen in love and sired offspring. They would have lived lives which mirrored their worshippers. Does this sound familiar? Could this be the bizarre world the Egyptians were describing with their myriad of gods, enigmatic beliefs and extraordinary tales?

Egyptian society was founded on a belief in the existence of a fine line between order and chaos. The Egyptians believed that the universe could fall into chaos at any time and it was therefore a constant threat. However, was this a primitive myth or a tenet born from actual events? If cosmic chaos was based on fact, could it explain why the Egyptians lived in constant fear? After all, if Egypt had experienced large scale death and destruction as a result of a meteorite impacting Earth, it is no wonder they lived in fear of impending chaos.

We are aware of the threat of asteroids in our present day, but we do not live in constant fear of imminent destruction. But what if we had experienced centuries of celestial bombardment where meteorites were a daily threat which caused devastation and death. Perhaps there had been a period of peace followed by complete and utter carnage as a meteorite crashed to Earth. Would we believe in a fine line between order and chaos?

Without the benefit of 4,000 years of science, ancient cultures would have had no concept of space or time and their understanding of the cosmos was naïve: the Earth was a flat body at the centre of the universe; the Sun and Moon were gods that travelled around the Earth; astral bodies were real, superior beings. Accurate knowledge of our ancestors can help us understand their thoughts and fears. As a psychologist, Velikovsky took the beliefs of our ancient forebears and concluded that the solar system has experienced chaos in the history of man.

When I first read Velikovsky's *'Worlds in Collision'* it made complete sense. It was clear that ancient Egypt and cosmic chaos went hand in hand. The Egyptians were not living in a surreal world of make believe but rather a world dictated and shaped by incredible events in the heavens. Yet why were Velikovsky's ideas so vehemently dismissed? If the solar system is a smoking gun of recent chaos, why do our history books make no mention of it? Has anybody followed up on Velikovsky's research?

The internet, with its many search engines, reveals very few catastrophe sites. This is because catastrophe is a subject that is little understood. Nevertheless, Velikovsky has built up a small but dedicated following and his ideas are going through a modern revival which is fully deserved.

One website inspired by Velikovsky is the Society for Interdisciplinary Studies (SIS). It includes a number of Velikovsky's unpublished works and has some intriguing articles on cosmic chaos (www.knowledge.co.uk/sis/). Another excellent website is CIAS – the California Institute for Ancient Studies (http://www.specialtyinterests.net/). Although it provides little reference to planetary chaos, it contains references to Velikovsky's research on the chronology of ancient history and in some instances reaches the same conclusions.

Some websites come close to Velikovsky's proposals while others suggest different timescales or attempt to physically identify prominent mythical gods by matching them with the proposed planets in chaos, notably Mars and Venus. I have thoroughly researched these sites and feel they offer nothing new in support of Velikovsky.

I would like to draw attention to an incredible piece of research written by a physicist called John Ackerman who resides in the US (http://www.firmament-chaos.com/). Using the pen-name Angiras, John Ackerman wrote two books entitled *'Firmament'* and *'Chaos'*. Both books were inspired by Velikovsky's controversial book *'Worlds in Collision'*. (I will refer to these works as Ackerman or the V/A Scenario or simply V/A). Following a study of space-probe planetary data and the *'Rig Veda'* and other Hindu myths, Ackerman developed his own interpretation of the myths and solar system history under the collective title *'The Velikovsky/Angiras Scenario'* (The V/A Scenario). They are great scholarly works, full of intelligent insight, and arguably the best books to have been inspired by Velikovsky. I will provide a brief overview of Ackerman's work because his research is closely aligned with my own beliefs concerning cosmic chaos in ancient times.

The Velikovsky/Angiras Scenario (V/A)

Prior to Bronze Age I (BA I) there existed only two terrestrial planets, the Earth and a planet which I call priori-Mars. Both were full of life. Mercury and Venus were not present. Priori-Mars, the more ancient of the two by some 800 million years, orbited closer to the Sun than the Earth in an orbit similar to that of Venus today and was covered with vegetation, requiring rain and a thick oxygen atmosphere. The Earth was in an orbit similar to its present one. Jupiter was a calm, bluish ice-planet which was similar to Uranus and Neptune as currently shown in NASA Voyager photographs. Saturn was the brightest planet in the heavens because its ring system was younger and larger than it is now.

About 6,000 years ago, a massive galactic 'traveller' entered our solar system at very high velocity and impacted Jupiter, releasing at least 10^{43} ergs. Its impact vaporized an enormous mass of material which rebounded into space at high velocity. The resulting plasma cloud was thousands of times the volume of Jupiter itself and glowed with a golden colour. Most of it escaped the gravitational pull of Jupiter and went into an eccentric orbit around the Sun. The plasma contracted rapidly, forming a star-like body or proto-planet. This was the birth of proto-Venus. The evidence of this event can still be seen on Jupiter as the Great Red Spot. Iits temperature excess is due to a continuing nuclear conflagration still taking place in the impact crater.

Proto-Venus' initial perihelion distance was probably less than the current radius of Venus' orbit, while its initial aphelion was near the orbit of Jupiter. Its orbit crossed that of the Earth and priori-Mars within a period of some five years. A large amount of its orbital energy was converted to heat at each perihelion passage as a result of tidal (gravitational) and electromagnetic forces exerted by the Sun. The net effect of the reheating events was to expel the lighter elements into interplanetary space, thus increasing the average density of the proto-planet to that of a terrestrial planet. But the much more abundant lighter elements that make up the atmosphere and oceans of terrestrial planets remain in the inner solar system awaiting capture as the proto-planet cools. Since all terrestrial planets are formed this way, this explains how the vast oceans of the Earth were acquired, not by trillions of comets as currently believed.

Proto-Venus passed close to priori-Mars on numerous occasions, transferring further orbital energy to the Red Planet. The combination of the solar braking and priori-Mars encounters reduced proto-Venus' eccentricity rapidly to the point that it only reached the vicinity of the Earth's orbit. At the same time the radius of priori-Mars' orbit was moved outward, bringing it closer and closer to the Earth. During this period the flaming proto-Venus passed extremely close to the Earth on two occasions, scorching the surface and causing tidal waves that swept across a number of continents.

Soon after this, a complex three-planet interaction occurred which involved priori-Mars, proto-Venus and the Earth. As a result of this encounter, sufficient orbital energy was transferred to priori-Mars to send it for the first time into an orbit which crossed that of the Earth. The same interaction further reduced the aphelion of Venus' orbit so that it no longer crossed the orbit of the Earth. This signalled the end of the most destructive phase of what we term the Vedic period. In this eccentric orbit, proto-Venus still came quite close to Earth every thirty years due to the correspondence of its aphelion to its inferior conjunctions (alignments in which proto-Venus was between the Earth and Sun). Its powerful gravitational force had a profound effect on the release of priori-Mars from its geosynchronous orbit at these times.

Under the periodic influence of proto-Venus, priori-Mars began engaging in a series of amazing encounters with the Earth. For some 3,000 years, priori-Mars engaged repeatedly in 'dances' with the Earth, each of which lasted fourteen or fifteen year with intervening periods of separation of the same length. These dances of priori-Mars and the Earth were such that the smaller body, priori-Mars, was captured in a geosynchronous orbit around the Earth – the two planets actually revolved about their common centre of mass like a lopsided dumbbell with a period of exactly one day. In this configuration, priori-Mars remained over the same place on the Earth – the Himalayan-Tibetan complex, with its north pole oriented toward the Earth.

'Firmament' explains how this configuration was established and maintained. The orbits of the three planets were in a unique resonance with one another for about 3,000 years. The capture and release of priori-Mars occurred again and again. It was this very repetitiveness that indelibly etched the cosmic events in the minds and souls of the people, stimulating the systematic record-keeping exemplified in the Rig Veda and Hindu myths, and less systematically in the myths of many other cultures. This

repetitiveness was also the origin of the notion of reincarnation in the eastern religions.

The tidal events that took place on priori-Mars during each dance encounter followed a similar pattern. First, all the surface and sub-surface waters in the northern hemisphere of priori-Mars were drawn toward its North Pole forming the outflow channels and the northern ocean, or Oceanus Borealis still visible on Mars. The tidal force of the Earth melted sub-surface rock and the magma was gradually drawn toward the surface through the ocean until it shot into the air. The lava hardened into vertical tubes which allowed the fragile structures to extend higher and higher, partially supported by the tidal force of Earth.

At this time seven large volcanoes roared into action which is why this number was viewed as mystical in the myths of many cultures. The most prominent feature, which took months to develop, was an enormous lava fountain at the north pole of priori-Mars, which comprised millions of lava tubes hardened on the outside. It extended 'down' toward the Earth and was the most prominent feature. This was the 'axis mundi', the axis of the world in ancient myth. It was surrounded by a number of concentric landmasses with water between them (Atlantis). This and lesser forms on the surface were anthropomorphised and called by different deity names. This great stage was called the 'firmament,' the 'astral plane', Olympus, Argo, Atlas, Horus, etc. These events were repeated to such a uniform degree that the Vedic hymns specifically divided each encounter into four 'kalpas' of gradually decreasing length, giving the progression of events in terms of the appearance of the bodies which were ejected from volcanic vents.

The bodies ejected from deep within priori-Mars comprise all Near Earth Asteroids while those containing aquifers comprise all short period comets. The storms of smaller rocks comprise all meteorites, the remaining meteor showers and the kilometre thick layer of regolith on the near side of the Moon. The entire northern third of Mars today is some seven kilometres below the Martian datum because of the vast mass of rock ejected into space during these encounters.

As the two planets revolved about one another, they frequently passed through alignments with the Moon. This caused enormous convulsions in the interior of priori-Mars, and many large hot rock bodies were shot into space from volcanic vents and volcanoes, carrying with them great storms of surface rocks, soil, atmospheric gases and water. Most of this fell to Earth but a large amount spiralled out and landed on the Moon, creating the regolith which covers its near side. Much material also went into various orbits around the Sun and comprised the Near Earth Asteroids, short period comets and all meteorites and were the cause of the meteor showers we see today.

The enormous mass lost during the entire 3,000 year Vedic period was so great that the entire northern plains are some seven kilometres below the datum level on Mars. As a result of these frequent convulsions, priori-Mars lost almost its entire complement of water and atmosphere to the Earth, leaving a dry, barren planet incapable of supporting life. Although it seems likely that a massive body like priori-Mars revolving about the Earth once a day would have had traumatic effects on the Earth, 100 generations of humans managed to survive.

Although enormous ocean tides were raised on both bodies, their orbits and spins were oriented in such a way that the tides on both bodies remained stationary. This configuration, once established, was one of equilibrium, or minimum energy dissipation, and therefore relatively quiescent. Nature favours such configurations. The greatest trauma for the Earth occurred during the engagement and disengagement of the two planets, the latter under the auspices of the close-approaching proto-Venus. At these times Earthquakes were continuous and tidal floods occurred. But these were not nearly as traumatic as the earlier close encounters of proto-Venus which destroyed most animal life on Earth.

Priori-Mars' mass was more than one tenth that of the Earth and it orbited about 33,000 kilometres (surface to surface distance) from the surface of the Earth. As a result, it produced an enormous stationary ocean tide 5,000 feet high inundating northern India. This radically changed the sea level around the Earth, lowering it in a circular band about 90 degrees from the Transhimalayas. The worst flooding occurred upon the priori-Mars approach. The most populous area which experienced the flooding and the lowered sea level was the Middle East.

Early flooding involved clear water, and was the origin of the Fertile Crescent. At the beginning of each dance encounter, the Mediterranean and Red seas were almost completely emptied as their water was drawn right across the land mass toward northern India. The residual water in them evaporated during the fourteen year encounters, leaving a layer of evaporites currently misinterpreted as the Messenian Salinity Crisis by geologists. At the same time, all of northern India up as far as the foothills of the Himalayas was inundated by some 5,000 feet of sea water.

The pyramids, tells and ziggurats of the Middle East were all built to provide their cultures with sanctuaries from these 30 years of floods.

The flooding in our scenario was more complex than the mere shuttling back and forth of the waters due to the arrival and departure of priori-Mars. Throughout the Vedic period there was also a continual increase in the sea level on Earth due to the influx of water from priori-Mars. In fact, the Earth was revitalized by the infusion, on a planetary scale, of all the volatiles on priori-Mars during the 3,000 year Vedic period. As a result priori-Mars is bone dry. Scientists ponder the question of where all the water went. Ironically, it makes up a part of every living thing on Earth, including the scientists.

The internal convulsions of priori-Mars were caused by sudden alignments of the pair with the Moon, or worse yet the combined effect of the Sun and Moon at the time of eclipses. After fifteen years of these convulsions, when priori-Mars was greatly weakened and compromised, Venus approached its closest point at the vernal equinox. The tidal forces of these nearby bodies drew its solid core right out of the planet, through what is now called the Valles Marineris (on Mars).

This solid core dropped into a lower orbit and circled the Earth to the east as the shell drifted away from the earth over the Middle East, but the two rejoined as they entered a planetary orbit for the next fifteen years. The rapid motion of the solid core was the origin of the myth that tells of the great speed of Mercury (Hermes).

The final release of Mars occurred when the solid iron core of priori-Mars came out through its lithosphere and was deflected by the Moon and Venus into the interior of the solar system. After interacting for approximately 300 years, the solid core, now called Mercury and Venus settled into their current orbits. That is why 'paleo-dynamacists' find a 'resonance' between Mercury and Venus, as well as the more obvious spin orbit coupling between Earth and Venus.

When the solid core failed to return, the lithosphere of priori-Mars drifted out to its current orbit and contracted into the small, low density 'planet' Mars. It left the Earth's vicinity in 687 BC. That is why the evidence of water on its surface seems fresh and why the surface rocks reveal the former presence of a global magnetic field, the residual of which has been found within Mercury.

The end of the Vedic period was signalled by this final breakaway of priori-Mars from the last dance encounter. In myth this coincided with the death of Romulus, dated about 687 BC. Romulus was not a human but was a name for priori-Mars or the largest feature on its surface. The end of the Vedic Period was noted by Jehovah, speaking through the prophet Isaiah:

'For as the new heavens and the new earth, which I will [do] make, shall remain before me, saith the Lord, so shall your seed and your name remain.'

Reproduced courtesy of John Ackerman

Basic differences between Velikovsky and Angiras

Velikovsky and Ackerman are both catastrophists; they both believe the solar system has experienced a radical change in the history of man during the last 5,000 years, and both believe the main perpetrators were Mars and Venus. Nevertheless, there are significant differences between their theories which I will now outline.

The V/A scenario proposed that a *'galactic traveller'* smashed into Jupiter which resulted in the birth of Venus. Velikovsky proposed the ejection or eruption of Venus from Jupiter. According to the V/A theory, Mars was originally on an inner orbit to that of Earth and was closer to the Sun than Earth. Due to cosmic chaos and the introduction of Venus, Mars was knocked into its present day orbit between Earth and Jupiter in a process that took thousands of years. There are also significant differences regarding dates. Ackerman believes the genesis of planetary chaos and the birth of Venus occurred some 6,000 years ago in 4,000 BC. Velikovsky places these events around 3,450 years ago, or 1450 BC.

The major difference between Velikovsky and Ackerman concerns Ackerman's proposal that Mercury was originally the core of Mars. This is an incredible hypothesis. Ackerman is proposing that the solid iron core of Mars was sucked out to become the planet we now know as Mercury. The evidence for this can be seen today in the form of the *Valles Marineris,* an enormous scar that dominates the Martian landscape. This, as Ackerman points out, is roughly the same diameter as Mercury. He follows this proposal with a wealth of scientific data all of which can be found in his books. Ackerman goes on to make a further astounding statement concerning the two gas giants, Saturn and Jupiter. He states that they are not gaseous giants but solid planets which appear as gas giants because of the high velocity winds encircling them. In other words, they are still in turmoil.

Ackerman's books have been available for a number of years and he has built up a small following. However, as with Velikovsky, he is still struggling to gain serious recognition, particularly in the world of academia. This opposition is surprising when you consider Ackerman's excellent knowledge of physics. Therefore, if Ackerman's proposals are to gain credibility we need to ask the following questions: Why haven't his theories been generally accepted by the academic world? Why isn't cosmic chaos common knowledge? If Mars loomed larger than the Moon and entered into regular 15-year 'dance encounters' with Earth, shouldn't astronomers be fully aware of this fact?

What of the outrageous proposal that Mars gave 'birth' to its solid iron core which became the planet Mercury? If such an event occurred in close proximity to Earth just a few millennia ago, why has it remained hidden and where is the evidence to support this proposal? Surely spectacular phenomena such as these would have been recorded by ancient cultures, and the common thread linking this 'genesis' would be easily recognisable today. Why would Ackerman, as a qualified physicist, spend ten years researching and writing two books that mainstream science dismisses without a second thought?

To answer these questions it is necessary to examine four basic reasons why catastrophe is struggling to gain acceptance. I will therefore list each reason briefly to provide a broad overview of the difficulties facing catastrophism before discussing them in more depth.

Ancient history

The testimony of ancient man does not speak of planetary chaos. If it did, this book would not be necessary and planetary chaos would be common knowledge.

1. Mythology

This will never be accepted as proof. There are too many grey areas, interpretations and variables.

3. Science

The ultimate judge and jury, science is largely being ignored; Ackerman clearly demonstrates this in his two books.

4. A Circular problem

Any scientific proof will always struggle to gain acceptance because history does not speak of planetary chaos and mythology is far too vague.

We will examine each of these points in more detail as this will help us understand why catastrophe has not gained substantial recognition.

IN SEARCH OF CHAOS

Ancient history

Fact: Recorded history only goes back 5,000 years.

Ancient history *is* ancient Egypt; this is generally accepted by historians because of the wealth of information available regarding this great civilisation. The god-kings, magnificent monuments, temples, tombs and hieroglyphs provide a sequential order of pharonic times which is used to measure all other ancient cultures.

Ancient Egypt spanned over 3,000 years beginning with King Narmer around 3100 BC and ending around 30 BC with the legendary Cleopatra. Throughout 3,000 years of history, where are the references to planetary chaos? It could be argued that chaos was shrouded by Egyptian myths and legends and was not historically recorded. For example, where is it recorded that Mars, Venus, Mercury and the Moon danced with Earth for several years at a time over several millennia? Where is the literal and visual corollary evidence of cosmic chaos, or the fusing of the written word and artwork with planetary chaos?

Velikovsky and Ackerman propose that planetary chaos occurred during historical times, in other words during pharonic times. Were such incredible events recorded solely by this magical world? Even though ancient cultures were naive in their understanding of the cosmos, we should be able to find some physical evidence of celestial chaos.

The planets Mars, Venus, Mercury and the Moon all bear the hallmarks of cosmic battles. They have all been pulverised by space debris including asteroids and comets. The Moon is also covered with space debris which in certain areas is several kilometres thick. Conventional wisdom believes this occurred billions of years ago but most catastrophists believe this bombardment occurred only a few thousand years ago. If catastrophists are correct, where is the written record? Where are the historical words and pictures depicting the planetary battles between Mars, Venus, Mercury and the Moon, or the accounts of the comets that collided with planets as well as with one another?

Most pharaohs were warrior kings; they fought many battles to keep Egypt's enemies at bay and conquered foreign lands to extend Egypt's mighty empire. Two of the most familiar warrior kings are Ramesses the Great and Tuthmosis III – the 'Napoleon of ancient Egypt'. Their legendary battles at Kadesh and Megiddo are amongst some of the most well-documented battles in the ancient world and they are gloriously celebrated many times on temple walls. The 'sacred' hieroglyphs detail how 'his majesty' gloriously defended Egypt's borders and vanquished the enemy. Accompanying these historical words are iconic images of the pharaoh with arm raised in readiness to 'smite the enemy'. This is an example of pictures and words celebrating a magnificent event – this is history. Yet, are we to believe that the battles of mere mortals took precedence over wars in the heavens? How could this be if the Egyptians believed in 'divine order'?

The Egyptian Sun god was Re. His most common symbol was a solar red disk which is found on almost every monument, tomb and temple wall throughout Egypt. It forms part of the hieroglyphic script and also appears as a pictorial representation of the Sun. Its prominence clearly reveals how highly revered the Sun was in ancient times, but what of the other planets? If Mars and Venus came so close to Earth that they loomed larger than the Sun, where was this recorded? Where is the disk of Mars, the god of war, or that of Venus, the goddess of love and beauty? Are we to believe the Egyptians represented the Sun but chose to ignore other celestial bodies which at times appeared larger than the Sun and even blotted it out completely? Wouldn't such dominance demand recognition and warrant recording in writing and pictures?

The heretic pharaoh Akhenaten and his beautiful and famous spouse Nefertiti ushered in a revolutionary period in Egyptian history which scholars have dubbed the Amarna Period. It was a period when Akhenaten began a new monotheistic religion by vanquishing all other gods in favour of one god called the Aten, or sun-disk. Akhenaten established his new religion by moving the capital of Egypt away from Thebes so he could build an entire city dedicated to the Aten in middle Egypt. He called this city Akhenaten, the Horizon of the Aten. At the peak of Akhenaten's reign, over 20,000 people lived in this city. This is undoubtedly history, but what of planetary chaos? Where are the records of Mars giving birth to Mercury? Wouldn't such events have led to the start of a new religion in honour of the newly formed Mercury? Why was such an event ignored in favour of a relatively simple renaming of the Sun as the Aten?

The fact is historical records do not mention planetary chaos. We will not find written or pictorial evidence of chaos amongst the remains of any ancient culture. The 'historical word' does not contain words or pictures depicting 3,000 years of chaos when Mars, Venus, Mercury and the Moon visited the Earth. It is therefore not surprising that recent catastrophe is vigorously dismissed.

Mythology

The non-existence of historical reference has been the primary reason why catastrophists have turned to the mythological world to prove their proposals. Velikovsky used the myths of the ancient world to propose that the Solar System was a smoking gun of recent chaos. Ackerman chose the relatively obscure Rig Veda and other ancient Hindu myths to support his proposed sequence of events. However, using mythology to prove planetary chaos is the main reason why catastrophe has not been accepted. Delving into mythology in an attempt to connect gods and their deeds with certain rogue planets or phenomena associated with catastrophe is a major obstacle that has existed since Velikovsky's *'Worlds in Collision'*. Unfortunately, as history fails to provide evidence for close proximity planet-gods, and as science refuses to consider the possibility of recent planetary chaos, catastrophists have looked to ancient mythology which is at the very core of their proposals.

This major obstacle is further exacerbated by the fact that, although all catastrophists believe chaos is shrouded in mythology, they each have their own interpretations of these myths. For example, Ackerman identifies the Egyptian god Re with the early Mars (Firmament p 138) and Isis with the Moon (ibid p 137), while others believe Isis or Hathor was Venus and Horus was Mars. Velikovsky, in his book *'World in Collision'* (p 174) proposes that Osiris was Saturn, Amun was Jupiter, and both Isis and Horus were Venus (p 175). Velikovsky also believed that certain gods were 'transferred' to different planets. For example:

'Ishtar of Assyria-Babylonia was in early times the name of the planet Jupiter; later it was transferred to Venus, Jupiter retaining the name of Marduk.'

'Baal, still another name for Jupiter, was an earlier name for Saturn, and later became the name of Venus.'

'Ishtar was first a male planet, subsequently becoming a female planet.'

(Velikovsky, 1950, p 175)

It has also been proposed that Earth was once a satellite of the planet Saturn and the Egyptian Re (or Ra) was not the Sun but the name given to this planet. For further information please see 'The Saturn Theory' by David Talbott – http://www.maverickscience.com/saturn.htm.
It is clear that the use of mythology to prove recent chaos will never be accepted. The deities of ancient times and the legends attributed to them are open to many interpretations and permutations, and it is not surprising that catastrophe is so vigorously dismissed.

Science

Can we look to science to provide proof of recent planetary chaos? This is a possibility, but unfortunately scientific evidence is largely ignored.

If we refer back to Ackerman, he begins his prologue with the following:

'The solar system is a smoking gun. The atmospheres, clouds, surface features and interiors of Jupiter, Venus, Mars, Mercury and the Moon are a direct result of recent planetary chaos. None of these bodies remotely resemble what planetary scientists publish as fact – open your mind to the real solar system.'

(Ackerman, Chaos, 1999, p 1)

Here Ackerman has condensed the very essence of planetary chaos and recent catastrophe into one short paragraph. Let us briefly examine the various abnormalities surrounding these planets from a catastrophe perspective. In doing so, we will pinpoint a series of explanations which have been ignored by scientists.

Jupiter

According to Ackerman, the evidence for Jupiter giving 'birth' to Venus is found in Jupiter's Great Red Spot.

Jupiter is the giant of the solar system. It is 1,300 times the size of Earth and is home to the Great Red Spot (GRS). First discovered in 1664, the GRS is the most distinctive feature of the planet and is large enough to fit two planets the size of Earth inside it. The currently accepted view is that the Great Red Spot is a high pressure storm that has been raging for over 300 years.

Ackerman believes the GRS is not an upper atmospheric storm. He proposes that this enormous feature was created 6,000 years ago when an enormous galactic traveller cataclysmically collided with Jupiter. The aftermath of this collision resulted in the birth of Venus.

'The Great Red Spot marks the top of a high speed jet of vaporised material rising from the impact creator out of which proto-Venus rebounded'

(Ackerman, 1999, p 37)

It is commonly believed that the GRS has been raging for over 300 years, although there is no real evidence to prove the duration of this 'storm'. Scientists quote 300 years simply because that is when it was first discovered. It is quite plausible that Ackerman is correct and this so-called storm could have been raging for thousands of years ever since it gave birth to Venus 6,000 years ago.

Assuming Jupiter is a solid planet as Ackerman proposes, this giant has been catastrophically impacted leaving behind an enormous crater. The GRS is a massive hole over twice the size of Earth which is still smouldering and churning out dust and debris. This activity is causing a 'tornado' of debris which is meandering to the top of Jupiter's upper atmosphere where it manifests as the Great Red Spot.

The GRS has remained at the same latitude because, unlike a normal storm which would move over the planet and eventually die out, it originates from and is constantly replenished by a fixed location on the 'solid' surface of Jupiter. This enormous crater is the source of all wind bands on the planet and is directly responsible for Jupiter's appearance. In fact, the GRS is shrinking because its source, the enormous impact crater on Jupiter, is slowly settling down. It seems obvious that Ackerman's theory, along with the physical evidence, makes more sense than the current 'storm' theory.

Venus – a new planet

The physical evidence that supports the theory that Venus is a hot new planet is overwhelming. When discussing the abnormalities surrounding Venus, Ackerman begins with the following paragraph:

'The currently accepted view of Venus as an ancient 'sister planet' of Earth fails to explain almost every one of its unique characteristics, among them; its slow retrograde rotation; its near resonant spin-orbit coupling with Earth; its high, uniform surface temperature and pressure; the super-rotation of its atmosphere; the surplus energy which its radiates; its lack of magnetic field; the totally volcanic surface; the uniform planet-wide cloud and haze layers; the illumination level at the surface; the high deuterium to hydrogen ratio; and the malfunction of the sensor systems on all the pioneer Venus probes as they fell through altitudes of 12 to 14 kilometres.' (ibid p 85).

Before probes were sent to Venus, it was believed it had a temperature similar to that of Earth. However, Velikovsky predicted the temperature would be far in excess of this due to the planet's recent birth from Jupiter. He was proved correct when space probe data revealed that Venus had a surface temperature of 864 degrees Fahrenheit (464 °C). The surface of Venus is actually hotter than the surface of Mercury despite it being nearly twice as far from the Sun. In fact, its surface is hot enough to melt lead!

In attempts to explain this surprising abnormality, scientists have erroneously invented the 'green house effect' which we also know as global warming. Ackerman suggests this is very poor science as the real explanation is very simple.

Venus is the hottest planet in the solar system because it is a new planet which is still in the process of cooling down. It gives out far more energy that it receives from the Sun because it is a boiling hot cauldron of molten magma. It has no solid core and no magnetic field because it is a newly formed planet.

All abnormalities surrounding Venus can therefore be explained. They are linked to its recent birth from Jupiter and the fact that it has yet to fully join the rest of the planets in our solar system.

Mars

Mars was once a planet similar to Earth – it is now a desolate, reddish, frozen orb with no sign of life – yet!

Mars is the fourth rock from the Sun. More is known about Mars than any other planet in the solar system apart from Earth. It is generally accepted (and recent probes confirm this) that at some time in the past, Mars was a 'living' planet replete with an atmosphere, land masses, mountains, oceans and rivers. It had a magnetic field, an invisible protective bubble, driven by a solid iron core. In effect, Mars was similar to Earth, only half the size.

According to the current scientific view, Mars underwent a cataclysmic upheaval which led to its present desolate state. Its dynamo came to a grinding halt resulting in the failure of its protective magnetic shield. Its once great oceans, atmospheric gases and other volatiles have all but disappeared. Mars has the largest volcano in the solar system, the Olympus Mons, as well as thousands of others volcanoes. This evidence points to a time when Mars was systematically torn apart to become a dead, frozen planet.

Scientists believe the demise of Mars occurred billions of years ago whereas catastrophists believe Mars was torn apart in the last 5,000 years. Catastrophe theory states that recent encounters with the Earth and Venus (and the Moon and Mercury) devastated Mars and culminated when the iron core was sucked out to form the planet Mercury.

Evidence for the birth of Mercury from Mars

The Valles Marineris is an enormous gash on the face of Mars. The Grand Canyon is minute when compared to this great chasm. Just as the Great Red Spot dominates the face of Jupiter, the Valles Marineris, at 4,500 km long and 7 km deep, is a dominant feature of the Martian landscape and dwarfs all other such features in the solar system. Planetary scientists have yet to establish a satisfactory explanation for this enormous scar. However, Ackerman has put forward the incredible proposal that it was formed by the extraction of the solid iron core which formed the planet Mercury.

The most fundamental piece of evidence Ackerman points to in support of this theory concerns the length. At 4878 km long, the diameter of Mercury is virtually identical to the length of the Valles Marineris and Ackerman insists this is no mere coincidence. Further evidence shows that the density of Mercury is made up of a disproportionately large iron core covered by rocky space debris. Ackerman's evidence can therefore be summed up as follows: Mars is a planet which is missing an iron core, and Mercury is a planet which used to be the core of a much larger planet.

As a physicist, Ackerman comprehensively covers the science of how the solar system is a smoking gun of very recent events. He uses scientific data collated from planetary probes and, rather than twisting them to conform to the conventional understanding of our solar system, he takes them at face value. For those of you who are interested in scientific facts and figures, I refer you to Ackerman's excellent books.

Circular problem

Planetary chaos will struggle to gain acceptance unless it can be proved that it was recorded in ancient times. Currently, catastrophists look to ancient myths to support their theories but unfortunately mythology is not a valid source of historical data, hence the circular problem.

Catastrophists believe that one day science will support catastrophe and Velikovsky will be vindicated. They are certain that future scientific advances will persuade scientists that the Solar System has undergone a very recent catastrophic upheaval. The irony is, regardless of any future scientific discoveries, the theory for recent cosmic chaos will not be accepted due to the lack of ancient evidence. This is an important point and a major hurdle for catastrophists.

It is impossible to use ancient mythology to provide evidence of what occurred and when in relation to the ancient cosmos. That is why mainstream science will never be drawn into a debate regarding recent catastrophe; history makes no mention of planetary chaos and mythology is regarded as fiction created by ancient cultures to explain the world around them. It is obvious why catastrophe is vigorously dismissed from a mythological, historical and scientific perspective. In fact, it seems that catastrophe has hit a brick wall!

Is there a way forward?

I am a committed catastrophist. I believe Velikovsky was absolutely correct in his basic premise of recent cosmic chaos. I am also certain that Ackerman, in furthering Velikovsky's research, has come close to establishing what actually occurred. This proposal states that Mars and Venus visited Earth numerous times which resulted in the Martian core being sucked out to become the planet Mercury.

Having examined the proposals put forward by Velikovsky or Ackerman, what can I offer to improve the current understanding of cosmic chaos? Should I invent another extraordinary theory, or rehash old theories and claim them as my own? Could I present a new interpretation of an old myth? No, because I believe Velikovsky was a genius of the magnitude of Albert Einstein and I have no desire to detract from his great works. To consider my own interpretations as more valid than established theory would weaken the whole concept of catastrophe and encourage further ridicule. However, I would like to propose a theory which proves that planetary chaos was indeed recorded by ancient civilisations – a theory which is both unconventional and outrageous. To begin this extraordinary journey, I will briefly recap the order of cosmic events which will form the basis of this theory.

ANCIENT HISTORY IS COSMIC CHAOS

Overview of Cosmic Chaos

Approximately 5,200 years ago (3,200 BC), the solar system differed considerably from today. The planets Venus and Mercury did not exist and Earth had no Moon. Mars was a lush green planet replete with land masses, oceans and an atmosphere. Mars harboured abundant life (intelligent life, but that's another story!) and was a replica of Earth, only half the size.

Cosmic chaos began when a giant interloper entered our solar system and smashed into the largest planet, Jupiter. The force exerted upon Jupiter was enough to blast the Earth into smithereens many times over. It caused an apocalyptic explosion which resulted in the birth of Venus as well as unimaginable quantities of space debris and a Dark Age on Earth.

Among the debris was a small body we now know as our Moon. Our nearest celestial neighbour was born from debris blasted out from Jupiter only 5,000 years ago. The evidence for the initial cataclysmic explosion on Jupiter is still with us today in the form of Jupiter's Great Red Spot, erroneously believed to be a raging storm, and the asteroid belt which is a rocky band of debris between the orbits of Mars and Jupiter.

Shortly after its cataclysmic birth from Jupiter, Venus disturbed Mars from its once stable orbit and together they were slowly drawn in towards Earth. Mars and Venus took on highly erratic and elliptical orbits close to and in the vicinity of Earth's orbit which led to hundreds of encounters with Earth. Occasionally they orbited around Earth although they never actually collided with it. This 'celestial dance' lasted for 3,000 years and became a perennial cycle of death and rebirth as Mars and Venus moved back and forth to Earth

Mars was slowly and systematically transformed from a living planet to a frozen, desolate rock. Venus, which began life as a scalding hot, cosmic ball of molten magma similar in size to Earth, spent millennia cooling down. The surface temperature of Venus is a still a scorching 800 degrees Fahrenheit. In short, Mars spent 3,000 years battling itself to death as Venus cooled down.

After approximately 2,000 years of encounters with Earth, the gravitational and electromagnetic forces exerted upon Mars become so huge that something monumental happened. The tidal forces of Earth and Venus combined and literally tore out the heart of Mars. Its solid iron core, its working dynamo, was sucked out to become the planet we know as Mercury. A second 'glorious sun-disk of all lands' was born! However, Mercury's life as a glaring Sun was very short-lived due to its relatively small size. It rapidly cooled down after approximately 17 years and appeared as a hazy, reddish disk.

The evidence for the genesis of Mercury is still visible today in the form of the Valles Marineris. The extraction of the core of Mars signalled the beginning of the end of cosmic chaos. We can liken these events to a cosmic elastic band which snapped, allowing the planets to move away from the Earth and settle into relatively stable orbits around the Sun. Finally, Mercury joined Mars and Venus in their celestial encounters with Earth. All three planets moved back and forth in relation to Earth in an erratic and unpredictable cycle of death and rebirth which lasted a further 700 to 800 years. Planetary bodies were granted 'life' as they approached Earth, only to 'die' as they moved away to become gigantic stars.

The Moon now took centre stage and, assisted by Mars and Venus, it was slowly pulled into orbit around the Earth. Initially the orbit was erratic until it settled into its recognisable 28 _ day monthly cycle in a process that took several hundred years. Cosmic chaos stabilized and the planets slowly migrated to their current orbits. Mercury and Venus became the first and second rocks from the Sun respectively, while Earth became the third and Mars the fourth.

Cosmic chaos lasted 3,000 years. Mars and Venus were the main perpetrators as they moved back and forth to Earth. After approximately 2,800 years, they were joined by the Moon and Mercury. After the birth of Mercury, the planets migrated to their current orbits, leaving the Moon to become Earth's permanent companion.

The solar year prior to cosmic chaos was 360 days. After 3,000 years of cosmic chaos it was extended to 365 _ days as a direct result of Earth taking on extra baggage in the form of the Moon. The Moon fractionally slowed Earth's path around the Sun, thus allowing it to spin on its axis for an extra 5 _ days before completing a solar year.

Having established when and how these incredible events occurred, I will now prove that this information was actually recorded by our ancestors. I am not referring to hidden or encrypted messages imbedded in obscure mythological legends _ the evidence for cosmic chaos is staring us in the face via ancient history.

You may be wondering where these events are recorded. Where is it written that Mars and Venus visited Earth numerous times to dominate the heavens for thousands of years? Where does it say that this original divine couple were later joined by Mercury and the moon?

The key to cosmic chaos can be found within the 'bizarre world' of the ancient Egyptians. It is centred on the pinnacle of Egyptian society, the divine monarchy of ancient Egypt – the god kings or 'living gods'. This is the crux of the theory. The God King Scenario (GKS) proposes that in the first instance the monarchs of ancient Egypt were guises of the planets Mars, Venus, Mercury and the Moon each and every time they visited Earth; in the second instance they were represented on Earth via human doubles.

The Egyptians deified everything. From simple phenomena such as moisture (Tefnut) to our perennial Sun (Re) and the stars inhabiting the night sky, all were considered divine. The planets in chaos were no exception. Mars and Venus, who were later joined by the Moon and Mercury, entered into hundreds of encounters with Earth. Each time they approached Earth, they were perceived as divine entities. Yet these were not immortal, cosmological deities like Re or Amun, or the mothering goddesses Hathor and Isis. The planet-gods were mortal and became 'living gods' as they approached Earth, only to die as they moved away to become gigantic stars. However, this was only a temporary death because they were actually being transported to the next world. Although the planets were mortal, in the hierarchy of the divine cosmos they were awarded the second-highest accolade (the first being immortal godship). They were considered to be 'divine' kings and queens who were sent down from heaven by universal gods to rule the Earth. They lived, died, fought great battles and performed wonderful acts as the true royal family of ancient Egypt.

Ancient Egypt was a male dominated world. Mars, Mercury and the Moon were perceived as 'warrior' kings while Venus was regarded as the perennial 'passive' queen or 'king's great wife'. Mars, Mercury and the Moon ventured closer to Earth than Venus – a location that would see them take on the distinctly male trait of stirring up incalculable amounts of space debris while Venus, a beautiful and loyal queen, watched from afar.

The pharaohs reigned over Earth for varying lengths of time which accurately paralleled the chronological and historical record. When they dominated the heavens and ruled the Earth, they were given the familiar names and titles we recognise today. Ramesses the Great, Tutankhamun, and Akhenaten were names given to Mars; Tuthmosis III ('Napoleon' of ancient Egypt) and Horemheb were names given to the Moon; Nefertiti, Nefertari, Hatshepsut and Cleopatra were names given to Venus.

Mercury was initially born as a golden 'second Sun' ('disk of the Sun') referred to by the Egyptians as the Aten. However, after a short period of time, Mercury joined the divine royal bloodline of pharonic kings and was given the name Seti after Seth, the god of chaos. This is just a sample of pharonic names as history reveals there were at least 170 (possibly 300) pharaohs and just as many queens. They were first and foremost names given to planets sent down by the gods to rule the Earth. As such, they are all guises of planetary bodies which inhabited the skies some 4,000 years ago.

I am not merely proposing that the planets were the true god-kings and queens of ancient Egypt. The scale of the proposed chaos would have produced incalculable amounts of space debris such as asteroids, comets, dust and gasses. Everything was observed and deified including Moon sized bodies, asteroids and comets which orbited the planets. They were regarded as nobles, concubines, priests, priestesses, viziers, scribes, fan bearers, overseers and other dignitaries. The remaining space debris which littered the cosmos was perceived as the vile enemy of the monarchy and of Egypt itself. This evil debris threatened to blot out the Sun and bring the universe into chaos (Seth).

It was the role of the warrior god-king-planets of Mars, Mercury & the Moon to maintain 'divine order' (*ma'at*) by 'battling' up the space debris in an attempt to keep darkness and chaos at bay. This was a perennial conflict between good and evil that lasted for the duration of pharonic Egypt. Ironically, it was the godly planets that created the enemy in the first place.

We need to look among the dust, gasses and other solar phenomena to find the true 'physical' identity of many of the mythical 'sky-gods' who played such a prominent role in the lives of the ancient Egyptians. Sky gods such as Amun, Horus, Osiris, Seth, Isis and Hathor were not fictitious gods invented to explain the natural world; they were real, physical gods attributable to phenomena created as a direct result of cosmic chaos. These 'sky-gods' are no longer visible because chaos has now subsided and the phenomena attributed to certain deities is no longer visible.

The exploits of the 'astral monarchs' are meticulously recorded in history – in the glorious images and 'sacred' hieroglyphs adorning tombs and temple walls throughout pharonic Egypt. Every hieroglyph and image, right down to the smallest artefact, points to a time when the planets Mars and Venus (and later Mercury and the Moon) dominated the heavens as pharonic kings and queens. Hieroglyphs provided details of their births, deaths, legendary battles, marriages, coronations, elaborate state visits and their interaction with the universal sky gods. They also recorded the actions and movements of the planets as well as 3,000 years of cosmic chaos and have virtually no connection with events on Earth.

The bodies of numerous Pharaohs and their queens survive to this day and rest peacefully in the Cairo Museum. However, if these great Egyptians were guises or names given to planetary bodies, who is it that lies in these pharonic tombs? They were mortal 'doubles' _ humans chosen to represent and interpret the will of the planetary gods because they were considered to be 'at one' with astral bodies. These humans were believed to be the incarnation of divine astral kings and queens.

According to ancient Egyptian custom, when a planet such as Mars descended from heaven, it was perceived as a god-king on Earth. It was believed that such bodies were transposed entities of royalty and a human king was therefore chosen to be 'at one' with and act as a human manifestation of this planet. This concept also applied to

Venus, Mercury and the Moon _ each and every time they visited Earth they were represented with human doubles. The Egyptians believed that everyone was born with an astral twin or soul _ a real physical double that would unite with them at death before undertaking a perilous journey to a life of eternity among the stars

Although believed to be 'at one' with the astral bodies, the mortal kings and queens played no part in celestial events but were mere puppets to a far higher order. They were pawns in a world dominated by cosmic chaos. The true divine rulers of ancient Egypt were the planetary 'god-kings' who were 'rulers of everything encircled by the Sun'. They literally held the power of life and death in their hands and their very location deemed them intermediaries between heaven and Earth – gods among gods.

It was the kingly planets that had a direct line to the numerous sky gods and not humans. The ancient Egyptians could only follow and record the doctrine of Heaven, which is exactly what they did. By using 'sacred hieroglyphs', the Egyptians meticulously carved the life-history of the astral kings and queens for posterity on every tomb and temple wall throughout Egypt – this is the history that is staring us in the face!

The implications of my proposal are incredible and I am under no illusion that proving it will be a daunting task. However, the beauty of such a theory is that I will be using history to prove it. I will use accepted and recorded history as well as the occasional ancient myth (given the subject matter, this is unavoidable). My aim is to turn history upside down by using the most fascinating of ancient civilisations – Egypt. I will take the history of this great nation and transfer it to the heavens above. I will translate it as the Egyptians understood it which is how it was meant to be understood. I will show that pharonic Egypt actually recorded cosmic chaos. I will present a time when the planets Mars, Venus, Mercury and the Moon (and space debris) played havoc with the Earth.

History from the birth of civilization (approximately 3100 BC) through to the birth of Christ is all part of the legacy of cosmic chaos. Scholars have been unaware of the existence of this evidence because they were looking for answers to the mysteries of the past at ground level instead of listening to the ancient Egyptians and looking to the skies. A new world dawns in the heavens filled with astral kings and queens who lived and died and interacted with a myriad of enigmatic deities. This is the world of celestial pharonic Egypt and cosmic chaos.

Clarification of terms

Chaos

You will become aware I occasionally write 'chaos' in parenthesis. This is not a 'get out of jail' card. The reason for doing this is that cosmic chaos comes with many variables and it is impossible to cover every aspect. Therefore 'chaos' is merely allowing for variants.

Moon

I will occasionally refer to the Moon as a planet. I know the Moon is not a planet, but it is easier to refer to the four main perpetrators of chaos as planets and negate the need for constantly having to say: 'the planets and the Moon'.

Chronology out

The currently accepted chronology of ancient Egypt is inaccurate and therefore the entire chronology of ancient history is incorrect. For this reason I will take my dates from the CIAS website which was inspired by Velikovsky and is a serious study of the chronology of ancient history.

Any serious student of ancient history will realise there is something drastically wrong with the chronology of our ancient past. As the prime objective of this book is the GKS, I have formulated the dates myself by taking a lead from the CIAS website. Although you may disagree, many of the dates and the currently accepted chronology of the pharaohs are wrong and the timescales should be greatly decreased. When giving dates I will often use the abbreviation RC. This translates as 'revised chorology,' and will be discussed later.

THE TESTIMONY OF ANCIENT EGYPT CARVED IN STONE

Identifications

The GKS proposes that the monarchy of ancient Egypt were primary names given to Mars, Venus, the Moon and Mercury each and every time they visited Earth. However, attempting to identify numerous kings and queens with respective astral bodies is a complicated task. The fact is, the true planetary identification of many monarchs may never be known. This was especially true towards the end of cosmic chaos when Mars gave birth to numerous astral bodies. I have used a circular format drawn from certain synchronical points in Egyptian history as well as my own sequential order of events (and common sense) to explain the order of events in simple terms.

Mars and Venus were the original perpetrators of chaos and, because of their attributes, Mars was always perceived as a king while Venus was a devoted queen. Using my time frame, Mars and Venus reigned for approximately 2,000 years before the Moon and Mercury appeared. Therefore, for the best part of pharonic Egypt, we will associate the kings with Mars and the queens with Venus. The possibility of large rogue moons ruling Earth for certain periods cannot be ruled out, but this doesn't alter the fact that Mars and Venus ruled virtually unopposed for at least two millennia.

After approximately 2,000 years, at around 1000 BC RC, the New Kingdom was born and events became more complicated. The Earth slowly captured the Moon and joined the royal bloodline to rule as pharaoh many times. Around the 7\th century BC, Mercury was 'born' from Mars. This was a major synchronical point which can be attributed to an enigmatic period in Egyptian history and which scholars have dubbed the *Amarna period*. According to current thinking, it was a time when the Egyptians, in their 'infinite wisdom', decided to rename the Sun the Aten. This theory is absurd! The entire period concerns the birth of Mercury from Mars and has nothing to do with the Sun. Mercury began life as the Aten and rapidly joined the royal bloodline and was named and renamed many times over as pharaoh of Egypt.

It is difficult to identify Mercury, Mars and the Moon in relation to certain kings and I have therefore used logic to establish identities. I have drawn on lunar gods and Mercury's migration towards the Sun with Venus to help in my identifications. For example, historians believe that Ramesses II had over 200 children. At this time, after Mars had given birth to Mercury, the red planet continued to give birth to hundreds of smaller planetary bodies. These were the children of Mars, or more specifically the children of Ramesses II. I have reached this conclusion by a process of elimination. As a solid iron core, Mercury could not give birth. As a lump of rock, the Moon could not give birth. Venus, a planet in the process of cooling down, could not give birth. However, the systematic tearing apart of Mars, which was transformed from a 'working planet' into a desolate shell, led to the expulsion of tons of material which blasted out into space to become the numerous children of Ramesses II. Simple logic therefore leads to a more accurate identification.

Throughout this book I identify certain pharaohs with their respective bodies without an accompanying explanation. For example, Ramesses is occasionally referred to as a facet of Mars, Tuthmosis as the Moon and Mercury as the Aten. This is because some aspects of my theory need to be made clear before I can explain these identifications. Therefore it is necessary to mention certain pharaohs together with their respective planets.

Basic Purpose

The basic purpose of this book is to prove that the god-kings were first and foremost planets in chaos. I will explain the concept of 'double' as it existed between planetary bodies and humans and will identify where these details were written down in history.

Hieroglyphs (Greek: 'sacred carved letters')

Hieroglyphs are the testimony of ancient man – the uncorrupted word of history – the uncorrupted word of planetary chaos!

Earlier I made a bold statement and stated that planetary chaos is staring us in the face via ancient history. We therefore need to look at the method used to record ancient history – the written word of the Egyptians or 'sacred' hieroglyphs.

If you read a book or watch a TV documentary on ancient Egypt, or visit the Egyptian section at many of the world's museums (or even visit Egypt itself), you will immediately become aware of hieroglyphs. This is the Greek word for sacred writings, referred to by the Egyptians as *mdju netjer* meaning 'words of the gods'. Hieroglyphs were a system of writing that used recognisable objects such as animals, men, beasts, flowers, mountains, the Sun and other items drawn from the Egyptian world.

The whole range of human experience was encapsulated in hieroglyphs which were read left to right, right to left, horizontally and vertically. Animals, birds, people, serpents, and fish were drawn in profile in the same direction and this told the reader how to read the line. Hieroglyphs, as well as mummies, tombs and statues, were used to assist the deceased to the after life and were a vital part of the process of achieving immortality. Magical spells were placed on the bandages of mummies, the walls of pyramids and on coffins as it was believed they contained magical powers. For example, the Egyptians believed that whatever was written on a coffin would come true.

It wasn't until the decipherment of the Rosetta Stone (which is currently in the British Museum) by Jean-Francois Champollion early in the 19th century that Egyptologists were able to understand this script. Described as the single greatest event in the development of Egyptology, Champollion's work provided the key to understanding hieroglyphics and for the first time in 1,500 years these ancient voices could be heard. It led to a better understanding of ancient Egypt and a clearer understanding of the purpose of these ancient inscriptions.

Hieroglyphs provided the key to unlocking the mystery of the pharaohs and their gods and historians were finally able to establish a chronological order of events. They established accurate dates for each monarch's reign and revealed every aspect of the lives of the pharaohs. It was possible to discover details concerning the legendary victories of god-kings such as Ramesses and Tuthmosis. It enabled the identification of many gods and goddesses and brought the glorious images to life in a bizarre world of strange beliefs and weird customs. The history and intellectual achievements of the ancient Egyptians could now be examined in a new light.

It is interesting to note that the Egyptians were accustomed to viewing hieroglyphs as something 'sacred' which contained the history and power of the gods. This is because hieroglyphs were believed to be 'sacred letters' and 'words of the gods'. However, this does not explain which gods were being referred to in these inscriptions. The Egyptian world consisted of a myriad of deities; were these eloquently carved symbols the words of gods such as Amun, Hathor, Isis or Osiris? After all, these deities were among the principal gods of ancient Egypt and it seems reasonable to assume the 'words of the gods' were attributed to them. Further evidence can be gleaned from the glorious images of deities which accompany the hieroglyphs on every tomb and temple wall throughout Egypt.

Having considered the purpose of hieroglyphs, we are left with a problem. Egyptian gods and goddesses were essentially 'made up' entities and were invented to explain the universe and Egypt's place in it. Therefore, hieroglyphs are the words of fictitious deities. Surely this undermines them and renders them mythical in content.

The implications of this are incredible. Ancient history *is* ancient Egypt and the very foundation upon which Egypt is built is based on the translation of the sacred Egyptian script. Are we to believe that ancient history is built on the words of mythical gods? If ancient history was based on a script that was considered to be the 'words of the gods', how should this script be viewed if the gods were fictitious?

I believe there is an alternative explanation as to why the Egyptians considered hieroglyphs as sacred. The GKS proposes that hieroglyphs are real time 'recordings' of divine events above. Hieroglyphs are the 'words of the gods' because they are the historical account of a 3,000-year period of planetary chaos.

As Mars and Venus (and later the Moon & Mercury) approached Earth complete with entourage, they were naturally perceived as divine royal kings and queens. They lived and died and presided over the mortal Egyptians from different locations in the heavens. Sometimes they appeared to traverse in Re's solar barque as they tracked the Sun across the sky. They even married and had 'children', which were chunks of molten lava thrown out into space. They battled to clear the heavens of celestial debris, a role that saw them as upholders of divine order (*ma'at*) as they fought the forces of evil (Seth). From this astral location they interacted with very real sky gods such as Amun, Hathor, Isis and Osiris.

Such divine events could not be ignored. An array of 'sky' deities accommodating planetary kings and queens had to be appeased and placated. They demanded representation and their glorious deeds had to be recorded. After all, they held the power of life or death in their hands and therefore dictated whether one lived or died – they were upholders of divine order!

Ancient Egyptians appeased their gods by meticulously carving entire celestial scenes in stone thereby preserving history for all eternity – and so hieroglyphs were born! These sacred carvings recorded the deeds of the divine throughout 3,000 years of celestial chaos and a religion developed based on the 'words of the gods'. It is no coincidence that sacred hieroglyphs appeared at the birth of planetary chaos around 3200 BC, when the gods came down from heaven to take kingship on Earth for the first time. Similarly the glorious pictures and reliefs which accompanied the sacred script were images of battles, state visits and scenes of monarchs making offerings to the gods.

Deciphering celestial chaos

Just as the eloquent script of the Egyptians is the written record of events in the heavens, I also believe that many of the symbols were invented as a direct result of observations of celestial phenomena. In other words, the real world of celestial chaos dictated the form, shape and colour of the symbols. This was a distinctly symbolic representation because the ancient Egyptians did not understand the science behind these natural events. Celestial phenomena were therefore encapsulated in things drawn from the natural world of the Egyptians.

There were hundreds of thousands of cometary bodies of all sizes inhabiting the heavens during celestial chaos. The larger ones played host to the royal court as viziers and overseers while some of the smaller ones took on the attributes of a snake in the form of a nucleus and spiralling tail. On many occasions these bodies meandered across the heavens and the Egyptians, who didn't understand such phenomena, regarded them as divine snakes. Because of their threatening demeanour, they were also depicted as dangerous snakes. It is possible that this led to the invention of the 'horned viper' hieroglyph symbol.

Egyptians believed that hieroglyph names for gods, people and animals were capable of causing harm to their living entities and so hieroglyphs were linked to events in the heavens. For this reason many of the signs included in pyramid and coffin texts were deliberately abbreviated to neutralise the potential dangers within the royal tomb. For example, the horned viper was depicted cut in half to negate its deadly power which made the king's journey to the afterlife less hazardous. The ancient Egyptians were also convinced that the awesome potential of 'sacred words' was due to the chaotic universe where the divine held the power of life and death. By extension, the words of the gods were perceived to have special powers.

Hieroglyphic script first appeared during the birth of Pharonic Egypt with little more than 1,000 symbols. This number remained constant for over 2,000 years when, after two millennia, a further 4,000 symbols were created. It is believed that this increase indicated a change in the material culture of the ancient Egyptians. However, I would question this and suggest additional symbols were invented because celestial events intensified. It is no coincidence that these additional sacred symbols appeared prior to, during and after my proposed time frame for the birth of Mercury (Aten) around the 8th century BC (New Kingdom). It is reasonable to assume that this event produced an enormous amount of new celestial phenomena. As with the birth of chaos some 2,000 years earlier, all new phenomena had to be represented and therefore new sacred symbols were invented. It is important to note that although a total of more than 6,000 hieroglyph signs have been identified, the Egyptians used a core selection of basic signs.

Hieroglyphic script was not the only script to be used by the Egyptians. There were three other scripts: Hieratic, Demotic and Coptic. Hieratic, which translates as 'sacred', was a simplified form of hieroglyphics and was the first stage in the laborious process of creating the script. First, the hieratic text was written by one man before it was converted to hieroglyphics by a second man. This was followed by the sculpture as a third man followed the outlines of the first two scribes. Then a fourth scribe checked the sculpture to ensure there were no mistakes. Finally a fifth man, the painter, brought the hieroglyphs to life by adding colour. Coptic was introduced with the advent of Christianity towards the end of pharonic Egypt. In fact, the Coptic script sounded the death-knell for the hieroglyphic script and is of little interest here.

Demotic

The demotic script was a cursive (joined) form of writing derived from the Egyptian hieratic script, which was also a cursive form of hieroglyphic. Demotic comes from the Greek word 'demos' meaning 'for the people'. This was the writing of the people and, as an everyday form of writing, was used for items such as grocery or laundry lists, or receipts for the purchase of animals etc. It was also used for writing business, legal and religious documents and its obvious advantage was it was far quicker to write than hieroglyphics. The most famous example of demotic is the Rosetta Stone which is inscribed with texts in the hieroglyphic script as well as Greek and demotic. It first appeared in the 7th century BC and was one of the keys to deciphering ancient Egyptian scripts.

To summarise, hieroglyphs were the recordings of a chaotic sky dominated by divine planetary kings and queens and their gods _ Mars and Venus and later the Moon and Mercury; they had little to do with events on Earth. The celestial realm of divine kings, queens and their gods had to be placated. The gods naturally took precedence over events on Earth because the events above dictated the events below which led to the invention of hieroglyphs. These pictorial symbols were drawn from celestial events (albeit symbolically) and were meticulously carved on the walls of temples, tombs and great monuments, some reaching out to the heavens with their gigantic columns. This made sure the 'words of the gods' were immortalised for posterity.

Hieroglyphs were exclusively for the divine which is why they were considered sacred. For example, if they spoke of a pharaoh vanquishing the enemy in the north, this referred to a planetary body 'battling up' or hoovering up space debris in the northern skies. If the script referred to a battle in the south, east or west, then the same reasoning would apply. It referred to a planetary body in the act of upholding 'divine order' by vanquishing space debris in these locations. The script may have referred to a king or queen making a state visit to the south or another location; this was a planet performing the very rare action of downing his weapons to make a visit to the south. It is a similar situation with 'offering' scenes where the monarchy made offerings to the 'sky' gods, or coronation scenes where the monarchy interacted with the gods – these were actual recordings of real events in the heavens.

There will be many more references to 'sacred' hieroglyphs throughout this book because this is the history upon which the foundation of my theory rests.

A TWILIGHT WORLD

Re (Ra) the Sun god - the 'red' Sun god

In order to understand my proposal concerning the planets and hieroglyphs, you will need to strip yourself of all learned facts regarding the workings of the solar system and ancient history. You must transport yourself back in time to a world dominated by planets that appeared larger than the Sun. This was a time when Mars, Venus, Mercury and the Moon plus entourage ruled the heavens as divine kings and queens for an incredible 3,000 years. Apart from the Moon, these planets no longer dominate the heavens or preside over Earth. The divine royal family of ancient Egypt are now mere specks of light in the night sky or, as the Egyptians believed, divine stars in the 'kingdom of Osiris'.

Because of their ascension to the heavens, we are unable to see the planets as the ancients saw them. We no longer see Mars as Ramesses in his dutiful roll of upholding divine order by 'smiting the enemy' or battling up space debris. Venus, as the devoted and loving queen Nefertari, no longer stands by the side of this 'ruler of rulers'. There is nothing remaining to physically reference, no red orbs tracking a path across the heavens day and night. However, the Moon is one celestial object that played a very significant part in 3,000 years of planetary chaos. As our nearest companion, it is still clearly visible, although it has undergone many incredible changes.

I believe the Moon is a recent addition to our solar system and was captured by Earth only 4,000 years ago. This incredible capture, which was assisted by Mars and Venus, took hundreds of years and saw the Moon take on many guises and different names. Its behaviour in the skies was totally erratic and unpredictable until it settled down into its regular monthly cycle. Therefore the main perpetrators of chaos – Mars, Venus, Mercury and the Moon – have only recently settled down into their regular and predictable cycles and their current appearances and orbits bear little resemblance to those of millennia ago.

There is one glaring orb that hasn't altered its eternal path across the heavens or changed its shape and size. It is our one source of light, energy and heat and it appears today just as it did millennia ago. Of course I am referring to the Sun. Its perennial cycle across the heavens hasn't changed in 4,000 years. It rises in the east, arcs across the sky and sets in the west in a very predictable and measurable 24-hour cycle. As the Sun was present throughout periods of planetary chaos, it is the one planetary body we cannot ignore when discussing the GKS.

There are other points to consider regarding the Sun such as the close and personal relationship that existed between the pharaohs and the Sun god, Re. The Egyptian monarchy believed they were related to the Sun and the ubiquitous title 'sa-re' means 'son of Re' or 'son of the Sun god'. From the middle kingdom onwards all pharaohs were bestowed with this title. The throne names of the kings also refer to the Sun god Re and include 'appearing like Re', 'eternal like Re' and 'chosen by Re'. They are devotional tiles which appear many times for numerous pharaohs.

There is something unusual about the way the Egyptians represented our nearest star which is incredibly revealing when considered alongside planetary chaos. It is a perfect example of how the most obvious evidence can be overlooked. It shows how childlike observations can lead to incredible discoveries which irrefutably prove that planetary chaos is reaching out to us from the distant past.

We have established that the Sun in ancient times was referred to as the god Re (or Ra) and we can confirm this identification with some common epithets.

'Re (Ra) was the Egyptian sun god'
(http://www.touregypt.net/featurestories/re.htm)

Countless hymns extol him as the divine power opening each day.

'Homage to thee, O thou who risest in the horizon as Ra, thou restest upon law unchangeable and unalterable.'

'Thou passest over the sky, and every face watcheth thee and thy course, for thou hast been hidden from their gaze. Thou dost show thyself at dawn and at eventide day by day.'

(From the pyramid texts)

'Re is the great light who shinest in the heavens.'

'The lord of all lands ... praise Re when he riseth at the beginning of each day.'

Re is the 'great light who shinest in the heavens ... Thou art glorious by reason of thy splendours.'

Re was typically represented as a sun-disk, or as a falcon-headed man wearing a red sun-disk on his head. This imagery points to the god's solar character. With epithets such as 'opening the day', 'light', 'shinest' and 'lord of all lands', we are presented with traits which are consistent with the life-giving properties of the Sun we experience today. This makes perfect sense, until we turn our attention to Re's most common representation – the red disk.

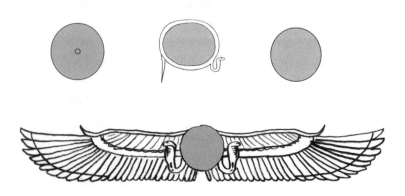

This is Re's solar disk. It features heavily in Egyptian art and there are hundreds of thousands of them adorning every monument, tomb and temple wall throughout Egypt. They can also be found painted on stela (round topped stones), decorated on the inside and outside of coffins and sarcophagi, and on artifacts, scrolls of papyrus, statues and even incorporated into Egyptian jewellery. Re's red disk can be found everywhere. As the Sun was the primary source of life in ancient Egypt, such ubiquitous representation is only to be expected.

Re's red disk appeared in a variety of sizes, and is most often seen forming part of the sacred text (hieroglyphs) whenever the Sun god is mentioned. The Egyptian kings were given various titles, many of which referred to the

Sun god Re. The names included 'powerful are the manifestations of Re', 'the souls of Re appear', 'eternal like Re' and 'chosen by Re'. Many pharaohs adopted these titles and they covered tombs and temple walls throughout Egypt. Wherever this title was found there was invariably a red disk. A famous example was Ramesses (Re-mesess) which translates as 'Re has fashioned him'. The 'Re' part of the name, and indeed all references to Re, was represented by a simple red disk (sometimes with a dot in the centre) and the remaining part was represented by corresponding hieroglyphs. The most well known identifying mark of a royal name is the cartouche, a magical, oval-shaped rope encircling the king's name. Peter Clayton's book 'Chronicle of the Pharaohs' contains almost every known name of the kings of pharonic Egypt complete with solar disks encircled by the cartouche.

The Pharaohs also had the title 'sa-re' which translates as 'son of Re' (son of the Sun god). The 'sa' part was represented by a duck glyph while the 're' part was represented by a red disk. This hieroglyph would normally precede the birth name of the kings and the walls of Egypt are covered with this title. Although many reliefs have faded and lost their colours over time, the stonework was once painted in stunning colours. At least 99% of Re's solar disks were painted red, and it is important to remember this when we are examining Egyptian reliefs.

Accompanying the sacred hieroglyphs were glorious reliefs including images of gods and goddesses interacting with the monarchy. Re's red disk featured strongly and many gods were portrayed with decorated red disks crowning their heads. The two mothering goddesses, Isis and Hathor, were adorned with red disks which were surmounted by a set of cow's horns commonly known as 'Hathor horns'. Some sacred bulls were also adorned with solar disks mounted with horns. Sometimes the god Amun wore a flat-topped crown with a sun-disk and two plumes or feathers. In the New Kingdom, the great royal wives, who had a close relationship with Amun, wore similar headgear consisting of a red disk surmounted by a set of Hathor horns and two plumes. Many pharaohs also wore elaborate headgear with solar disks incorporated into them.

Re's disk was also decorated with large wings and in such a guise it took centre stage and brought the scene together by arching over it. When it appeared in this form, it was known as a 'winged sun-disk'. Many examples can be found on tomb and temple walls and on top of steles, which are upright, round-topped stones with sculptured surfaces.

Whether used as part of the hieroglyphs or depicted in a separate scene, Re's red disk can frequently be seen with a cobra (sign of kingship) draped over or encircling it. When encircling Re's red disk, the cobra formed a very small ring which was typically yellow. However, Re's disk was also shown with a thin yellow ring around it. Both images are very common and can be found in books on ancient Egypt. It is interesting to note the absence of anything connected to the Moon as it had yet to settle into a regular and recognisable orbit. As we have examined Egyptian art and the use of red disks, there appears to be something wrong with Re's symbol, and by extension the Sun.

Always depicted as a red disk!

It matters little where Re's symbol is found. Whether used as part of the 'sacred' hieroglyphs or as a pictorial image,

Re's most basic form consisted of a simple red disk which was sometimes dressed with wings, cow's horns, plumes or cobras. Yet the Sun is a blinding, golden-yellow disk with emanating rays – a ball of glaring, golden light. As Egypt has one of the sunniest climates in the world, the Sun would have shone on ancient Egyptians with monotonous regularity.

Why did the Egyptians depict the blinding yellow Sun as a red disk which is a lifeless image by comparison? Ask a child to paint the Sun and they will paint a yellow circle with yellow rays. Why didn't the Egyptians portray the Sun as it appeared – a bright yellow disk with rays?

The full power of the Sun is not captured by a lifeless red orb which strips the Sun of its blinding light. In effect, this image is demeaning to the solar deity, Re. Would the Egyptians risk the wrath of this great god by ignoring its true form in this way? As one of the original creator gods, Re was 'the lord of all lands' and 'the great light who shinest in the heavens'. Life on Earth depended on Re and he was revered greatly. The early Egyptians believed that he created the world, and the rising Sun was their symbol of creation. As 'sons of Re', the pharaohs believed they were offspring of the Sun and bathed in its life-giving properties daily.

The abundance of glorious reliefs proves that the Egyptians were proud of their art. Many pieces took months, if not years, to complete as each hieroglyph was meticulously carved and painted. The colours were of paramount importance and many gods had their own sacred colours. It therefore seems bizarre that they carved a disk to represent the Sun and then proceeded to paint it red!

When discussing the Egyptians depiction of the red Sun, I would like to point out that I am excluding the Amarna period. This was the revolutionary episode in Egyptian history when the 'heretic' pharaoh Akhenaten left Thebes to form a new capital in Middle Egypt for the worship of the Aten, the 'disk of the Sun'. This is not because this was an age of yellow suns with rays. On the contrary, there were numerous red disks from this period which the Egyptians called the Aten and which scholars have erroneously assumed were aspects of the Sun. Shown slightly larger than normal, the Aten had one distinct trait that separated it from the millions of red suns before and after the Amarna period – it was shown with sunrays. They were not normal rays because they did not sweep around the circumference of the disk but protruded from the lower half only. Nevertheless, the Amarna period was the only time in Egyptian history when a 'sun' was depicted with rays.

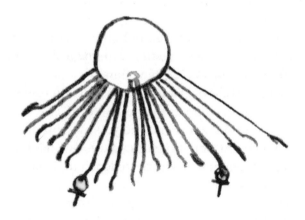

However, I am not excluding the Amarna period because of the existence of sunrays. I am excluding it because the Aten had nothing to do with the Sun! This whole epoch of approximately 17 years was a time when the combined gravitational forces of Earth and Venus sucked out the core of Mars which became the planet Mercury. This biblical event occurred in the skies above Earth and was witnessed by all ancient cultures. The Egyptians initially called Mercury the Aten – and so the Aten was Mercury. It was never a renamed sun and to suggest such a thing is totally incorrect.

Ancient cultures do not suddenly decide to rename one of their most important creator deities. Re was never the Aten. The Aten was portrayed as a large red disk with partial rays because that is exactly how Mercury appeared. It was a totally separate body to the Sun. In fact, the Sun was blotted out for at least 17 years because of the light from Mercury. As it cooled down, Mercury joined the royal bloodline of god-kings. Even the rare golden Aten on the back of Tutankhamun's throne was an image of the recently born Mercury of the first millennium BC.

Another interesting point regarding the Aten concerns certain TV documentaries on the Amarna period which depict the Aten and its rays as yellow. However, the reliefs at Amarna clearly show traces of red paint. Perhaps the producers struggled to accept a red Sun because their subconscious told them it must be yellow. This also happened with red suns from other periods whereas it would have been more accurate to depict the colours as recorded by history.

Although the Sun is portrayed as a red disk 99% of the time, there were occasional gold, orange, yellow and white suns and even the occasional blue one. However, non-red disks were rare and the red disk was predominantly depicted in ancient Egypt. Apart from the Amarna period, both non-red and red disks lacked sunrays, which is an unnatural way of representing the Sun. In ancient times, the Sun wasn't merely a bright orb in the sky – it was a perennial god, one of the original creator gods necessary for life. If these red disks were representations of the Sun, why were they coloured red and depicted without sunrays?

I believe that these discrepancies in relation to the Sun occurred because most coloured disks and red orbs were actually representations of different planet-gods as they appeared in the heavens. When a disk was depicted in a scene, perhaps incorporated into the headgear of the goddess Isis, it was not necessarily the Sun that was being represented.

Scholars automatically assume that all circular disks represented the Sun, but this shows a relatively poor understanding of ancient Egyptian culture. It is obvious that something is definitely wrong with our current understanding and it is surprising that this issue has never been questioned before.

The colour

'Red is also a colour given to the Sun, red at its rising and its setting.'
(http://www.touregypt.net/featurestories/colors.htm)

Is it possible the red Sun derives from observations of the Sun at sunrise or sunset? The Sun occasionally appears red on the horizon due to the disfiguring refraction caused by the layering of the air. At sunset, light travels through more of the atmosphere and appears to the observer as if the transmitted light from the Sun has an intense red hue, hence a red Sun.

To propose that the Egyptians depicted the Sun as a red disk because it occasionally appears red at sunrise and sunset is a ridiculous assumption. Where are the depictions of yellow suns with sunrays? Surely if red disks represented the Sun at sunset, we should also expect to find corresponding yellow disks which represented the Sun during the day. Furthermore, as the Sun occasionally appears red on the horizon, the percentage of yellow suns far outweighs red suns. There should be millions of yellow suns and only a few red suns, but ancient Egyptian art is dominated by the red disk.

Did the Egyptian palette contain yellow paint? Yes it did – yellow ochre was readily available and was used regularly by the Egyptians. There were many reliefs where yellow paint was used as well as the occasional yellow disk. For example, in 'The Art of Ancient Egypt' by Gay Robins, on page 173 there is a facsimile painting of a scene from the chapel of Isis in the Osiris complex. It shows King Seti I offering a platter of food to the seated figure of the goddess Isis. This mothering goddess is normally depicted crowned with a large red disk surmounted with black cow's horns. However, in this scene Isis is unusually shown with yellow flesh and a flat-topped yellow crown with white cow's horns and a large yellow disk. If this yellow disk represented the Sun, it is clear evidence that the Egyptians not only used yellow paint but also painted the Sun yellow. Therefore all disks that represented the Sun should have been coloured yellow. Yet this scene also contains hieroglyphic red suns and numerous images of cobras, each one crowned with a red disk.

The yellow disk of Isis was portrayed with a set of cow's horns. It seems odd that the colour was correct whereas sunrays were omitted. Many red suns had a thin, yellow ring around the circumference and this sometimes had a cobra attached. It would have made more sense to colour the entire disk yellow rather than red with a thin yellow ring around it. The situation becomes increasingly bizarre when we consider the precious metal gold which was regarded as the flesh of the gods. It was closely associated with the Sun as the following quotes highlight:

'With decorations in gold leaf or yellow paint to represent gold, which both form the flesh of the gods and as a colour had a close association with the Sun god.'
(Robins, quoting on the gold funerary mask of an elite woman, The Art of Ancient Egypt, 2000, p 146)

'Because of its warm glow and indestructibility, gold was thought to be the flesh of the Sun god Ra and contained supernatural powers.'
(Discovery Channel, Age of Gold, 2004)

'The colour yellow was often associated with the sun-disk and with gold, or nbw. Gold was not only associated with the Sun, it was also the flesh of the gods.'
(http://www.touregypt.net/featurestories/colors.htm).

Gold leaf and yellow paint were colours associated with the Sun. If gold was the flesh of the gods, and if this originated with our golden Sun, why didn't the Egyptians paint the Sun yellow? More importantly, why haven't scholars questioned this irregularity? It seems strange to ignore the golden flesh of the original creator god in favour of red flesh. It could even be argued that the Egyptians were contradicting themselves.

'Khenet, or yellow, was symbolic of all that is eternal and imperishable.' (ibid)

The Sun is eternal and imperishable; it rises and sets with ceaseless regularity and remains imperishable at the centre of the solar system. It has traversed our skies for billions of years; it was present at the birth of pharonic Egypt and at the end some 3,000 years later. As the Egyptians believed that yellow was symbolic of all that was eternal and imperishable, they would have used this divine colour to paint the Sun. Yet Egyptian images do not tally with their sacred words and there is no connection between gold flesh and the colour of the Sun. Is there any way we can reconcile such apparent contradictions?

THE SOLAR SYSTEM BESEIGED BY SPACE DEBRIS

Where are the sunrays?

Having considered colour, we will now consider the Sun's rays. We know that the Sun has rays of light streaming from it, so why didn't the Egyptians paint a few simple lines around the Sun to represent this glaring light? If we consider the skill required to produce certain intricate hieroglyphs, carvings and paintings, a disk with rays would have been effortless by comparison.

In the title 'sa-re' (son of Re), the duck glyph (son) took longer to carve than a disk with rays. What of the hieroglyphic texts which represented an owl, a crocodile, a bee or a boat with sails? All required expertise, time and patience whereas a novice could have carved a circle with rays. We know that the Aten from the Amarna period was clearly shown with partial rays emanating downwards. Although the Aten did not have rays all around, it provides clear evidence that the Egyptians were able to depict a disk with sunrays.

Many tomb ceilings were decorated with rows of five-pointed stars. Here the Egyptians depicted exactly what they saw with the five points representing the twinkling of the star as the rays emitted light. It therefore seems strange that they did not show rays of light emanating from the Sun.

The majority of solar disks were red, and we know that a red sun is a diminished sun which doesn't give off any glaring rays. When the Sun appears red on the horizon, it is possible to look directly at it because its power is diminished. Therefore a red sun would not have had rays, but this doesn't explain the lack of yellow suns. Why did the Egyptians depict the Sun in such a bizarre fashion? I believe there is a perfectly logical explanation which has been missed due to its simplicity..

The Egyptians portrayed the Sun as a red disk because it only ever appeared as a red disk! Ancient cultures throughout the globe never experienced a blinding, yellow Sun; they experienced a diminished red Sun. The Sun rose in the east as a red disk, traversed the heavens as a red disk and set in the west as a red disk, chaos permitting. The Egyptians didn't deliberately ignore the true power and colour of the Sun. The truth is they never experienced its full power and form as we do today. The Egyptians portrayed exactly what they saw – the Sun as a red disk. That is why the red disk dominated Egyptian art for 3,000 years.

Planetary chaos and a solar system besieged with space debris

It makes sense to suppose that 3,000 years of chaos would have produced trillions of tons of space debris made up of comets, asteroids, gigantic boulders, icebergs, fine grains of sand, frozen water droplets, dust and gasses. This debris scattered throughout the solar system to form a gargantuan, universal 'cosmic cloud' which affected every planetary body in the cosmos. It shrouded the Sun which, from the perspective of Earth, turned red for the 3,000 year-duration of pharonic Egypt. This mass of debris was eventually vacuumed up by the warrior god-kings (the planets) and the

Sun god Re. This process saw the forces of good (Horus) pitched against the forces of evil (Seth) for an incredible 300 centuries.

To understand the scale of the space debris at this time, we will examine some of the primary sources. A mass of debris was produced as a result of the initial impact on Jupiter and colossal amounts of debris were created by subsequent and ongoing planetary chaos involving the two main perpetrators, Mars and Venus. When we have examined the sources, we can identify where this debris went and the effect this had upon the Sun & the Earth.

When discussing our solar system, the numbers and sizes involved are infinite. What was once there has long since disappeared and as a result the implications of such phenomena has also disappeared. However, by using the Sun as a yardstick, and by considering a few basic facts and a little logical reasoning, I will show how a solar system littered with debris can help to explain the colour of the Egyptian Sun.

Space debris opens up other avenues such as the 'physical' identification of the so-called mythological 'sky gods' such as Hathor and Isis. It also helps to explain why the monarchy was thought to have such a close and personal relationship with the Sun god Re and why they were given the title 'sa-re' (son of Re). This will form a solid foundation for the entire GKS and the seemingly bizarre world of the Egyptians will be transformed into a world of chaos.

Initial source of debris – Jupiter

Some 5,000 years ago, planetary chaos began. A galactic interloper smashed into Jupiter resulting in the birth of Venus. To understand the incredible forces involved, I will refer you to Coast to Coast AM, an American radio show which featured Ackerman (V/A Scenario) in 2005. He quoted the following regarding the forces involved:

'And that force was so enormous (10^{42} ergs) that it was like a 1,000 times the binding energy of the Earth. In other words, it was a 1,000 times more energy than you would need to blow the Earth to smithereens.'

A cataclysmic event such as the birth of a planet roughly the size of the Earth from a planet 1,300 times larger would have produced colossal amounts of debris. Trillions of tons of space material were thrust out into space as Venus was born. Astral bodies, from the smallest grain of dust to bodies the size of our Moon, as well as clouds of dust and gasses swarmed around on a scale we can only imagine. It is from this debris that I propose we will find the origins of our Moon. I am convinced that our magical measurer of months, in the guise of the god Thoth, originated from the material ejected by Jupiter.

The impact on Jupiter was outstanding. Even after the birth of Venus, the Moon and trillions of ton of debris, Jupiter continued to billow out masses of dust and debris for thousands of years. The source of this material was the enormous volcanic impact-crater which formed as a result of the galactic interloper colliding with Jupiter. The evidence for this still remains visible today in the form of Jupiter's Great Red Spot.

The GRS is believed to be a complex storm that has being raging since its discovery some 300 years ago but this is not the case. It is the remains of the colossal impact of 5,000 years ago. It is still raging today, albeit on a much smaller scale, because the impact crater on the Jovian surface is billowing out a vortex of debris which manifests itself in Jupiter's upper atmosphere as a swirling red spot. Jupiter's GRS is so large it could swallow Earth three times.

Where did all this debris go?

Jupiter, as the second largest body in the solar system next to the Sun, exerts an enormous amount of gravitational pull. As this giant was involved in the genesis of chaos, it is sensible to assume it 'hoovered' up large quantities of space rubble. For thousands of years, the gravity of Jupiter pulled in gigantic chunks of space debris which catastrophically found their way back to the surface. It is likely there were further catastrophic explosions and eruptions as more material was expelled. Some of the debris subsequently created by Mars and Venus would have encountered Jupiter's immense gravitational pull. This sweeping up of debris by Jupiter is still occurring today and planetary scientists consider Jupiter to be the 'cosmic hoover' of the solar system. This massive planet protects the Earth by literally hoovering up trillions of tons of space debris every year.

When the comet Shoemaker-Levy 9 broke up into many pieces and collided with Jupiter in 1994, it provided many revelations about Jupiter and its atmosphere and highlighted Jupiter's role in reducing space debris in the inner solar system. Masses of space rubbish were

continually created by and swallowed up by Jupiter as it tirelessly cleared the heavens. It is ironic that the planet which produced the debris ultimately hoovered it up!
This was only the beginning. Galactic energy, powerful enough to blow the Earth to smithereens, blasted out colossal amounts of material and scattered it throughout the solar system. Fragments were propelled in all directions and rapidly drawn in line with the ecliptic plane, the same flat disk that the planets orbit. Debris catapulted outwards to the outer planets Saturn, Uranus and Neptune and blasted inwards to the inner planets Mars and Earth and the Sun (Venus and Mercury were not in this location at this time). It was a time of total devastation as debris encountered, engulfed and bombarded everything in the solar system including Earth.

It is no coincidence that Earth suffered a geologically accepted dark age around 3200 BC which was approximately 5,200 years ago. This dark age lasted for over 200 years and I believe this was entirely due to the initial cataclysmic explosion on Jupiter. I will therefore use this dark age as a fixed reference point for the birth of cosmic chaos.

To fully understand the effect of the impact on Jupiter, it would be beneficial to visualise how I believe the solar system looked shortly after this cataclysm 5,000 years ago. First, imagine a yellow sphere representing the Sun at the centre of a rotating flat disk, the ecliptic plane. Add a number of smaller spheres to represent the planets as they slowly orbit around the Sun and you have a simple model of the solar system.

Now cloak the entire scene with a huge, flat, hazy cloud, particularly around the Sun. As the Sun drew in tons of debris, it acted like a star 'kicking and screaming' as it constantly battled the enemies of Re. This is how the solar system looked shortly after the explosion on Jupiter. The force exerted on Jupiter was capable of destroying the Earth and the solar system was engulfed in a huge cosmic cloud.

Secondary source of debris – 3,000 years of chaos involving Mars and Venus

At this time, the solar system was hazed in space debris and an enormous, flat disk of dust and debris orbited the Sun and the planets. The cosmic cloud caused by the explosion on Jupiter lasted approximately 300 – 500 years. Therefore it would have taken approximately 500 years for the solar system to reach a stage much like today, with relatively clear skies and a cosmos littered with debris. However, the cosmic cloud that shrouded the solar system remained for an incredible 3,000 years! This was because it was constantly replenished by debris produced by the two main perpetrators of chaos, Mars and Venus. We will now examine this secondary source of debris which had more of an effect on the Earth and the Sun than the explosion on Jupiter did.

Shortly after its birth from Jupiter, Venus disturbed Mars and the two planets entered into numerous encounters with Earth. Mars dominated the heavens as a perennial warrior king while Venus took on the role of 'king's great wife' and remained placid in the background. Although they appeared as a divine royal couple, Mars and Venus were actually in complete turmoil. This caused total carnage on

Earth as Mars 'battled' itself to death and Venus cooled down. Masses of space debris were propelled into space in a process that lasted an incredible 3,000 years.

Venus 5,000 years ago

Venus was a planetary fireball – a flaming body of molten rock billowing out trillions of tons of dust and gasses. The source of this torrent was thousands of volcanic vents that formed on the Venusian surface shortly after its birth. As a new planet, Venus spewed out mainly gaseous debris, unlike Mars which has a solid, rocky outer shell like Earth. The surface of Venus was, and still is, a bubbling caldron of molten lava and each active vent billowed out sulphur-based gasses like bubbling mud pots. Venus took 2,700 years to travel from the vicinity of Jupiter to its present location of second rock from the Sun. As it billowed out incomprehensible amounts of gaseous debris along its way, it took on the attributes of a gigantic comet exactly as proposed by Velikovsky.

Venus continues to billow out gasses but they are now contained within its dense atmosphere which formed as Venus cooled down and settled into a stable orbit. Although Venus has rapidly cooled down since its birth 5,000 years ago, its surface temperature today is still a massive 800 degrees Fahrenheit, which is hot enough to melt lead! This extremely high temperature is the legacy of its recent cataclysmic birth from Jupiter.

Mars

During three millennia of cosmic chaos, Mars has undergone enormous changes and has expelled staggering amounts of space debris as it was slowly torn apart in close proximity to Earth. Until 5,000 years ago, Mars was identical to Earth. It was a lush, blue-green planet replete with an atmosphere, land masses, oceans and life. (It once harboured human life, but that's another story!) The only difference between Mars and Earth was size – Mars was approximately half the size of Earth. But cosmic chaos changed everything. Mars was transformed from a planet thriving with life into a dead, desolate, frozen planet.

Earth, at twice the size of Mars, was the chief perpetrator in the destruction of the red planet. The tidal forces of Earth combined with the gravitational pull of Venus were no match for Mars. Its once great oceans and atmosphere were sucked out into space and captured by Earth and its flora and fauna were wiped out. It no longer holds a magnetic field as an invisible protective bubble because its solid iron core was sucked out to form the planet Mercury (Aten). Mars is now a shell of its former self.

It is a frightening analogy to imagine the slow destruction of Earth by a planetary body twice its size. The tidal forces of the larger planet would gradually tear Earth apart over thousands of years. Earth's atmosphere and great oceans would be sucked out and all life would be destroyed. Eventually the larger planet would suck out Earth's working dynamo – its solid iron core. This is exactly what happened to Mars. While Venus has spent the last 5,000 years cooling down, Mars has been slowly and systematically torn apart.

This slow and systematic destruction of Mars caused trillions of tons of debris to be thrust out into space forming asteroids and comets as well as dense clouds of dust, gasses, water and ice. As planetary chaos has now subsided, it is not possible to observe Mars in the act of churning out debris. However, we can glean an idea of the extent of this by looking at the primary source of debris that still litters the Martian surface – volcanoes.

There are many thousands of volcanoes on Mars. Although now extinct, 4,000 years ago they were highly active. The immense tidal forces of Earth and Venus caused them to throw out immeasurable amounts of lava, rock debris, ash, gases and great chunks of landmass from the sides of mountainous volcanoes. Much of it fell back to the surface, although large quantities were blasted out into space.

To understand these events we will examine the largest volcano in the solar system – Olympus Mons on Mars. Rising 16 miles above the surface, this monster is three times taller than the tallest mountain on Earth (Mount Everest only rises 5 miles) and stretches some 370 miles – the distance from Boston to Washington DC. It makes the largest landform on Earth look like an anthill! If we travel back some 4,000 years to the peak of planetary chaos, this incredible monster would have churned out trillions of tons of debris.

As the largest volcano in the solar system, there was nothing to compare with the debris expelled by this incredible structure. Although large quantities fell back to the surface, the tidal forces of Earth and Venus assisted in the extraction of insurmountable quantities of material into space. Cosmologists are puzzled by the lack of outflow from this monster. Considering its size, there should be far more debris surrounding Olympus Mons and more evidence of outflow. This enigma is very easy to explain.

There is a lack of outflow because it was blasted out into space during the many encounters with Earth.

The genesis of Mercury was witnessed in the skies above Earth and was meticulously recorded in history; it was responsible for one of Egypt's most enigmatic periods – the Amarna period. This was when the 'heretic' pharaoh Akhenaten, in his worship of the Aten, moved the capital of Egypt away from Thebes to build a new one in the middle of Egypt called Akhetaten (horizon of the Aten), modern day El Amarna. We have established that the Aten was the core of Mars, the planet Mercury. Due to its recent birth, it initially appeared as a 'dazzling sun-disk' but rapidly cooled down and joined the royal bloodline of god-kings.

We have examined the evidence for the birth of Mercury in the form of the enormous canyon on Mars, the Valles Marineris. We can only imagine the forces that shaped this gargantuan scar and the colossal amounts of debris created as Mercury was sucked out from Mars. The rotating core gives a planet its protective magnetic field and once this ceases to function there is little to hold a planet together apart from gravity. Atmosphere, oceans, dust and gasses would be vulnerable. The turning point in cosmic chaos was the extraction of Mars' core; in effect, the cosmic 'elastic band' snapped. It took approximately 600-700 years for cosmic chaos to slowly subside which resulted in the solar system we see today.

Where did this debris go?

The debris from Jupiter merged with the debris from Mars and Venus and chaotically swirled around the flat disk of the equatorial plane. Mars and Venus churned out debris close to Earth, and by extension close to the Sun, for 3,000 years and constantly replenished the cosmic cloud which engulfed the inner solar system. Mars and Venus provided an endless supply of debris that superseded anything caused by the initial impact on Jupiter. But exactly were did the debris go?

The planets and the Sun hoovered up the debris and continue to do so today. The planets were a hive of activity as they set about clearing up the cosmic mess. They used their orbital paths and gravitational powers to draw in and hoover up swarms of space rubble in a process that took many thousands of years. This clearing up process was extended by subsequent and ongoing cosmic chaos. For evidence of this clearing up operation we can look to the surfaces of the inner planets – Mars, Venus, Mercury and the Moon. They bear the hallmarks of asteroid and cometary impacts and are covered with hundreds of thousands of impact craters and incalculable amounts of space rubbish. This is clear evidence of a past epoch when they were pummelled by swarms of space debris.

The Moon is a silent witness to a catastrophic past. Its surface is littered with thousands of impact craters and it is covered with space debris several kilometres thick in some areas. This is the legacy of recent cosmic chaos when the solar system was besieged with debris. It is not evidence of catastrophic events billions of years ago as orthodox science asserts. It occurred in historical times and was clearly recorded in history as the battles of the pharaohs when the god-king planets were 'at war' as they cleared up the debris.

The planets are still clearing our solar system. Earth collects about 40,000 tons of celestial debris each year, mainly tiny grains produced by shooting stars. There is a mass of debris that has not been cleared up which is suspended between Jupiter and Mars forming the asteroid belt. This ring of debris contains the remains of the initial explosion on Jupiter.

Planetary Rings

As the clean-up operation progressed, many planets developed planetary ring systems. This occurred as the centrifugal force caused by the spinning planets congregated debris around the equatorial regions and formed rings similar to the ones that orbit Saturn. Cosmic chaos combined with the rotating planets to produce this phenomenon.

It is not widely known that at least four planets have rings – Jupiter, Saturn, Uranus and Neptune. Saturn's rings are the brightest and the most familiar so we will use Saturn as an example. Saturn's rings consist of chunks of rock, icebergs and dust that slowly encircle the planet's equator like a swarm of moonlets. This is similar to the debris we have already discussed but in a more diluted state. It is generally accepted that these rings formed either from captured asteroids and comets or from celestial bodies that impacted the surface of the planet. The gaps in Saturn's rings are caused by small moons sucking up material from the orbiting debris. If Saturn's moons were larger they would probably have been vacuumed up eons ago.

According to astronomers, Saturn's rings formed within the past few hundred million years. I disagree and suggest they are the legacy of recent cosmic chaos from only 4,000-5,000 years ago. They are the fragmented remains of infinite numbers of cometary bodies that broke up and collected around Saturn's girth shortly after the explosion on Jupiter. The rings today are thin and diluted because they are no longer fed by cosmic chaos which has long since subsided. The erratic bodies responsible for the rings have fragmented and dispersed leaving behind the defined rings we see today. We can no longer see tons of space debris bombarding and congregating around Saturn's equator. However, if we could turn the clock back 4,000 years, Saturn's rings would appear much thicker, denser and intensely active as swarms of space debris were drawn in to form an enormous, hazy cloud of debris swirling around Saturn's girth. Armies of asteroids and comets collided with one another to fragment and cause further debris. As dust and gasses were drawn in to join this melee, Saturn looked like a gigantic spinning top.

I believe that 4,000 years ago, most planets were home to hazy bands of debris. Earth was home to a gigantic ring of debris that formed shortly after the initial explosion on Jupiter. Trillions of tons of space debris were captured in orbit and formed a gigantic ring around Earth's equatorial regions. Asteroids, comets, chunks of rocks, icebergs, water droplets, dust and gasses and fine grains of sand (and eventually our Moon) congregated around Earth's girth. This cosmic ring of debris was constantly replenished for 3000 years by the ongoing chaos involving Mars & Venus, and later the Moon and Mercury. Earth took on the appearance of a gigantic spinning top as a ring of rubble span around its equator. From the perspective of Earth, this cosmic ring arched across the heavens from east to west and occupied the same path as that tracked by the Sun and the planets. On many occasions it took on the appearance of a giant cosmic mountain arching across the heavens

There was a sequential order of events which led to Earth developing a ring of debris. We can use our Moon as an example to explain how events unfolded. If our modern Moon was impacted by a celestial body large enough to sends tons of debris into space, it would initially be scattered out in all directions before rapidly forming a hazy ring around Earth's equator. The debris would eventually be vacuumed up by the Moon or fall to Earth as meteorites. The size of the ring would depend on the amount of the debris created by the initial impact. For example, if the Moon were blasted to smithereens, Earth would be home to a relatively thick hazy band of debris. Alternatively, a small impact would create very thin rings consisting of fine dust particles similar to those orbiting around Saturn, albeit on a smaller scale.

The currently accepted theory regarding the formation of the Moon is that a planetary body the size of Mars collided with Earth which resulted in debris being scattered around the Earth to form an equatorial ring which slowly coalesced to form the Moon. However, I believe this theory is incorrect.

Jupiter was hit by a force powerful enough to blast the Earth into smithereens. Mars and Venus subsequently danced with Earth for thousands of years. Such events would have created debris on an incomprehensible scale and large quantities would have been pulled by the gravitational force of Earth to orbit around its equatorial regions. Cosmic chaos was therefore responsible for planetary rings. We know that Earth was home to a gigantic ring of debris because it was clearly seen, particularly at night. It played a crucial role in the lives of the astral monarchy and the mortal Egyptians on Earth. Arching across the heavens as a whitish hazy band, Earth's ring of debris took on numerous aspects.

The main role of Earth's ring was to nurture and suckle the royal family as they lived and died amidst it. In this aspect, the ring would be known as the mothering goddess Hathor (and to a large extent Isis). Hathor was one of the principal deities of ancient Egypt and the incarnation of Earth's gigantic ring of debris in the heavens. The name Hathor translates as 'house of the king' (hat-hor). This translation should be taken literally as the Earth's milky ring of debris was the home of the kings who suckled on the milk of Hathor.

Earth's ring also played a pivotal role in the Egyptian belief in 'divine order' (*ma'at*), as it had the power to bring the whole world into chaos. This happened during intense periods of planetary chaos when Earth's ring became so thick and dense with space debris that it blotted out the Sun and bombarded the Earth with planetary debris causing total carnage. Earth's ring was therefore known as Sekhmet, a destructive form of Hathor. Sekhmet was a goddess associated with war and retribution as well as disease and plague. However she was also endowed with the 'power' to cure ailments.

When the skies were overrun with chaos, it was the duty of the pharaohs as upholders of 'divine order' to step in and bring about some kind of order. The god-kings tirelessly and perpetually cleared the heavens of debris. They relentlessly vacuumed up trillions of tons of evil debris (foreign invaders) that threatened to engulf the skies in a perennial battle that saw the forces of good (Horus) pitched against the force of evil (Seth). This was ironic because it was the god-kings themselves who produced the debris. References to the pharaohs 'battling up' debris refers to Mars, the Moon, and Mercury. Venus also assisted in clearing the heavens but was rarely observed as she remained in the background. These planetary bodies, in the guise of celestial god-kings, played their part in battling up Earth's cosmic ring.

The Moon played an important part in regard to the debris encircling the Earth. As it was slowly captured in orbit around the Earth, it loomed so large in the heavens that it became the ultimate warrior astral king, Tuthmosis, and took on the onslaught of evil foreign invaders. Today, the Moon has been left behind to finish off the task of clearing up Earth's ring. I believe the Moon has prevented the Earth becoming home to a ring of debris because it is unusually large compared to other planets and their moons. It is over a quarter of the size of Earth and as a result has sucked in more debris. Saturn's rings still remain because its many moons are small in comparison and cannot complete the clearing-up operation. Also the rings are slowly dissipating over time.

Sun

The largest ring of debris was around the Sun. Although the planets played a major part in drawing in and sweeping up masses of rubble, the Sun contains 98% of the mass of the solar system and therefore dictated where the majority of space debris was deposited. The planets are mere specks of dust in comparison to the Sun and its interior could hold over 1.3 million Earths! The enormous gravitational forces of Jupiter and other planets pale into insignificance compared to this 'nuclear beast.' It is the gravity of the Sun that holds the whole solar system together. Any space debris that escaped the tidal forces of the planets ultimately succumbed to the immense power of the Sun as it drew in trillions of tons of debris.

The distance between the Earth and the Sun is approximately 93 million miles or 150 million kilometres. If you travelled in a 747 jumbo jet at full throttle, it would take you 17 years to reach the Sun. Shortly after the birth of Venus, this expanse became engulfed with incalculable amounts of space material and the Sun became home to the largest ring of debris in the solar system.

The haze of debris was constantly replenished by subsequent cosmic chaos involving Mars, Venus, Mercury and the Moon. The chaos intensified during the New Kingdom (1000 BC RC), and I propose this was when Venus, as the 'king's great wife', crossed the obit of Earth to move to the Sun side (between the Earth and the Sun). Venus, en-route to its present day orbit, billowed out masses of dust and gasses as it slowly migrated to become the second rock from the Sun.

Huge amounts of debris were swallowed up by the Sun ('curse of Re'). The Sun, as the ultimate judge and jury of our solar system, dictated the fate of thousands of bands of space rubble which were sucked into its atmosphere. The Sun still acts as a giant vacuum cleaner as it sweeps up around 100,000 tons of micrometeoroids per day.

Cosmologists are puzzled because if this debris was created at the birth of the solar system some 4.7 billions years ago, it should have long since dissipated. Once again, the answer is simple. The bulk of this debris was created in the last 5,000 years!

We have established that a cosmic cloud once cloaked our solar system as a result of cosmic chaos. This was due to the effects of chaos which caused a haze of dust and debris to besiege the solar system. We will now examine the visual effects of this phenomenon on the Sun from the perspective of the Earth.

EARTH'S RING OF DEBRIS

If we could observe the Sun the way it was 4,000 years ago, our view would be affected by Earth's hazy ring and the debris orbiting around the Sun. How did the Sun appear through the incalculable amounts of debris that orbited the Sun and the Earth? For a simple answer we need to look to the hundreds of thousands of suns adorning every temple, tomb and monument throughout Egypt.

The Sun as a red disk

The ancient Egyptians portrayed the Sun as a red disk simply because it appeared as a red disk. Huge amounts of dust and debris around the Sun and the Earth, as well as dust in the Earth's atmosphere, distorted the image of the Sun and transformed it from a blinding golden disk to a red disk. The Egyptians did not inhabit a bizarre world of make believe and strange practices where the Sun's true colour was ignored. They lived in a real world of cosmic chaos where the Sun appeared as a red disk and was portrayed accordingly. This is the reason for the absence of yellow suns with sunrays in ancient times because this Sun did not exist. Cosmic chaos ensured our ancestors never experienced a blinding golden Sun as we do today; they experienced a diminished red-Sun.

The Sun god Re was one of the original creator gods. He was '*lord of all the lands*' the '*great light shinest in the heavens*'. The Egyptians believed he created the world and the rising Sun was the symbol of creation. Re was recognised as the driving force behind all life on Earth and without Re all life would cease to exist. As sons of Re (sa-re), the pharaohs believed they were offspring of the Sun. It therefore seems unlikely that the Egyptians would dare portray Re's most basic symbol, the Sun itself, in the wrong colour. Re was shown as a red disk, and the religious Egyptians would not demean Re's glorious golden power or risk the wrath of this almighty god by getting his colour wrong.

Sunset comparison

The red colour of the rising and setting Sun is due to the atmosphere that its rays pass through before reaching our eyes. Our thick, impurity-laden lower atmosphere only allows the red tones to pass through and the Sun therefore takes on a distinctly reddish hue. The same principle turned the Sun red in ancient times.

Our forebears were not merely looking at the Sun through Earth's dusty atmosphere. They were also gazing through a hazy band of debris and a wall of rubble, dust and gasses some 93 million miles thick. To explain this principle, imagine you are on the surface of Saturn looking towards the Sun through its dusty rings. The Sun's light would be diminished and the Sun would appear as a hazy red disk. Therefore a haze of dust and debris turns our Sun from a golden Sun to a diminished red Sun.

History

I believe a red Sun existed from the birth of pharonic Egypt and the birth of cosmic chaos some 5,000 years ago. Therefore historical man never experienced a glaring golden Sun. As we find a golden Sun perfectly normal, so too a diminished red Sun was normal to ancient cultures.

Even when cosmic chaos entered periods of calm and Earth's ring of debris began to dissipate, there were still trillions of pieces of debris orbiting the Sun.

Re's most common symbol, a red disk, was therefore the true representation of the Sun in ancient times. It can be found in every corner of pharonic Egypt because it is a 'sacred' representation of the Sun exactly as it appeared in the heavens 4,000 years ago. The Sun appeared red from the birth of pharonic Egypt until its demise sometime around 300 BC. Only when the divine planetary gods retreated back to the heavens did the Sun's true golden brilliance begin to burst through. This true golden appearance neatly coincided with the introduction of golden coffins during the Greco-Roman period.

The clean-up in the heavens and the emergence of the true colour of the Sun was a slow process. The gods left the Moon behind to speed up the process of clearing Earth's ring. The Moon was extremely effective at clearing Earth's ring once the planets retreated and it has swallowed up trillions of tons of debris in 'recent' times. If you look at the surface of the Moon on a clear night, you will see the Moon's surface layer of regolith which is almost certainly the vacuumed up remains of Earth's ring.

It seems likely that Earth's rings were cleared up long before the debris orbiting the Sun because a huge amount of debris would have filled the 93 million mile space between the Sun and the Earth. Therefore the unmasking of the Sun undoubtedly took many thousands of years. Prior to the New Kingdom, there were no planets between the Earth and the Sun – no large bodies represented resident kings or queens to assist the Sun in vacuuming up the debris. It wasn't until Venus (and later Mercury) migrated to the Sun side that they could assist Re in clearing the heavens. Although on a much smaller scale than the Sun, Venus and Mercury have assisted the Sun in removing debris between the Earth and the Sun. If Venus and Mercury had not moved to their currents obits, it is possible that the red Sun of antiquity would have remained for longer and we would still be living in a twilight world.

Implications of a red Sun

The implications of a red Sun are far reaching, profound and incredibly exciting! Just as we can look at a red sunset today, ancient cultures could look directly at the Sun during the day as there was no blinding glare. They could watch the Sun god Re as he journeyed across the heavens in his celestial 'boat of millions of years' without any fear of being blinded. However, for ancient Egyptians, a 'sunset' Sun existed throughout the entire day, which led to incredible observations of solar phenomena.

We have only recently discovered phenomena such as solar flares, prominences, coronal mass ejections and sun-spots by means of space-craft (Solar and Heliospheric Observatory Project). These were all clearly observed with the naked eye by ancient Egyptians and were named and deified. In fact, the Sun as Re was a 'living and breathing', highly active red orb. If we look to solar activity and the red Sun, we will find the answers to the many enigmatic beliefs that were attributed to the solar deity Re such as Re battling the demons of the underworld. We will see how a red Sun makes perfect sense by examining the main effect of a perpetually hazed Sun – the effect upon the climate.

No rain?

Less energy reached the Earth from a diminished Sun. This had a drastic effect upon the Earth's climate – less energy from the Sun meant little or no evaporation of the oceans and in turn no rain. Does this imply there was no rain for 3,000 years? We know that rain was vital in ancient times (and still is), yet the Egyptians had neither a god nor a hieroglyph to represent it. There was a god of moisture (Tefnut) but no god of rain. In fact, rain in ancient Egypt was considered bad and was referred to as the 'evil that comes from the sky' (Kinnaer – Ancient Egyptian Site http://www.ancient-egypt.org/). Human survival was of paramount importance, yet we are led to believe that ancient people considered rain to be evil. The only plausible explanation for such a view points to toxic or acid rain. Toxic rain would destroy crops and livestock, and acid rain would pollute the Nile and make it undrinkable. It is possible that we are looking at a toxic liquid that fell to the Earth as a result of planetary fallout.

Egyptian clothing

It is puzzling that ancient Egyptians wore nothing more than a loincloth. Look at any Egyptian relief, whether depicting workers in the field or soldiers following the pharaoh into battle, and you will notice the figures are shown wearing loincloths. Even Hollywood movies and documentaries take their lead from these reliefs and depict the Egyptians in this distinctly odd attire.

Egypt today has one of the hottest and sunniest climates in the world. During the summer months its average daily sunlight is 12 hours a day; it is incredibly hot and sunny.

The intensity of the summer heat is such that it requires the population to cover themselves from head to toe for protection. Even the Egyptian tourist board advises extreme caution against the Egyptian Sun.

If the population of modern Egypt emulated the attire worn by the ancient Egyptians, they would be severely burnt. How was it possible to wear nothing more than a loincloth in such intense heat? Scholars have pondered this many times and have reached the same conclusion – that it would have been impossible to wear this attire in such a hot climate. Therefore they have suggested that the artwork depicts an idealistic or preferred world, not the physical world that existed back then. In other words, scholars reason that ancient Egyptians depicted themselves engaging in battle or otherwise in the most impractical attire possible – attire better suited to a beach in the Bahamas!

This explanation is ridiculous and demonstrates a poor understanding of ancient Egypt. It also raises many questions. Are these scenes real or are they idealised? Did this idealised world really exist? After all, not one relief depicts the Egyptians wearing anything that would be considered practical for today's climate. How do we explain this? If this represents an idealised world, something is seriously wrong. Are we expected to believe their idealised world included marching for many months, fighting great battles, spending many months marching home, all wearing nothing more than a loincloth under the searing Egyptian heat? Despite the fact that some Egyptologists attempt to dismiss the wearing of a loincloth as idealistic, a little research reveals that the ancient Egyptians did actually wear loincloths or short kilts. How do we explain this?

'In general, Egyptian clothing was very simple; men working in the fields or involved in craftwork often wore little more than a loin-cloth or short kilt...'

(Shaw & Nicholson, Dictionary of Ancient Egypt, 2002, p 66)

On page 67 of the same book there is an illustration of three triangular loincloths taken from the tomb of Tutankhamun which are now in the Cairo museum No. 50b. The explanation is obvious. Ancient Egyptians lived under a red Sun and this meant no damaging rays which in turn meant no sunburn! The ancient Egyptians wore nothing more than a loincloth because the climate allowed them to.

A diminished red Sun resulted in a totally different climate to that of today. It was a climate devoid of a scorching hot Sun, with no burning rays or intense heat. This twilight world allowed the ancient Egyptians to endlessly work the fields, build great monuments, and march across the deserts for months on end. Such activities could be carried out at any time during the day as there was no scorching Sun to impede their work. Temples such as the Vatican of ancient Egypt, the temple complex dedicated to the king of the gods Amun at Karnak, could be worked upon every daylight hour as there was no intense heat.

The loincloth was not an impractical article of clothing. On the contrary, it was totally practical and was dictated by the climate of 4,000 years ago. There was no need to wear clothing from head to toe, or protective hats and scarves, sunglasses or sun cream. The diminished red Sun and mild climate lasted for the duration of pharonic Egypt. Now the proposal for a solar system in chaos starts to make sense.

It's important to note that although the Sun's energy that reached the Earth was greatly reduced, the Sun was far more active and churning out far more energy than anything experienced today. The Sun was 'feeding' on incalculable amounts of space debris caused by cosmic chaos in a process that lasted 3,000 years.

Hathor

It is totally implausible to propose that ancient Egyptians understood the science of the solar system and there is no evidence to prove the ancients were aware of a spherical Earth with a ring of debris orbiting its girth. In fact, they believed the Earth was flat and placed in the centre of the universe. A band of haze and rubble arched across the heavens and, as with all celestial phenomena, it was deified. This haze played a prominent part in the lives of royalty; it had the power to destroy mankind and, due to the infinite permutations of chaos, it manifested in countless forms. It is therefore understandable that such a phenomenon was embodied as the universal goddess Hathor.

All references to this deity are mythological in context. For example, when Hathor was mentioned in connection with the monarchy, she was referred to as the 'mythical' mother of the king or queen in an epithet that was similar to that given to Isis. Although this may imply that the ancient Egyptians invented a very complicated and 'invisible' goddess to take on the role of divine mother to the mortal kings and queens, this reasoning is incorrect.

This enigmatic goddess should be granted a real 'physical' status; a divine, celestial status as understood by the ancient

Egyptians. By examining the attributes of this deity, it will become clear that the connection is related to Earth's rings. I will therefore place Hathor where she belongs – in the very real world where god-kings were planets. I will then be able to demonstrate that planetary chaos is staring us in the face.

Earth's band arching across the heavens was deified in the form of the goddess Hathor and it was observed during the night and also at dusk and dawn. Depending upon the intensity of 'chaos', Hathor was periodically observed during the day, although it is likely that the goddess Isis presided over the daytime hours.

To support this ground-breaking identification, we will examine two of Hathor's manifestations.

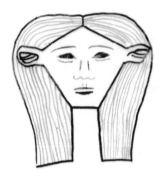 

'Important bovine goddess worshiped in three forms; as a woman with the ears of a cow, as a cow, and as a woman wearing a headdress consisting of a wig, horns and Sun disk. Her associations and cult centres were among the most numerous and diverse of any of the Egyptian deities'. (Dictionary of Ancient Egypt, Shaw & Nicholson p 119)

If we look at a selection of Hathor's titles, we can find a link between Hathor and Earth's ring of debris. These titles include the following:

- Lady of the sky
- Daughter of Re
- The mistress of heaven
- Lady of the stars
- Goddess of love, music and beauty
- Goddess of fertility, children and childbirth
- The Mothers of Mothers, the celestial nurse
- Goddess of the dead, lady of the west
- The mistress of life
- The great wild cow
- The golden one
- Mistress of Turquoise
- Lady to the limit of the universe
- The powerful one
- Mistress of the desert
- Lady of the southern sycamore
- Lady of malachite
- The great one of many names

There are many others as Hathor's epithets were among *'the most numerous and diverse of any of the Egyptian deities'*.

Perennial Hathor

Hathor, in the form of Earth's ring, formed shortly after the birth of celestial chaos and remained for the duration of pharonic Egypt. The historical record supports this as Hathor is among the most ancient of Egyptian deities. She featured prominently in the creation saga with Re and maintained a constant presence in the history of Egypt. The historical record reveals she was among the most important of Egyptian deities which was to be expected of one who dominated the heavens. We have established that Earth's ring started to dissipate as celestial events began to settle down. This coincided with the period when Hathor and the rest of the Egyptian deities were demoted from real physical deities to mythical figures.

Forms

Hathor traditionally took on more forms than any other Egyptian deity, many of whom were limited to only one or two shapes. In terms of imagery, she is the most fluid of all the Egyptian deities, rivalled only by the god of chaos, Seth. For example, the goddess Bastet appeared in two forms – as a cat and as a woman with a cat's head. Hathor took on innumerable forms: woman, goose, cat, lion, malachite, sycamore fig etc. This is consistent with the infinite number of forms displayed by the hazy band of debris over the millennia. Earth's band was a hive of activity as asteroids, comets, dust and gasses of all shapes and sizes combined to create a variety of manifestations. It is similar to the way in which pictures appear in the flames of an open fire or the way shapes are formed by clouds in the sky.

It is important to remember that Earth's band was formed and fed for millennia by chaos and it was impossible for it to keep a uniform shape for 3,000 years. Earth's magnetic field would also have had an effect on the shapes that were formed. Recently, Saturn's magnetic field produced 'spokes' which appeared as dark, ghostly shapes within Saturn's rings. Something similar would have occurred within 'Hathor'. As well as forging different shapes, at certain times of the day Hathor appeared in a kaleidoscope of colours due to the refracted light from the Sun. It would have been a spectacular sight and it is no wonder *'her associations and cult centres were among the most numerous and diverse of any of the Egyptian deities'*.

Destroyer of Humanity

'In one myth Hathor was said to have been sent to destroy humanity...' (ibid)

There were at least three major dark ages during pharonic Egypt as well as many shorter periods of 'Seth' destruction. There were other difficult times which were not recorded and some of them may have been attributed to Hathor. History reveals that Hathor occasionally took on an uncharacteristic destructive aspect and in this manifestation she was known as 'Hathor Sekhmet'.

It is logical to assume that Earth's band had the ability to destroy mankind. During times of immense chaos, Hathor was 'fierce and terrible' and had the power to totally blot out the Sun and cause complete devastation on Earth. Hathor also sent space debris crashing to earth which caused further chaos.

There was also 'fallout' from chaotic events such as acid rain and, although Seth was the major contender for such evil deeds, it is also possible they were attributed to Hathor. Although some dark periods were caused by other sources such as the close passing of Venus or Mars, from the perspective of the ancient Egyptians the female goddess Hathor may have been held responsible.

Chaos resulted in a melee of huge asteroids, comets, gigantic lumps of rock and ice, all colliding with one another in a pea soup of dust and gasses orbiting Earth's girth. The number and ferocity of so many collisions was audible from earth.

'Her connection with the music was particularly represented by the sistrum, ceremonial examples of which were often endowed with Hathor heads, sometimes surmounted by a naos, and frequently shaken by the priestesses of the cult of Hathor. She was also portrayed on the menat counterpoise attached to necklaces.' (ibid)

It is not surprising that Hathor was also the 'goddess of music' and I believe the faint 'clatter' emanating from the heavens was heard on Earth and was attributed to Hathor. Noises from heaven were perceived as the divine music of the gods and it is likely that the ancient Egyptians invented an instrument to emulate the actual sounds they heard as accurately as possible.

This divine music was represented by an instrument called the sistrum. This was an ancient Egyptian percussion instrument consisting of a thin metal frame with rods or loops that jingled when shaken. On top of the handle was the carved figure of the goddess Hathor. The sistrum was called *shesheset* by the ancient Egyptians and was a favoured instrument in many religious ceremonies and rites, particularly those associated with Hathor. The distinctive shape of the instrument is found in many contexts ranging from small mortuary objects to the columns of temples such as those at the Temple of Hathor in Dendera. I believe this instrument was invented as a result of Earth's hazy band which arched across the heavens producing audible noises and it was used to placate the deities, particularly Hathor.

'Each evening she (Hathor) was considered to receive the setting Sun, which she then protected until the morning. The dying therefore desired to be 'in the following of Hathor' so that they would enjoy a similar protection in the netherworld. Hathor was also one of the deities who was thought to be able to determine the destinies of new born children.' (ibid - my parenthesis)

This was Hathor (Earth's band) which came into prominence in all her glory as the Sun set in the west. Hathor appeared to enshroud Re as the Sun set. She wrapped her protective haze around the perennial solar deity, perhaps turning Re a deeper shade of red in the process, and protected him until he rose rejuvenated in the east.

Re was the perennial father to all. The divine relationship between the Sun and the haze was such that Hathor was considered the daughter of Re in a relationship that continued for the duration of pharonic Egypt. There follows a perfect example of this divine relationship, which also exemplifies the red disk theory of a non-glaring Sun without sunrays:

'Nekht, the captain of soldiers, the royal scribe, singeth a hymn of praise to Ra, and saith: Homage to thee, O thou glorious Being, thou who art dowered [with all sovereignty]. O Tem-Heru-Khuti (Tem- Harmakhis), when thou risest in the horizon of heaven a cry of joy goeth forth to thee from all people. O thou beautiful Being, thou dost

renew thyself in thy season in the form of the Disk, within thy mother Hathor.'

(From the Papyrus of Nekht, British Museum No. 10471, Sheet 2)

Nekht praises Ra as a disk and not as a blinding Sun. The 'disk' is referred to as being within Hathor and I would therefore suggest that Nekht was a celestial body. This would also explain Hathor's funerary role as 'goddess of the dead' or 'lady of the west'. The Sun was perceived to die each night as it set in the west and Hathor received the dying Sun as well as other large celestial bodies. There were references to the deceased being 'in the company of Re' and the dying who desired to be 'in the following of Hathor'.

The name Hathor and the god-kings

'The literal meaning of Hathor was 'House of Horus', and it was written in the form of a falcon contained within a hieroglyph representing a rectangular building. Since the pharaoh was identified with Horus, Hathor was correspondingly regarded as the divine mother of each reining king, and one of the royal titles was 'son of Hathor.' (ibid)

It is interesting to note that there are no personal names mentioned among the names given to Hathor – they are all titles. This correlates with my identification as it is impossible to give a personal name to such a vast, constantly changing phenomenon. There is further evidence which identifies Earth's celestial band as Hathor, and by extension it supports the GKS. Hathor's name translates as *'house of the king'*. This can be broken down into 'hat' which means house and 'hor' which is Horus, the embodiment of kingship or another name for king.

The planets in chaos (Mars, Venus, Mercury and the Moon) dwelt in this 'house' and therefore Hathor was 'the house of the king'. The kings lost their giant 'star like' guise (Osiris) as they moved closer to Earth. They became 'living breathing gods' as hazy surface features and red disk outlines were observed. This incredible transformation, from star to 'living god', occurred many times within Hathor as she played her part as mother-goddess by giving birth to divine celestial bodies. Hathor played host for varying lengths of time, paralleling the chronology of ancient Egypt as the planets ruled earth as god-kings. Therefore, Earth's band in the guise of Hathor was exactly as history reveals – the house of the king.

'Mysterious One who gives birth to the divine entities...'

'You from whom the Divine Entities come forth in this Your Name of Mut-Aset.'

(Excerpts from a hymn dedicated to Hathor at the Temple of Horus and Edfu)

This quotation is explicitly clear. If we examine the orthodox belief, Hathor as house-king makes no sense at all in a human context. For example, if Hathor was a mythical sky goddess, how could the 'house of the king' be in the heavens when the king or queen inhabited the earth? It is evident that we must take the translation of Hathor's name quite literally as 'the house of the king'.

The mothering aspect of Hathor is self explanatory and referred to the divine haze that arched across the heavens to 'house royalty'. This conjures up a familiar image as mothers throughout the ages have nursed and housed their offspring. This also explains why one of the titles given to the pharaohs was 'son of Hathor' which was a title befitting this divine relationship in heaven.

HATHOR AND ISIS

Hymn to Hathor from Denderah

The King, Pharaoh, comes to dance,
He comes to sing;
Mistress, see the dancing,
Wife of Horus, see the skipping!

He offers it to you,
This jug;
Mistress, see the dancing,
Wife of Horus, see the skipping!

His heart is straight, his inmost open,
No darkness is in his breast;
Mistress, see the dancing,
Wife of Horus, see the skipping!

(http://www1.hollins.edu/Docs/academics/divisioni/classica l%20studies/saloweyca/clas%20260/HATHOR.html)

The emergence of royalty amidst Hathor and the subsequent 'mothering' can be supported by looking at a very common image of Hathor. If you look at the illustration on page 123, this particular image of Hathor with cow's horns and an unusual hairstyle was standard and ubiquitous. It is regularly found on architectural columns and was traditionally used to decorate Hathor's musical instrument, the sistrum.

Hathor's hair was so distinctive that scholars have dubbed it the 'Hathor hairdo'. It was not a heavily bejewelled or elaborately braided hairstyle as was typical of ancient Egyptian imagery or custom. It was simplicity in the extreme and took the form of a simple quiff which was frequently parted down the middle and wrapped around Hathor's face as part of an elaborate style.

I believe this particular trait, and in fact Hathor's entire image, was wholly symbolic of Earth's celestial 'haze' as it wrapped itself around the 'royal' celestial bodies. A universal cosmic phenomenon enveloped the kings as they were born to earth – the 'lady to the limit of the universe' enveloped the kings as they took the throne as 'sons of Hathor'.

How else could the ancient Egyptians represent such a manifestation? The planets were gods; they were 'swathed' by a phenomenon that remained for millennium and this divine relationship demanded representation. Hathor was given a human face which symbolically represented the face of the king.

The debris which enshrouded the kings was represented by the 'curling' hairdo. The ancient Egyptians could not portray the king's face within Hathor's hair as this would merely be the king with the same hairstyle as Hathor which would be totally confusing. The kings did not become Hathor – they were merely nurtured by this goddess; they did not take on her attributes but emerged from within them. When the kings died and moved away from Earth to become stars (star attribute = Osiris), they were occasionally portrayed in the image of Osiris (Seti). This was understandable because they took on this god's 'star' attributes.

Bovine attribute

'Her role as royal mother is illustrated by a statue of Hathor in the form of as cow suckling the pharaoh Amenhotep II (1427 CC) from a chapel at Deir el Bahri (now in the Egyptian museum Cairo).' (ibid)

Hathor's most famous manifestation is as a cow. Even when she appeared as a woman, she often wore cow's horns, or a pair of cow's ears. Hathor is frequently depicted suckling the pharaoh, whether in the guise of the cow or as a sycamore fig, a tree that exudes a white milky substance. At the Shrine of Hathor; Hatshepsut (Venus) and Tuthmosis III (Moon) are depicted bringing offerings to Hathor. Hatshepsut (Venus) is also seen nursing from the divine cow.

If we examine this image in more detail, we will see that Hathor is depicted as a very large cow with horns. There also appears to be a large sun-disk between the horns.

Hatshepsut is shown at least a quarter of the size of Hathor and is kneeling below Hathor's rear legs sucking milk from her udder.

This imagery may seem strange and unfamiliar to us. Are we to assume that ancient Egyptians lived in a world of giant cows? Why did they portray such a surreal scene? By using the GKS, I will show that such images had a purpose. To explain this further we must revisit Saturn's rings.

Saturn's rings broke up into countless narrow ringlets which resembled the grooves of an old-fashioned gramophone record. Although there are countless rings, it is possible to make out bands with distinctive, bright features. Planetary scientists have sectioned out a least seven 'bands' and have labelled them A to G. Some of the gaps separating the bands have also been named. There is the narrow 'Encke division' and the larger 'Cassini division' which spans 5000 kilometres and separates the A and B rings. It is believed that these gaps were created by tiny satellites as they swept out bands of particles. For example, the two 'shepherd' moons, Pandora and Prometheus, orbit in gaps either side of the narrow F ring. They are known as shepherds because they prevent the ring particles from straying.

A recent space probe called Cassini was sent to study Saturn's rings and its moon, Titan, in September 2004 and made a remarkable discovery. It went through a gap in Saturn's rings and captured an incredible image of the moon Prometheus 'sucking out' some of the dust particles from Saturn's F ring. An image of this can be found on the Nasa web site. It clearly shows a faint stream of material or 'streamer' connecting the moon to the ring. The moon is gravitationally perturbing the material as the satellite passes near to the ring. Although this was not mentioned, it is common sense to assume that Prometheus is slowly 'clearing up' Saturn's F ring.

Imagine you are on the surface of Saturn gazing up at its glorious rings arching across the heavens. Would you be able to observe Prometheus interacting with the rings? What of Saturn's numerous other satellites? Other moons similar to Prometheus would also assist in 'clearing up' Saturn's rings, but would any of them be visible?

Although the satellites within the rings are very small, it is possible they would be seen because the rings are wafer thin in places. It is also possible that any interaction with the rings would also be seen. If we added larger satellites or planets, they would definitely be seen just as our Moon is seen. I believe they would also be observed 'sucking up' Saturn's rings. If we deify Saturn's rings as Hathor and treat any celestial body orbiting Saturn and interacting with the rings as divine, the result is divine entities 'suckling' from Saturn's 'Hathor'.

These incredible events were observed by humans long before we sent space probes to Saturn. They were observed thousands of years ago by ancient cultures throughout the world. Such events were common place and took place on a far grander scale due to the heightened celestial events of 4,000 years ago. Earth's band, as Hathor, was far thicker and denser than it is today. It housed numerous satellites and at times these satellites were observed 'suckling' Hathor's milk. The god-kings or royal family 'suckled' Hathor as the divine celestial cow. As well as battling up large debris, the living-gods periodically sucked in fine dust and gasses and this phenomenon was perceived as Hathor suckling the pharaohs. This was a natural and understandable perception as the planets were the true god-kings.

It is clear that the nourishing manifestations of Hathor can easily be understood, and the iconography surrounding this goddess can be taken at face value. There is a statue in the Cairo museum that depicts Hathor as a cow suckling Amenhotep II. This represents Amenhotep as a facet of Mars within Earth's rings 'sucking' in the finer dust and debris – Mars suckling Hathor. The same reasoning applies to the scene depicting Hatshepsut suckling Hathor; this is Hatshepsut as an aspect of Venus taking advantage of the nourishing generosity afforded by Hathor.

If we examine Hathor in the guise of giving milk as 'the lady of the sycamore' this too can be explained. This represents many satellites feeding from the edges of Earth's ring. Hathor's great cosmic band arches across the heavens on an east/west axis with many small divine moons in the southern sky 'suckling' from the hazy edges of Hathor. This gives the illusion of a gigantic cosmic tree with small celestial bodies sucking from its branches.

The sycamore fig exudes a white milky substance which is why this tree was used to assist Hathor in her bovine guise. Ancient peoples had to draw on the natural world around them to represent events in the heavens. If the sycamore fig tree excreted 'milk' and Hathor was known to give milk, then the milk-producing tree could represent one of Hathor's many guises.

Titles such as 'the lady of turquoise', 'the golden one' and 'the gold that is Hathor' logically referred to the colour of Hathor as she appeared during the night, at dusk, at dawn or during the day. We have established that Hathor was a band of debris that once surrounded Earth. If the ancient Egyptians occasionally referred to her as golden or turquoise, then it is likely that at some point she appeared gold and turquoise. There were also references to Hathor adorning many colours:

'The Beautiful, with numerous colours...'

(Naville, Edouard, The XIth Dynasty Temple at Deir El-Bahari, Part III, p. 8, pl.IX)

It is puzzling that scholars, when referring to Hathor as the golden one, erroneously refer to her close relationship with Re (daughter of Re) as the likely source of this title. Remember that Re was depicted as red-coloured and not golden, so there is no connection between a golden Hathor and a red Sun.

The attributes and imagery of Hathor (and all gods) do not descend from a 'bizarre world' of infinite imaginary gods or fairytales. They point to actual events and a real world of chaos; they are all symbolic of celestial phenomena which has since disappeared.

One interesting point concerns a late king called Nakhthorheb which may have been represented by our Moon. His birth name was 'beloved of Hathor' which implies that this particular king ruled Egypt from within or amidst the hazy band of debris which arched across the heavens.

Isis

Hathor's countless manifestations were mainly observed arching across the heavens at night and during dusk and dawn. Considering the infinite permutations of celestial chaos, Hathor was probably observed enshrouding and nurturing the monarchy for extensive periods during the day. However, there were undoubtedly prolonged periods when Hathor was not visible during the day. These were times when, as the Sun rose, Hathor slowly disappeared due to the power of Re's diminished red light.

The god-kings were clearly observed but were not in the company of Hathor. This situation was true of the New Kingdom (1000 BC RC) when major events switched to the Sun side during the day when Venus, Mercury, Mars and the Moon dominated the skies. There were also occasions when the god-kings ruled Earth during the night from a location outside of Earth's ring (Hathor), as it seemed they were not within Hathor.

Hathor was 'physically' observed nurturing the monarchy and was perceived as a 'mother goddess' who looked after royalty when Hathor wasn't seen. Who took on the role of 'great mother' when royalty was not enshrouded by Hathor and who would tend to the 'house' of the kings? It was the Egyptian goddess Isis.

Isis and Hathor were sometimes indistinquisable. This is because they were both forms of Earths ring of debris. They were both home to the red disk of the monarchy.

Isis was one of the most important goddesses of ancient Egypt, and she remains one of the most well known of this era. Isis appeared as a beautiful woman in magnificent clothing, sometimes wearing the red sun-disk. Unlike Hathor, she had almost no variant forms and her colours were white, gold, and cobalt blue. As with Hathor, Isis was a 'goddess of countless names' such as the Lady of Heaven, the Great Enchantress, Goddess of Magic, the Goddess of Love and War, the Giver of Life, Queen of the Gods, and Goddess of Marriage and Protection. She was revered as the great protector, prayed to for guidance, and beseeched for peace in the world. Temples to Isis are found everywhere in Egypt and many houses had shrines to her devotion.

Many scholars suspect that beneath her multiple guises there is only one goddess, one underlying concept upon which a wide spectrum of variations freely evolved. Yet, even in the most well established instances, the goddess seems to be everywhere and nowhere. Egyptologists have alternately explained the goddess Isis as the Earth, the starry sky, the Moon, the planet Venus, the star Sirius and more. Catastrophists have mainly alluded to Isis as the planet Venus. In the hieroglyphic texts, the goddess appears as a throne, the 'eye' of the Sun god, a serpent, an egg, and even a lock of hair. One must surely wonder if an accurate representation of the goddess is possible.

'Her origins are uncertain.'
(Shaw & Nicholson, 2002, p 142)

Identification

Isis is one of the few deities that cannot be attributed to a definitive natural phenomenon such as 'Hathor's haze' although later she may have been associated with the star Sirius. She was a mythical figure, but not to the extent that scholars believe. As with Hathor, Isis was closely associated with the monarchy and had a real physical presence.

Certain attributes of Hathor and Isis are interchangeable and logical reasoning dictates there must have been a connection between the two. We have established that Hathor was Earth's ring and this phenomenon must therefore be connected to Isis. If we take a look at some of the attributes of this goddess, this identification will become very apparent.

In the first century AD, Greek philosopher Plutarch believed that Hathor and Isis were one and the same (Mariette, op. cit, p. 142). We can think of Isis as an invisible form of the goddess Hathor. Isis was the 'Great Mother Goddess' to the monarchy when they were not being nurtured by Hathor. This was mainly during the day when the incredible power of the light from the Sun deemed Hathor's phenomenon invisible. Unlike Hathor, who could physically be observed enveloping the monarchy, Isis was part of the sky during the day. As the day represents light, so Isis was connected to the light. Hathor could be seen whereas Isis, in the form of light, was transparent. As a sky goddess she took on an almost omnipresent role and granted visibility, birth, growth development and vigour to the royal family. By doing this, Isis herself was granted a divine presence.

The monarchy were temporary 'kings' of the Earth and came under the umbrella of universal 'mothers & 'fathers'. Where possible, this role was given to the celestial bodies (Re as father) or celestial phenomenon (Hathor as mother) that remained for millennia. If the royal family was not 'wrapped' in Hathor, a mother goddess was invented to care for them. As the main events occurred within the same portion of the sky that Hathor resided in, a beautiful great goddess was invented with similar attributes. According to the ancient Egyptians, they were two separate deities although it could be argued that Isis was indeed the transparent Hathor.

'She [Isis] shines into her temple on New Years Day, and she mingles her light with that of her father Ra on the horizon.'
(From the Temple of Isis at Denderah)

Isis, through her connection with the light, could have been associated with the advent of daylight which is in the east, whereas Hathor could have been associated with the west.

This is because Hathor became visible as the Sun set in the west and Isis took over as the Sun rose in the east.
Name

The name Isis comes from the hieroglyph of the throne with a female ending reading 'Mistress of the Throne'. Her name may originally have meant 'seat' and the emblem she wore on her head may have been the sign of a throne. I believe this has a similar meaning to Hathor's 'house of the king' because 'throne' has the same connotation as 'chamber' or 'house'.

Isis and Hathor 'housing' the red disk of the Sun

'From the new kingdom onwards, she was closely connected with Hathor and so sometimes wore a solar disk between cow horns.'

(Shaw & Nicholson, 2002, p 142)

There is a direct correlation between Hathor and Isis as sky goddesses 'housing' royalty which can be found by examining a common guise. Hathor, whether in the guise of a cow or a goddess, was often depicted with a headdress consisting of a red disk surrounded by cow's horns. Isis as goddess would often be depicted in this fashion also. The image of the red disk with horns is a ubiquitous image and other goddesses were portrayed in this fashion.

We have established that not all red disks were representations of the Sun; Mars, Venus, Mercury and the Moon appeared as red disks many times. I believe the red disks, when portrayed in this fashion, symbolised the act of playing host to the predominantly 'red' disks of the royal family and this 'sheltering' included the red Sun. The royal family appeared amidst Hathor or Isis which warranted representation; Hathor was mother and 'the house of the king' while Isis had a similar role during the day. What better symbol could be used than the ubiquitous red disk of the monarchy?

Isis as mother & sky goddess – similar trait to Hathor

'Praise to you, Isis, the Great One, God's mother, Lady of Heaven, Mistress and Queen of the gods.'

(From the Temple of Isis at Philae – translations by Louis Zabkar in Hymns to Isis in Her Temple at Philae)

'The king however was also described as the son of Isis, who appears to have usurped Hathor's role when the legend of Isis, Seth and Osiris was conflated with that of the birth of Horus.'

(Shaw & Nicholson, 2002)

'Goddess who encapsulated the virtues of the archetypal Egyptian wife and mother. She was the sister- wife to Osiris and mother to Horus and such became the symbolic mother of the Egyptian king, who himself regarded as a human manifestation of Horus.'

(Shaw & Nicholson, 2002, p 142)

Royalty, when it manifested as Horus, was both 'Son of Isis' and 'Son of Hathor' as there were references to both. Such contradictory beliefs can be extremely confusing. However, if we use the GKS, this can easily be explained. Kings appeared amidst Hathor or the monarchy simply by appearing during the day. A king could also be born amidst

Hathor during the night, only to move into position as a 'living god' during the day.

Similar bovine connections were related to Isis and her maternal roles. These included the 'Isis cow', mother to the Apis bull and the 'great white sow of Heliopolis'. She was commonly portrayed with cow's horns and a red solar disk. Such traits were consistent with her identification as a goddess who was responsible for a transparent form of Earth's ring of debris and therefore we would expect similar nurturing traits to be observed as those associated with Hathor. The reference to Isis as the 'great white sow' may be a reference to the colour of Isis during the day – a white, ancient sky, or a white band which arched across the sky.

'Isis, giver of life, residing in the Sacred Mound...'

(From the Temple of Isis at Philae – translations by Louis Zabkar in Hymns to Isis in Her Temple at Philae)

This highlights a connection between the colour of milk and the milky colour of Hathor during the night. Royalty were 'born' during the day amidst a white sky and the monarchy appeared amidst Hathor's whitish band during the night. Isis, as the great mother goddess, nurtured the kings and queens of Egypt as they ruled the heavens during the day.

It is possible that similar scenes such as the 'suckling of royalty' were observed during the day. Such phenomena wouldn't have been as visible during the day and were therefore attributed to the beautiful goddess Isis rather than Hathor cow. Many statues show Isis as she suckled the infant Horus on her knee. Horus was the embodiment of kingship, and such depictions symbolised royalty inhabiting the day. It was a recurring image, particularly during the New Kingdom, which represented the numerous appearances of the royal entourage during the day.

Here is an image of Isis suckling Horus. All pharaohs were Horus 'god on Earth' and this image represents Isis as Earth's daytime hazy band nurturing the god king planets.

Isis rose to prominence during the New Kingdom (1000 BC RC) when she usurped the role of Hathor. This rise to prominence parallels the time frame when many main celestial events switched from the night (space side) to the day (Sun side); the monarchy now principally appeared during the day.

Royalty initially consisted of facets of Mars and Venus and later (8th century BC) Mercury and the Moon. All dominated the day and night and were granted life by Isis in the form of light, the sky or both. It is logical to assume there was a reason why Isis usurped Hathor. According to the GKS, there was a significant change in the heavens as a new order was born which coincided with the time Isis rose to power.

According to orthodox belief, mortal kings believed they were nurtured by a mythical sky goddess. However, the GKS explains that these god-kings were in fact planets in close proximity to Earth. They loomed larger than the Moon and were clearly seen during the day courtesy of the red-sun, and were nurtured by the great goddess Isis. It was these 'living gods' that granted Isis divine presence and the cult of Isis and Hathor eventually died out when the god-kings no longer inhabited the skies above.

Red Sun – Red Planets – divine relationship with the Sun god Re

The Sun wasn't the only red orb inhabiting the heavens; the planets also had a distinctly reddish hue when reigning over Earth which was understandable as they were planets in turmoil. This distinctive trait held a direct and physical association with the Sun which led to them being perceived as directly related to our perennial red Sun. According to the ancient Egyptians, the divine astral kings and queens were perceived as 'offspring' of the solar deity Re.

It is important to note that we are discussing the appearance of the royal family when in close proximity to Earth. They were in the position of being born to Earth. They also came alive as the hazy outline of the planets was observed.

When they were at a distance or moving away from Earth, these planets took on the attributes of a star (Osiris). In this 'star-like' form, they were either journeying to the next world, or living an eternal life in the heavens above. Therefore, the heavens were inhabited by a red sun and red planets.

Mars, the red god of war

We have established that the red Sun coincided with 3,000 years of chaos when Mars was slowly and systematically torn apart. It was in turmoil, blasting incalculable amounts of dust and debris into space which turned our glaring golden Sun into a diminished red Sun. Any planet in a state of chaos and in close proximity to the Earth would appear as a reddish orb. There were internal convulsions as thousands of volcanoes simultaneously erupted and covered the surface of Mars with scalding hot molten lava. Tidal friction and catastrophic bombardments all contributed to give Mars a distinctly reddish hue.

Mars now appears as a peaceful, twinkling 'star'. If it moved closer to Earth so that it loomed larger than the Sun as it appeared in ancient times, it would appear as a red disk, a red king reigning over Earth. Mars is known as the red god of war and NASA refers to it as the red planet. Most people understand a little of the science connected with the heavens and recognize that Mars has a stable orbit. However, back in ancient times they did not understand the workings of the cosmos. As Mars constantly moved back and forth to Earth in the form of a red orb it was given many pharonic names. The other main perpetrators of chaos also appeared as red orbs.

Venus is a scalding new planet recently born from Jupiter only 5,000 years ago. It is still in the process of cooling down and its surface temperature is a whopping 800 F. What was its temperature some 3,000-4,000 years ago at the height of planetary chaos? Common sense dictates it must have been far hotter than today. Given such basic traits, how would Venus have appeared when close to Earth other than as a reddish orb? After the red Sun, I believe Venus was the perennial red disk. Mars battled itself to death while Venus cooled down. Therefore the appearance of Venus would have been far more constant than Mars.

Mercury, born sometime in the 7th century BC from the solid iron core of Mars, reached temperatures hotter than the Sun. It began life as a glaring golden sun, Aten, and rapidly cooled down to become an incandescent red orb.

The Moon, although a speck of dust in comparison to the other bodies, took on the form of a red orb on many occasions. Because of its size, it would have cooled down long before it reached the vicinity of Earth. My belief is that the tidal forces of the planets as they tugged on the Moon caused intense friction, or tidal heating. This friction, along with catastrophic bombardments which still affect the Earth today, caused the Moon to heat up and glow red many times. It is worth noting that the Moon today can take on a reddish hue, although this is due to atmospheric conditions and light refraction.

If my theory is correct and events occurred as described, the planets would have appeared as red orbs many times. The Moon is a sphere, as are all other planets, and spheres in chaos would predominantly appear red. But Egyptians did not view them as red orbs or planetary bodies as we understand them – they were gods – divine kings and queens named and renamed as they moved back and forth to Earth.

I have suggested that the millions of red disks that adorn almost every tomb, temple and monument were not all representations of the Sun. This is because many of them were images or symbolic representations of the main perpetrators of chaos – Mars, Venus and later the Moon and Mercury. This was true of the numerous red disks incorporated into the headgear worn by the monarchy and the gods. Not all were red suns – many symbolically represented the red-disked monarchy.

The monarchy did not appear red on every occasion because, unlike the immovable Sun which was always a red disk, the planets occasionally appeared in other colours such as black, blue, yellow, green and white as depicted in the art of the Egyptians. The colour contrast and appearance of the planets depended on many variables such as location, light refraction and the internal state of the planets. The planets were god-kings and god-queens and the colour of such divine entities was of paramount importance. Many statues and images were commissioned to represent the basic colour of the kings while they reigned over Earth. For example, if a king reigned for a number of years with distinctive colour traits, this would be reflected in the art, particularly in the statues of the monarchy. Ramesses the Great is a prime example and by examining the statues we can deduce that two of the most basic colours associated with Mars/Ramesses were red and black.

Many statues were carved from black or red granite, and some were carved from natural rock and painted red. This tells us that Mars appeared predominantly red but occasionally appeared black. In the case of black statues, the Egyptians traveled many hundreds of miles to find suitable rock to match the colour of the king because the god-kings had to be appeased.

Sometimes statues of Ramesses were made of red granite with a blue crown, although the crown wasn't actually coloured blue. This is because the red granite was maintained and no colouring was added to the crown. The blue crown indicated that Mars/Ramesses appeared as a red orb with perhaps a blue tinge to it.

The same basic principle applied to all kings and queens and other royal dignitaries. If they appeared red, red stone was used; if black, black was used; if white, white was used etc. If a stone or rock couldn't be found to match the colour of the royal figure, sandstone or limestone was used and painted in the matching colour.

There are many avenues to explore regarding the colour of the planets and the way they were directly reflected in Egyptian art. However, despite the variety of colours adopted by the monarchy, the most basic form of a planet in turmoil when it ventured close to Earth was a red disk or red orb. This is why the red disk dominated Egyptian art.

In summary, when reigning over Earth, Mars and Venus dominated the heavens in the form of hazy red disks. They were later joined by the Moon and Mercury and they took on a similar appearance. When close to Earth, these planets appeared many times larger than the Sun – perhaps two metres at arms length. Although the heavens were littered with dust and debris, these planets were clearly seen, particularly in Egypt where it did not rain due to less energy from the Sun. When they moved away from Earth (when temporarily dying), the planets took on the attributes of gigantic stars.

CHILDREN OF THE SUN

Sa-Re 'Son of Re' (offspring of the red-Sun)

The pharaohs were given many sacred names and titles. I believe these were titles given to planetary bodies as they dominated the heavens and they were of the utmost importance. In fact, the significance of these names and titles cannot be stressed enough and we will therefore examine a selection of them.

Sa-Re (son of Re)

From the Middle Kingdom onwards, the kings were given the title '*Sa-Re*' which indicated that the king was the 'son of Re' and his heir on Earth. This title can be found preceding the king's cartouche, an oval shaped rope that magically encircled the king's name. It was a common title which denoted the king's birth name. Typical examples were as follows:

Tuthmosis III
*'The Good God, Lord of the Two Lands, King of Upper and Lower Egypt, Menkheperre, **Son of Re**, Thutmosis, given life eternally.'*

(Davies, 1987, p 45)

Sesostris I
*'Kheperkare', **Son of Re** 'Sesostris', (may he be) granted life, stability, and wealth like Re eternally.'*

(Gardiner, 1957, p 71)

'The relationship of the Egyptian gods with human beings however was generally benign. Humans were part of that richness of creation, and they were connected to the divine through the pharaoh, who himself had a divine decent from Re.'

(Chapman, 2002, p 34)

There are other similar references which confirm that pharaohs were considered offspring of the solar deity Re. We have mentioned that many queens also made reference to Re as their father. Examples included Hatshepsut and the legendary Cleopatra.

We are all children of the Sun. However, according to the GKS, this title holds much more substance than the belief that mortals were related to the Sun. This ubiquitous title arose because of a direct and physical association between red planetary bodies as they inhabited the same arena as the red Sun, forming a divine 'celestial family'.

Assuming there were no global catastrophes, Re (the red Sun) perpetually rose in the east, traversed across the heavens and set in the west in a very predictable and easily measurable cycle. His epithets confirm he was one of the original creator gods and was thought to have created the universe. He appeared as a living, breathing red disk, never altering his size and always remaining at the same distance. The red solar disk of Re presided over the cosmos as an immoveable and eternal god; a father to all.

The god-king planets, however, were different; they were neither immortal nor immovable. Their size and appearance changed as they moved back and forth to Earth in a cycle of death and rebirth. They began life as gigantic stars in the heavens above, became 'living gods' (Horus) as they dominated Earth's skies, and eventually died (albeit a temporary death) as they moved away and journeyed to heaven.

Although not immortal, the god-king planets had much in common with Re – two distinct traits that physically connected them to the Sun. Firstly, they inhabited the same arena as the Sun. Secondly, when reigning over Earth, they adopted the same basic appearance as the Sun – a red orb. It therefore seems obvious that these divine bodies were perceived as 'offspring of the Sun'.

Red orbs visited the Earth in unpredictable cycles and were considered children of the almighty and steadfast red Sun. They were regarded as bodies taking kingship over the Earth under the divine authority of Re, the perennial father. Re watched over his celestial children and dictated and granted kingship to his offspring and heirs. This was true whether or not the planets appeared during the day or night or in a variety of locations; when reigning over Earth they were all perceived as 'sons of Re'.

Re would always be the father to these 'mortal' astral entities and it was Re who was the 'opener of days' and who dictated times and solar years. The planets could not compare to the light emitted by Re (a light which had no glare) as they were mere children in comparison to the almighty Sun god.

No Moon!

It is puzzling that we have the title *Sa-Re* ('son of Re') but no titles alluding to the Moon. The Moon is closer to the

Earth than the Sun, and it dominates the night sky and even has the power to blot out the Sun during a solar eclipse. However, the Egyptians never associated earthly kings with the Moon. There were no titles alluding to the pharaohs as being 'son of Thoth' which was one of the many names given to the Moon. The Sun and Moon have not altered their paths across the heavens for millennia and therefore we should find a title similar in meaning or of equal importance to those relating to the Sun. Did the Egyptians completely ignore their nearest celestial neighbour?

There were no titles such given to the Moon or Thoth because the Moon had not yet settled into its regular monthly cycle. The Moon was born from Jupiter around 5,000 years ago and the process by which it was captured took several millennia. During pharonic times, the Moon was an erratic body that did not rise or set in an orderly or predictable monthly cycle. Unlike the Sun, the Moon could not be counted on to measure time. In fact, it was so erratic it took on many guises before falling under the gravitational spell of the Earth. The only predictable celestial body that existed 4,000 years ago was the Sun. The planets and all other bodies were totally unpredictable because they were in chaos.

One guise of the Moon was the lunar god Thoth, a deity who acted as a scribe to the gods and a measurer of the heavens. Thoth was a magical deity who settled into orbit around the Earth and assisted in judging the deceased by recording the results of the 'weighing of the heart'. If the deceased had led a good and just life, they were allowed to pass to a life of eternity amongst the stars. This involved a perilous journey through the heavens due to ongoing cosmic chaos.

King or Queen

We have established that the numerous kings and queens of ancient Egypt were first and foremost names given to the planets Mars, Venus, Mercury and the Moon each and every time they visited Earth. Furthermore, Mars, Mercury and the Moon were perceived as male warrior god-kings while Venus was always the 'great wife' or queen to the god-kings. But what criteria dictated the gender of the planets, the sexuality of Re's offspring and the gender of the red disked monarchy?

Mars was never perceived as a queen and Venus never appeared as a king. Is it possible that thousands of years of reincarnation allowed Mars to reign as a king only to be reincarnated a few years later as a queen? Perhaps the pharonic name 'Ramesses the Great' referred to Venus while Nefertari (wife of Ramesses) was Mars? What of the other main perpetrators of chaos, Mercury and the Moon. Although they appeared two thousand years after Mars and Venus, is it possible they changed gender? If we consider cosmic chaos, we cannot rule out the possibility of gender change or occasional mistaken identity. However, I believe there were little or no mistakes with the gender of the four main bodies _ Mars, Venus, Mercury and the Moon.

There were three basic factors which dictated the gender of the planets. The first and most significant was the behavioural traits of the planets. However, this was closely connected to their location and appearance. For example, a red orb in close proximity to Earth which encountered and fended off space debris before being catastrophically bombarded by this debris was perceived as a fearless warrior king maintaining divine order (ma'at) by battling the forces of evil (Seth). A large red orb which remained serene in the background and which didn't take part in these events was perceived as a divine queen or a 'great wife' to the battling god-kings. These traits were drawn from the antiquated natural world where men did the fighting while the women kept house. For example, the main perpetrators of chaos, Mars, Mercury and the Moon, came very close to Earth numerous times and were perceived as warrior kings. Meanwhile Venus remained predominantly in the background, acting as a beautiful divine queen.

Mars and Venus were the original 'divine couple' whereas Mercury and the Moon appeared two thousand years later. Mars and Venus were sent down from heaven by the gods to reign over Earth for the 'first time', a phase which is found in the mythology of most ancient cultures. As a result, they gave rise to the birth of pharonic Egypt and played a major part in shaping Egyptian religion and the many beliefs related to the monarchy. They set many precedents which lasted for millennia and if we examine their basic attributes we will identify the origin of their masculine and feminine identities.

Mars the god of war – the original warrior king

Throughout the entire 3,000 years of chaos, Mars was an aggressive planet; a red-blooded male; a king 'ready for battle'; a fearless warrior pharaoh.

Cosmic chaos created unimaginable amounts of dust and debris which turned the glaring Sun into a diminished red disk. Although Venus belched out billions of tons of gasses, Mars churned out the bulk of space debris. Mars has been slowly and systematically torn apart, and has literally battled itself to death. Great chunks of Mars have blasted out into space via its hundreds of thousands of volcanic vents. Even its heart, the solid iron core, was sucked out to create Mercury. This resulted in the loss of its protective magnetic field, its atmosphere and its once great oceans. Dust and debris amassed and, from the perspective of Earth, the Sun was turned red for hundreds of centuries.

An aggressive demeanour is associated with masculinity and the traits displayed by Mars gave it a masculine identity. As Mars was pulverised by space debris, it also churned out incalculable quantities of its own debris and this intense bombardment was the key to its identity. Mars vanquished the evil debris using qualities which could only ever be associated with a red blooded male.

In one of its many encounters with Earth, Mars appeared as a hazy red sphere, a 'son of Re'. It loomed many times larger than the Sun and was clearly observed day and night courtesy of the diminished red Sun. It became a living, breathing, fiery orb as internal convulsions and incessant electrical discharges were observed through a haze of dust. As it traversed the heavens it encountered huge amounts of asteroids and comets that had accumulated around the Earth. Mars fearlessly faced this evil material head on. Like a raging bull, it charged through the vile debris and catastrophically blasted it to smithereens.

Because of its planetary size, nothing could defeat this Horus of the heavens. It dealt with the evil enemy with ruthless efficiency and swept up billions of tons of debris in the process. This period of 'smiting the enemy' continued for an incredible 3,000 years as Mars moved back and forth to Earth hundreds of times in a conflict between the forces of good and evil. The evidence for these cosmic battles can be found in the millions of impact craters that still litter the surface of Mars. They are a silent witness to a very recent and catastrophic past when Mars created debris via its volcanoes and also cataclysmically cleared it up.

It is appropriate that Mars was always perceived as a male warrior – a fearless god-king. For 3,000 years, in the guise of the many pharaohs of Egypt, Mars fended off the evil that threatened to bring the whole world into chaos. Even when Mars was not observed in the act of vanquishing the enemy, its internal 'aggressive' convulsions and incessant electrical discharges established Mars as a red blooded male. Today, as a speck of light residing in the heavens, Mars still remains undefeated.

It is ironic that Mars was slowly being destroyed, battling from a vibrant planet to a lifeless ball, although this was not recognised by ancient cultures. They had no understanding of physical science and regarded Mars as a warrior king fearlessly clearing a path to the heavens and the afterlife. If we could observe Mars as it appeared to our ancient forebears, what gender would we assign to it?

Venus –goddess of love and beauty – the perennial passive queen; divine of body – the beautiful one

Venus has not experienced the changes Mars has undergone. Throughout 3,000 years of chaos, Venus appeared as a placid body; a divine and beautiful queen and a loyal and devoted consort to the battling Mars.

Venus was a new addition to the solar system and, since its cataclysmic birth from Jupiter, it has been cooling down for the past 5,000 years. It was never a working planet like Earth or Mars. Because of its recent creation, Venus had nothing to tear apart or destroy. There were no great land masses, vast oceans or atmosphere to dissipate or blast out into space, no invisible magnetic field to tear down, no solid iron core to suck out. Unlike Mars, Venus was unable to battle itself to death because it was, and still is, a gigantic ball of scalding hot rock in the process of cooling down.

During pharonic times, Venus was observed at greater distances than Mars because it is roughly twice the size of the red planet. Queen Venus was a red ball of magma that appeared as an incandescent red disk. It saw little activity as it cooled down and settled into orbit around the Sun. It appeared far more stable, uniform and serene than Mars as it exhibited female traits as a beautiful, divine queen of Egypt.

There were times when Venus appeared in a seductive, translucent 'skirt' which emphasised her femininity. This was produced as Venus slowly cooled down and developed a thin atmosphere. Sulphur clouds formed and combined with the tidal extraction of volatiles from Mars which included carbon dioxide and other gases. This gave Venus a thin, translucent veil shrouding its red disk. From the perspective of ancient cultures, Venus was wrapped in transparent clothing as worn by a divine queen.

The appearance of Venus in see-through attire is clearly reflected in the art of the Egyptians, particularly in relation to the queens of the New Kingdom (with Venus Sun-side in respect to Earth). Many queens were shown wearing seductive, transparent attire. Hatshepsut, Nefertari (wife of Ramesses), Nefertiti (wife of Akhenaten) and the great seductress, Cleopatra, and many others were regularly portrayed wearing seductive, transparent clothing. It is logical to identify these queens with Venus and the transparent attire is undoubtedly a symbolic representation of Venus adorned with a hazy atmosphere.

Such images mystify scholars who conclude that the ancient Egyptians were extremely open about their sexuality because the queens of Egypt wore transparent clothing. I feel this is incorrect because such a male dominated world would not have tolerated queens parading through the land half naked. However, it is reasonable to assume that the beautiful red disk of Venus wearing a seductive, hazy veil made of see-through linen represented queens such as Cleopatra.

There is similar transparent 'skirt' iconography depicted on some Babylonian cylinder seals which show the goddess Ishtar (Inanna/Venus) wearing the same seductive apparel. Hatshepsut belonged to the early part of the New Kingdom whereas Cleopatra was the last queen of pharonic Egypt and they were both depicted wearing translucent attire. As 600 to 700 years separated them, we can conclude that from the beginning of the New Kingdom through to its demise, Venus regularly appeared with a thin veiled atmosphere. This is consistent with the sequential order of events. During cosmic chaos, the erratic movements of Venus prevented it from sustaining a thick atmosphere. However, Venus now has a dense, choking atmosphere because it no longer has an erratic orbit. It has stabilised to become the second rock from the Sun and its self-generated sulphuric gasses are gravitationally tied to Venus.

The way in which Egyptian queens were portrayed provides additional support for the GSK. The wearing of translucent clothing inexorably links the early New Kingdom queens and later queens with a common theme. It was not a traditional fashion statement as scholars believe. Queens were portrayed in such attire because they were personifications of Venus. However, it is important to note that Venus manifested itself in many forms. If we could observe Venus as a beautiful, red orb adorned with a transparent skirt, what gender would we ascribe to it?

Mars in the foreground, Venus at a distance

Venus was always identified as female although it was pummelled by incalculable amounts of space debris. In fact, Venus, Mars, Mercury and the Moon were all subjected to a constant barrage of space rubble. However, the bombardment of Venus was rarely observed by humans for a number of reasons. Firstly, Venus was further away from Earth than Mars and was therefore rarely observed in the act of 'smiting the enemy'. Although it was clearly seen because of its size, it was too far away for the Egyptians to see the trillions of tons of debris crashing to its surface. Venus was observed through dust and debris and this formed a cosmic haze which obscured the view. It had a newly formed, hot, molten surface and debris that crashed into this viscous layer had less of a devastating effect than debris that impacted a solid rock like Mars.

I will offer a brief explanation as to why the very masculine Mars came closer to Earth than the beautiful and very female Venus. The key is electromagnetic forces and simple magnetic attraction. Earth is twice the size of Mars and is home to a gigantic electromagnetic system. A spinning iron core at the centre of the Earth generates an electrical current that exits the South Polar Region, travels up and around the Earth and enters the North Polar Region. This creates an invisible magnetic shield (magnetosphere) that protects us from the deadly radiation emanating from the Sun and outer space. Having magnetic north and south poles, Earth is a huge magnet and this can be confirmed with a compass. The reason a compass needle points north is due to Earth's north magnetic pole. Mars was once a working planet the same as Earth, only half the size. It was once home to a very similar electromagnetic system as that found on Earth. Generating a magnetic field via its spinning core, Mars once had the attributes of a very large magnet. This came to an end sometime in the 7th century BC when the very source of its magnetic field, its solid iron core, was sucked out to become the planet Mercury.

Venus presents a totally different scenario. Although it is roughly the same size as Earth, Venus has never had an electromagnetic system due to its recent birth. It is and always has been devoid of any magnetic properties. It has no spinning core or protective magnetic field, no magnetic north and south, and absolutely nothing associated with an electromagnet.

In essence we have three bodies: a large magnet in the form of Earth; a smaller magnet in the form of Mars; a body devoid of any magnetic properties in the form of Venus. As Mars is only half the size of Earth, I believe the superior electromagnetic force of Earth attracted the smaller and inferior electromagnetic force of Mars. In simple terms, we had two magnets – one large and one small and the larger magnet attracted the smaller one. Venus had no magnetic properties at all and was unaffected by Earth's powerful electromagnetic force. Although gravity played a part, Venus was not attracted to Earth. Venus therefore kept a watchful eye on proceedings from a distance.

It is important to note that when Mars was magnetically drawn in towards Earth, these planets never collided. This was probably due to the Sun, gravity and inertia, i.e. the planets orbited around the Sun and were held on the ecliptic plane. The north pole of Mars may have tilted towards Earth due to electromagnetic attraction but it never collided with it.

For two thousand years, Mars orbited on or close to the orbital path of the Earth. Earth, acting as a large magnet with strong gravitational forces, pulled Mars back and forth to Earth many times in a process that produced numerous god-kings of ancient Egypt. This divine arrangement could not continue. The electromagnetic forces of the highly charged iron core were sucked out through the Martian crust and caused a huge scar called the Valles Marineris. It was the beginning of the end of Mars which was now devoid of any magnetic properties. Mars died as a working planet and became a shell of its former self. Gravitational forces took over and its core (now Mercury) slowly began its descent towards the Sun while Mars migrated out towards its present day orbit.

Throughout this time, Mercury and Mars visited Earth many times in the guise of various pharonic kings. Venus, having never possessed an electromagnetic system, was far less attracted to Earth and rarely came as close as Mars did.

Venus therefore remained in the background as a beautiful, divine queen to the god-king pharaohs.

It was only after the magnetic core of Mars was sucked out to become the planet Mercury and its electromagnetic system was destroyed that planetary chaos began to subside and the planets settled down into their current orbits. It is logical to assume that electromagnetic forces played a part. If gravity was the only force involved, Venus would have ventured as close to Earth as Mars, but it did not.

Certain catastrophists believe Venus travelled around the solar system on a highly elliptical orbit, but I disagree. Although Venus was pushed and pulled around the cosmos, I believe her erratic movements as observed from Earth were much more casual and relaxed. Venus, representing the many queens of Egypt, appeared as a distant reddish orb and moved in a manner similar to the passage of the Sun. As the Sun moves slowly across the sky, it appears serene and almost motionless. Likewise Venus, as a beautiful goddess, was reincarnated hundreds of times in the guise of divine queens such as Hatshepsut, Nefertari and Cleopatra. Venus never appeared as an 'aggressive' god charging across the heavens in her chariot to vanquish the enemy. This was the job of the warrior king Mars, and later Mercury and the Moon.

Venus was in the process of cooling down, although its surface had solidified and formed a rocky crust. Around 4,000 years ago at the height of cosmic chaos, the surface of Venus was far hotter and more molten than it is today – it was a planetary body covered with vast oceans of red hot lava. Any large rock that smashed into Venus caused less damage than a rock that smashed into a working planet like

Mars because the molten surface of Venus swallowed up any impacting space debris. Asteroids, comets and meteoroids plunged into the surface of Venus and rapidly disappeared without trace. Even huge masses of debris or great cosmic clouds of giant asteroids were absorbed with little effort. The consequences of impacts on a 'working planet' such as Mars resulted in cataclysmic explosions, carnage and utter devastation on a global scale. However Venus, being in such a viscous state, was a perfect vacuuming machine and cleared up huge amounts of space debris.

Evidence that Venus swallowed trillions of tons of space debris without a trace is found on the Venusian surface. Despite scalding hot temperatures, Venus has a variety of surface features including mountains, canyons, and valleys. About 65 percent of the surface is covered by flat, smooth plains which contain thousands of volcanoes. However, there is a distinct lack of impact craters. The Moon, Mars, and Mercury are covered with millions of impact craters, whereas Venus has about 900. This scarcity of impact craters is an enigma to cosmologists and geologists and has led to the conclusion that the present Venusian surface is less than 1 billion years old.

Cosmologists argue that Venus was born at the same time as the other planets around 4.7 billion years ago and they should all bear hallmarks showing the same intensity of impacts. However, the absence of craters has led scientists to reason that its surface must have renewed itself billion of years ago, ridding itself of any evidence of cosmic bombardment. They add that the craters we see today formed in the last billion years. This is a ridiculous scenario because there is no evidence for this and no explanation as to how Venus renewed its surface.

If we consider planetary chaos, there is nothing enigmatic about the shortage of impact craters on Venus. Remember that Venus was born only 5,000 years ago and was pulverised by space debris. There is little physical evidence of this bombardment because the scorching molten surface swallowed up any impacting bodies without a trace. Meteorites melted into the Venusian surface and the 900 or so impact craters we see today were formed after Venus cooled down and formed a solid, rocky crust. In other words, as Venus cooled down it began to bear the hallmarks of cosmic impacts and it slowly took on the same battered appearance of other planetary bodies. As there are so few impacts craters, I believe the formation of a rocky crust on Venus occurred towards the end of planetary chaos. This was when Venus had settled down in its present orbit and much of the space debris that coloured the Sun red had been cleared up.

As Venus lacked a magnetic field and had no established atmosphere, any debris destined to collide with this planet had a direct route to the Venusian surface and its sea of molten rock. This was in stark contrast to debris that encountered Mars which had to negotiate the well-established Martian atmosphere and magnetic field. This resulted in some meteoroids burning up or exploding in its upper atmosphere before falling to the surface as meteorites.

This same phenomenon occurs every day on Earth as space debris encounters Earth's upper atmosphere and magnetic field resulting in shooting stars. These are fragments of space debris which burn up and glow white hot in our upper atmosphere. Around 4,000 years ago at the height of planetary chaos, Mars lit up the heavens in a great battle as debris broke up in the Martian atmosphere or crashed to the surface causing catastrophic eruptions which rebounded out into space.

Mercury – the Moon

We have established that the gender of a planet is primarily related to its behavioural traits in respect to Earth. That is, a planet observed battling space debris close to Earth was deemed to be male, while a red orb with passive attributes which observed events from a distance was perceived as female. Mars was always recognised as a warrior king and Venus a divine queen. These original perpetrators of chaos set many precedents, particularly in regard to gender.

The actions of Mars and Venus also dictated the gender of the other two main perpetrators of chaos which were relatively late editions to the pharonic bloodline _ the Moon and Mercury. When reigning over Earth, the Moon and Mercury were predominantly perceived as male pharaohs. I say predominantly because, unlike Mars and Venus who were always god-king and divine queen, the Moon and Mercury had slightly different attributes and were not always viewed as kings.

The Moon is a new addition to the solar system. Venus and the Moon were born from Jupiter around 3200 BC. The Moon was tossed about by Mars and Venus for millennia before slowly falling under Earth's gravitational spell to reincarnate itself many times over as a 'living god' _ a god of Earth. Despite having the same point of origin, the Moon bears little resemblance to the female Venus. The Moon's relatively small size enabled it to cool down rapidly and develop a rocky crust. Although it probably resembled the black and white orb we are familiar with today, cosmic chaos and numerous impacts resulted in an ever-changing appearance. In its initial 2,000 years of magical wanderings, the Moon's presence was a lifeless orb in comparison to the 'living and breathing' Mars and Venus. Although its involvement as a major player or king in earlier times cannot be ruled out, I believe the Moon was given a variety of lesser identifications due to its relatively small size and erratic movements. One such identification was the enigmatic ibis-headed god, Thoth. This deity was regarded as the patron of knowledge, secrets, writing and scribe to the gods and its epithets were completely consistent with an early erratic Moon.

Only after the Moon fell under Earth's gravitational spell and it loomed larger than the Sun did it join the royal bloodline and become a warrior pharaoh. When the Moon ventured close to Earth, it glowed red due to the tidal forces of the planets which caused the Moon to heat up internally and glow the traditional pharonic colour. As it grew in size and took on the traditional reddish hue, the Moon literally transformed itself from the enigmatic deity Thoth (and other roles) into a divine god-king, a warrior pharaoh. Due to its size and location, after reigning as king on a number of occasions, the Moon continually switched between pharaoh and far lesser roles until the end of cosmic chaos. It transformed itself from a gigantic hazy red disk into a hazy silvery orb as gravitational forces tossed the Moon back and forth.

In a similar way, Mercury did not immediately take to the pharonic stage as a fully fledged god-king. Initially born from Mars sometime in the 7th century BC, Mercury was initially known to the Egyptians as the Aten. It was a glorious new orb whose energy was so powerful it blotted out the solar deity Re and all other sky gods and was the only glaring Sun in ancient times. However, after 17 years it cooled down and its energy diminished. Mercury shed its blinding manifestation and adorned the traditional and instantly recognisable pharonic look _ that of an incandescent red orb. It joined the lineage of pharonic kings and was given the name Seti (He of the god Seth) which was very apt given the mayhem this planet caused shortly after its birth.

We cannot compare the red spheres of the Moon and Mercury with Venus. The Moon and Mercury became members of the royal family as a direct result of their close proximity to Earth. Our wandering Moon was snared by Earth's gravity and Mercury was sucked out of Mars as a result of the electromagnetic and gravitational forces of Earth. When it moved away from Earth, the Moon cooled down and lost its pharonic status as a dominant red disk and either reverted to the god Thoth or became lost in the mass of cosmic haze because of its small size. It is likely that Mercury did the same. Being the larger of the two, it probably maintained its pharonic aspect for longer and at greater distances. This was in complete contrast to Venus. Its large size and the fact it remained a boiling hot ball of molten lava for longer meant that it perpetually glowed at vast distances and oozed a passive demeanour highlighting its distinctly female qualities.

Mercury and the Moon's movements were far more erratic and unpredictable than those of the distant Venus because they were closer to Earth. There was nothing serene about Earth's capture of the Moon and, as it fell under Earth's influence, the Moon moved in a chaotic and irregular manner. Equally, Mercury's movements were haphazard and changeable as it demagnetized and extricated itself from Earth's gravity to take its place as the third rock from the Sun. This is in total contrast to Venus' female trait of remaining predominantly motionless and serene.

There was one basic characteristic that both the Moon and Mercury had in common with the original warrior king Mars which was a distinctly masculine trait. This was the sweeping up of unimaginable quantities of debris otherwise known as cosmic battles. The Moon and Mercury bear the hallmarks of intense celestial battles and their surfaces have been shaped by the impact of hundreds of thousands of meteorites.

If our Moon was captured in orbit around Earth, it must have 'battled' the debris from the giant planetary ring system countless times as its capture took centuries to complete. The Moon, as the only remaining 'king' of Earth, has ultimately finished the job of clearing up Earth's ring. For this reason the Moon in one of its many guises was dubbed the greatest warrior pharaoh of ancient times. This pharaoh was Tuthmosis III. The name Tuthmosis was one of many names given to the Moon and means 'born of the god Thoth' who was a lunar deity. To be 'born of Thoth' meant the Moon grew in size to loom larger than the Sun and other planets and was subsequently deemed pharaoh. This pharaoh was known as the 'Napoleon of ancient

Egypt' because of the superhuman battles attributed to him. History records that this pharaoh's sole purpose was to fight the enemy and return with the spoils of war. His actions and numerous battles extended Egypt's borders and were totally consistent with its masculine image.

Mercury was also observed battling the forces of evil very close to Earth and so was deemed masculine. It was the tidal and electromagnetic forces of Earth that culminated in the genesis of this planet and this incredible event occurred close to Earth. Mercury must have remained in the vicinity of Earth for many centuries due to the same forces that caused its birth. Subsequently Mercury revisited its point of origin numerous times before it was dragged away from Earth and in towards the Sun by Venus.

WHO WAS KING?

We have established a basic gender structure for the four main bodies involved in recent cosmic chaos. This should provide an image of the hazy but prominent red orbs either battling up space debris or appearing almost motionless. It is important to remember that the predominately red-disked monarchy was not alone in the cosmos. Any planetary body in chaos was surrounded by an infinite number of satellites, asteroids, comets, dust and gasses. While some were children of the royal family, most were deemed right-hand men, courtiers, viziers, concubines, fan-bearers and scribes – collectively known as the royal court. When considering the gender of planetary bodies, I suggest that asteroids were male and comets were female. This is because of the plain, rocky, 'male' appearance of asteroids as opposed to the more decorative 'female' comets.

If we consider the army of pharaohs, rocky red asteroids, and the red Sun trailing behind Mars, it is likely they were the rank and file male soldiers. Comets took on a more flowery and decorative appearance due to their long tails, and they were deemed female. The skies were buzzing with activity and our divine royal family were forever accompanied by an entourage of erratic moons, asteroids and comets of various shapes and sizes and they all indelibly stamped their mark on history.

The Egyptians had no rule for becoming king

From medieval times until the present day, royal families throughout the world have had precise guidelines for determining who is next in line to the throne. For example, in England there are strict rules which determine what happens if the monarch dies. This was not so in ancient Egypt – there were no rules for determining who would become king or queen because they believed the gods would decide.

This practice is completely understandable, particularly when we consider the GKS. How did the Egyptians predict who was next in line to the throne given that the kings were guises of meandering planets? 'Divine order' was effectively cosmic chaos and it was this that dictated the throne of Egypt – mortals had no say in the matter.

The naming of kings couldn't take place until a planetary body had moved close enough to become a 'living god'. It came so close to Earth that it discarded its star-like image and took on the traditional hazy red disk, or 'son of Re' appearance. Only then could a particular aspect of a planet be adorned with a 'sacred' name in fitting with its attributes. For example, names for Mars included Narmer 'The striking catfish', Hor-aha 'The fighting hawk' or Den 'Horus who strikes'. Queen Nefertiti was a name for Venus and meant 'The Beautiful one has come'. Names were chosen out of deference for astral bodies that were, by their very location, intermediates between the mortal world and the divine.

An example of a time when the Egyptians followed the doctrine of heaven was with the 19th dynasty pharaoh Horemheb (chosen of Re). Little is known of Horemheb's origins. He became Great Commander of the Army and first served under the Akhenaton before being appointed King's Deputy by Tutankhamun. After the death of Ay (Tutankhamun's successor), Horemheb declared himself king. There are two burial tombs attributed to Horemheb. As with most Egyptians, Horemheb planned for his journey to the next world long before he had any inkling he would become pharaoh. The Egyptians built a relatively small, private tomb at Saqqara, the walls of which were superbly carved with scenes of Horemheb's military and court career. Later, upon declaring himself pharaoh, work began on a larger tomb in the most prestigious and sacred of locations, the Valley of the Kings. Therefore the Egyptians constructed two tombs for Horemheb. Workmen then returned to Horemheb's first tomb at Saqqara and added the royal uraeus (cobra) to his brow which was the symbol of kingship.

Horemheb was associated with the moon because of his association with the ibis-headed lunar deity Thoth whereas Akhenaton and Tutankhamun were both guises of Mars. This gave rise to a situation where the Moon and Mars jockeyed for position of King. Because of its size, the Moon/Horemheb initially played a small but vitally important role of battling up space debris, first under the rule of Mars/Akhenaton and then in the presence of Tutankhamun/Mars. Mars then moved out of sight, leaving behind the Moon/Horemheb to dominate the skies and declare himself Pharaoh.

How did the Egyptians decide who was king?

The answer to this question was quite simple – it was size. The largest planetary body from the perspective of Earth dictated who would be king or queen whereas the physical size was not important. For example, Venus is the same size as Earth, Mars is approximately half Earth's size, the Moon is a quarter of the size of Venus and Mercury is about a third of the size of Venus. However, these dimensions were not important because it was the largest red orb from the perspective of Earth that dominated the cosmos and was deemed king. It can be argued that the Egyptians adopted a childlike psychology in believing that big is best.

Mars and Venus, the original divine couple, reigned unopposed for at least 2,000 years and gravitational and electromagnetic forces brought Mars closer to Earth than Venus. This location gave Mars its masculine, warlike personality and Venus its beautiful, female traits. Because Mars ventured closer to Earth than Venus, it appeared far greater in size. Mars was the dominant body and was regarded as god-king of Earth. Therefore, the gods in their infinite wisdom chose Mars as god-king and Venus as queen.

If we examine the size of the Sun and Moon, we know the Sun could hold 65 million Moons. However, as the Moon orbits close to Earth, it appears roughly the same size as the Sun. Despite is minuscule size, the Moon can blot out the Sun in a solar eclipse and to ancient cultures the Sun and Moon were perceived to be similar in size. At such close proximity, the fearless Moon regularly crashed head-on into masses of space debris. Therefore, the Moon as Tuthmosis III kept the forces of darkness at bay by battling up trillions of tons of dust and debris which threatened to blot out the Sun.

The Moon and Mercury joined Mars and Venus during the New Kingdom (1,000 BC RC) in what was the finale of cosmic chaos. As these four main bodies jockeyed for position as king, it was a confusing time for the Egyptians.

It is possible that other large bodies born from Mars were also visible and the Egyptians were mystified as to what 'divine order' had in store for them.

The GKS enables us to consult ancient history to reveal who ruled and when. There were many variables relating to Egypt's monarchy. For example, if Mars, Mercury or the Moon were not visible, then the easily recognisable Venus ruled as queen. Egypt was ruled by a number of queens throughout its history and the last queen to sit upon the throne was Cleopatra (Venus). There was also a period in Egyptian history when Venus ventured so close to Earth that she ruled as king and not queen – in other words a female pharaoh. This episode tested the resolve of the Egyptians in what was essentially a male dominated world.

Hatshepsut (Venus)

Hatshepsut was a New Kingdom queen who, having ruled as regent with Tuthmosis III, declared herself pharaoh. Rather than immediately appearing as pharaoh, she gradually took on this kingly role. She discarded the titles that only a woman could hold and adopted those of a pharaoh. She slowly took on the appearance of a male by wearing the shendyt kilt, the nemes headdress with its uraeus (cobra) and the traditional false beard. She ruled for approximately twenty years before enigmatically disappearing like many other members of the royal family. It is not known if she was murdered, died or retired from politics. After her disappearance, Tuthmosis III (Moon) became Pharaoh.

The Egyptians built a magnificent temple in honour of Hatshepsut at Deir el Bahri. It stood three levels high and was known as Djeser Djeseru, the 'holiest of holies'. This is where the inscriptions of Hatshepsut's life and achievements can be found. It is fronted by many statues of Hatshepsut and traces of vivid red flesh can still be seen. It also has chapels dedicated to the gods Hathor, Anubis, Ra-Horakhte and Amun-Re.

This queen who would be king has astounded Egyptologist. They are puzzled as to how a female became pharaoh. It seems illogical that, having ruled as queen, Hatshepsut suddenly declared herself king? Hieroglyphs occasionally refer to her as a man. Why did she not continue to rule as queen, and why did she take to wearing male attire including a male headdress and false beard? No Egyptian queen had ever done anything like it. Was it due to transexuality or political necessity? Furthermore, how could such a prominent queen disappear off the face of the Earth?

The GKS can help us understand this enigma. Hatshepsut was one of the many names given to Venus and the whole enigmatic period was related to size.

'daughter of the Sun god'

'her beauty is unsurpassed'

'like a god she brings peace and prosperity to Egypt'

(Inscriptions from Hatshepsut's temple at Deir el-Bahri)

This was the only time that Venus/Hatshepsut ventured so close to Earth that she was physically transformed from a passive, red orb into a dominant, large red sphere. She appeared larger than ever before and so demanded the title of a king. This was the only time that Venus /Hatshepsut entered the location normally reserved for the pharaohs. Hatshepsut/Venus was portrayed as slowly shedding her female gender and adorning kingly regalia as a direct result of outsizing and outranking all other planetary bodies. Mars was pushed into the background to take on a far lesser role _ that of chief architect and government official Senemut. Mars was located close to Venus and may also have been perceived as Hatshepsut's lover. Senemut was another pharonic figure who enigmatically disappeared from the annals of history.

The 'out-sizing' of Mars (and any other possible rogue bodies) by Hatshepsut/Venus is recorded on the walls of her mortuary temple at Deir el-Bahri.

'***Her majesty grew beyond everything***; *to look upon her was more beautiful than anything; her [unknown] was like a god, her form was like a god, she did everything as a god, her splendour was like a god; her majesty (fem.) was a maiden, beautiful, blooming, Buto (goddess) in her time. She made her divine form to flourish, a favour of him that fashioned her.*'

(Translation from J. H. Breasted, Ancient Records of Egypt (New York, 1962), vol 2, p 81-98 - my bold emphasis)

Is this a description of a young royal female being transformed into a very 'large' young queen? It does speak of the rapid growth of a divine queen, but this was the 'outsizing' of Mars by Venus. This was one of the very rare occasions when Venus outranked Mars to become the true Horus of the heavens.

Although Hatshepsut is often portrayed as a peaceful queen, she did enjoy some conquests, as did the rest of her war-loving family. There are references to military activity at her temple, one of which refers to a campaign in Nubia. Another inscription says that Hatshepsut led one of her Nubian campaigns and this calls to mind the viscous surface of Venus. This planet was rarely caught in the act of battling the enemy because impacts on Venus resembled pebbles sinking into thick mud. Venus occasionally ventured close to Earth to take on the enemy, and the scant references to Hatshepsut's military actions point to the close observations of Venus encountering space debris.

Once again, it was size that dictated who would be king. Most of the time this was not relevant because Mars and Venus reigned unopposed for two thousand years. Things changed in the New Kingdom as the Moon and Mercury appeared. The three bodies now jockeyed for the position of warrior pharaoh battling the forces of evil while Venus remained in the background as the beautiful supportive consort.

This explains the one occasion when Venus outsized all other planetary bodies and had to be given the title 'King of Egypt'. Venus ruled Egypt as queen prior to and after the reign of Hatshepsut because of the absence of the other bodies and not because of her distant location. Cosmic chaos occasionally gave rise to a situation where Mars, Mercury and the Moon took a break from fighting the enemy and thereby left the easily recognisable Venus to rule Egypt unopposed as queen.

The GKS therefore offers a very plausible explanation for Hatshepsut's reign. Even enigmas such as the mysterious disappearance and reappearance of Tuthmosis III before and after Hatshepsut's reign can be explained. Tuthmosis was the Moon and appeared before Hatshepsut took to the throne. It then disappeared as Venus ruled as king for twenty years and reappeared again as Venus moved away from Earth. The record shows there were many similar appearances and disappearance during pharonic times which were the result of 'divine order' or cosmic chaos.

Horus (Heru, he who is above)

The Falcon-god Horus can be traced back to the dynastic period around 3100 BC and is one of the most famous gods of ancient Egypt. Usually depicted as a hawk or as a man with the head of a hawk, Horus was not only a god of the sky but the embodiment of divine kingship and protector of the reigning pharaoh. Gradually the cult of other hawk gods merged with that of Horus, and a complex array of myths became associated with him.

According to one of the most common myths, Horus was the child of the goddess Isis. In this role (later known as Harpocrates) he was usually depicted in human form with the sidelock of youth and a finger to his mouth, often seated on his mothers lap. As a son of Isis and Osiris, Horus was also worshiped under the name of Harsiese. This was the god who performed the rite of 'Opening of the Mouth' on his dead father, thus legitimising his succession to the throne. In a similar vein, as Horus Ium-Mutef, priests or eldest sons wore panther-skin costumes and ritually purified the path of the deceased's coffin.

(Shaw & Nicholson, 2002, p 133)

Catastrophists, in an attempt to give physical presence to Horus, have tried in vein to identify him with certain planetary bodies. For example, Velikovsky identifies Horus as Jupiter (Velikovsky, Worlds in Collision 950, pp. 51-52) while Ackerman (V/A scenario) suggests Horus was Mars (Firmament 127). Neither are correct, certainly not in the context presented. Horus was never Mars per-se and Jupiter was too far away to play such a prominent role. Any other planetary identifications are also incorrect. If we consult the conventional understanding, it reveals Horus was the 'embodiment of divine kingship and protector of the reigning pharaoh'. Egyptologists arrived at this identification by consulting the sacred hieroglyphs. They reveal the pharaoh as the 'living Horus,' as follows:

'His majesty (Tuthmosis) is Horus, assuming his (i.e. Horus') kingdom of myriads of years.'

(Thutmose I inscription, Breasted, Ancient Records of Egypt, Part Two, p 73)

'Year 1, Akhet (month) 4, day 19, under the majesty of Horus…'

'Lord of the words of the gods, who appeared on the Horus throne of the living daily like his father Re.'

'All their life and health was (from) the nose of the mighty king, the Horus, who repeats births, the beloved son of Amen-Re, king of the gods, who had begotten him so that he would be created, of the king of Upper and Lower Egypt.'

(Tutankhamen's Restoration Stela)

'Grant that he rest upon thy throne as Horus, the Mighty Bull, beloved of Ma.t'

(Papyrus Harris, Breasted, *Ancient Records of Egypt*, Part Four, p 351)

The above inscriptions show that the basic role of Horus was that of guardian of the living pharaoh and they reveal that Horus was the living pharaoh. In identifying Horus, scholars are not theorising but are merely reiterating the written word and are recalling the 'sacred words' as recorded by history. I do not disagree with this reasoning as the written word is not in dispute. The reigning kings were exactly as described – the falcon god Horus. However, to understand Horus in his truest form and to understand the whole Pharaoh/Horus relationship as understood by the Egyptians, we must invoke the GKS.

The god kings of ancient Egypt were first and foremost guises of planetary bodies and Horus was the protective umbrella by which all planetary bodies would reign over earth. The symbol of Horus, the falcon, became an emblem for the kings because planetary bodies took on the same basic attributes as a falcon. With little effort, they too would soar the heavens like a bird.

As offspring of the solar deity Re, planets descended from heaven to reign over Earth. In doing so a variety of gods watched over them, and nurtured and protected them. The great sky god Amun gave his authority to the throne. Hathor suckled the kings many times as they moved close enough to suck material from Earth's planetary ring system.

Isis, the daytime nurturing goddess, took on a similar role and encompassed the red disks of the kings. Horus appeared as a 'good and just' god, a patron of the kings and a deity who provided protection for the 'living gods' from within as they battled the forces of evil.

It is not possible to identify a specific body as Horus as some catastrophists have attempted to do and it could therefore be argued that Horus was a mythological god. However, although not physically seen, Horus had true physical presence through the ruling planets. Every single guise of Mars, Mercury and the Moon (and Venus at least once) became an incarnation of the god Horus. This deity was granted physical presence each and every time the planets were born to Earth. This was a divine relationship where the kings needed Horus as much as Horus needed them.

In simple terms we can use the formula:

Horus = ruling pharaoh = planet ruling the sky above

By applying this simple formula, it is possible to understand the many enigmas surrounding this deity. There is ample evidence which points to Horus as the ruling planet. The name Horus stems from the word 'hr' (her) which in its simplest form was the preposition 'above', 'upon', 'that which is above' or 'he who is above.' This is perplexing in the conventional sense, for if the kings were Horus, how are we to explain 'that which is above'? A human king could never be 'that which is above' or a falcon of the skies, whereas a rogue planet could.

The Egyptians chose a falcon, a majestic bird of flight, to represent planetary bodies because they soared into the heavens just like a planet. Secondly, they called the falcon Horus (hr), meaning 'above' because planetary bodies are 'above'. Regardless of location, any planetary body which loomed larger than the Moon was naturally 'that which is above'.

A good example of this and one of the most famous scenes of Horus as the guardian of the kings can be found in the Cairo Museum. It is a seated statue of Khafre (Mars) with a falcon (Horus) perched on a throne behind the head of the king. The falcon embraces the king with its wings and such symbolism signifies the king as the incarnation of Horus ruling the heavens. It clearly reflects planetary bodies as the living incarnation of Horus. The falcon embraces the king with its wings as a gesture of protection towards the pharaoh Mars as it soars like a bird in the skies. To honour the sky god Horus and the celestial pharaohs, the royal titulary of the Egyptians included a Horus name as well as a golden Horus name and both included the falcon symbol.

Horus took on many enigmatic forms, most of which are not understood. Scholars are able to translate the names but do not understand their true meaning. We will briefly examine some of the titles and, by applying the GKS, it will become evident that most are self-explanatory.

The infant Horus (*Harpokrates*) – This is a reference to the infant stage of a planetary body when it is approaching Earth.

Horus the elder (*Haroeris*) – A reference to a planetary body which is mature in years. It is a collective reference to astral bodies which have travelled back and forth a few times.

Horus, 'son-of-Isis' (*Harseisis*) – As two similar aspects of the same phenomenon (i.e. Earth's hazy band of debris) it was the role of Hathor and Isis to nurture divine bodies when born to Earth. Hathor was the bovine goddess of the night and Isis looked after the throne during the day. Because astral kings were the incarnation of Horus, and as they were born amidst Hathor and Isis, both goddesses were considered mothers to Horus. Both were said to suckle Horus, the living pharaoh, hence the title 'son-of-Isis.'

Horus in the horizon (Horemakhet) – This is a reference to planetary bodies literally 'in' the horizon. It has nothing to do with the Sun as is currently believed because the Sun is unlikely to be 'in' the horizon (on or above, but not in). As proposed by Ackerman, Mars locked on to Earth many times above the Tran-Himalayas complex. From the viewpoint of Egypt, the god kings were literally 'in' the horizon. Similarly, the name 'Horus of the Two Horizons' (Harakhty) is a reference to the astral kings as the embodiment of Horus traversing the heavens, probably rising and setting just like the Sun.

There are many more variations to Horus such as 'Horus of two eyes' (*Harmerty*) and his syncretism with Re to become Re Horakhty. If we remember that Horus equals the current ruling body, it is possible to understand the majority of its guises. Some aspects of Horus will never be understood because they derive from the infinite permutations of celestial chaos and the astral kings, as Horus incarnate, were directly responsible for many of them.

PLANETS RULED AS GOD KINGS

Co-regency

There were occasions when celestial bodies appeared to be roughly the same size. This led to a shared throne and is clearly recorded in history. Scholars have dubbed this as co-regency or co-rule. Co-regency is the modern term applied to periods when two rulers were simultaneously in power. This usually consisted of an overlap of several years between the end of one sole reign and the beginning of the next. (Dictionary of ancient Egypt – Shaw & Nicholson) Co-regency is exactly as the term implies – two monarchs sharing the throne as recorded in history, or more specifically two planets sharing the throne. Co-regency occurred when two red orbs, irrespective of their actual size, appeared to be roughly the same size from the viewpoint of Earth.

We have established that size mattered to the ancient Egyptians because it determined who would be king. Size occasionally dictated a shared throne when divine monarchs appeared to be the same size. There were many variations of co-rule – Mars with Venus; Venus with the Moon; Mercury with Mars. According to the GKS, it is possible to consult history to establish who ruled together. Co-regency rose to prominence during the New Kingdom (1000 BC RC) when four main bodies, and possibly other smaller bodies, jockeyed for the position of king. To understand how this worked we will look to the most renowned co-regency of this period _ that of the pharaoh Tuthmosis and Queen Hatshepsut.

Historical sources reveal that Tuthmosis I ruled for six years. When he died, he was succeeded by Tuthmosis II. He was young in years and the son of a minor royal wife, and to strengthen his position he was married to his half sister Hatshepsut, the apparent daughter of Tuthmosis I. Together, Tuthmosis II and Hatshepsut co-reigned for about 14 years until Tuthmosis II died early in his thirties. When Tuthmosis II died, his son and successor Tuthmosis III was heir to the throne. However, because he was too young to rule, Hatshepsut acted as regent for the young king. After seven years of co-regency with the child-king, Hatshepsut took the unprecedented step of declaring herself King (the queen who would be king). She reigned for about 15 years after which she disappeared and Tuthmosis III (Napoleon of Ancient Egypt) took to the throne and reigned for over 30 years.

This situation may seem confusing, although the official version is more complicated. In simple terms, Hatshepsut was Venus (also the Queen of Sheba) and Tuthmosis I, II and III were all guises of the Moon (Solomon = Solo Moon). In the early part of the New Kingdom, Venus (with the Moon) crossed the orbit of Earth to move Sun side and deposited the Moon in the vicinity of the Earth leading to a situation where Venus/Hatshepsut and the Moon/Tuthmosis manoeuvred for the position of kingship. This was because they appeared similar in size on at least two occasions which led to co-regency occurring at least twice.

To simplify the above, I will retranslate history and transfer it to the heavens. The Moon/Tuthmosis came closer to Earth than Venus/Hatshepsut and therefore the Moon/Tuthmosis I ruled as the Horus of the heavens for about six years. The Moon/Tuthmosis I died, either because it moved away from Earth for a short period of time or because the human double died. Either way it was enough to warrant the introduction of Tuthmosis II – the Moon kept its birth name 'born of the god Thoth' but took on a different secondary name.

Hatshepsut/Venus loomed large and was magnified to such an extent she was considered wife of Tuthmosis II. More importantly Hatshepsut (Venus) and Tuthmosis (the Moon) appeared to be roughly the same size which resulted in a co-regency or shared throne. They ruled Egypt together for 14 years until the Moon either moved away or the mortal representative died which led to a slight renaming of the Moon to Tuthmosis III. Again this was the same birth name but a different throne name. Venus/Hatshepsut ruled alongside the Moon/Tuthmosis III for a few years although Venus had other plans for kingship.

In an unprecedented move due entirely to its size, Venus declared herself pharaoh and not queen. Hatshepsut/Venus took to the throne as sole ruler for approximately 15 years after which she disappeared either by rapidly moving away from Earth or disappearing below the horizon. It is possible that Venus didn't disappear but changed her attributes so much that it warranted a renaming and this is the likeliest explanation. Either way, Venus/Hatshepsut vacated the throne and left the Moon to rule as Tuthmosis III. The Moon became Egypt's greatest warrior pharaoh as it began to fall under the gravitational spell of Earth.

Where was Mars during this period? Mars at this time was Senemut, the royal Stewart and Hatshepsut's supposed lover. Research reveals that during Venus/Hatshepsut's reign, Tuthmosis III (Moon) actually disappeared. It is assumed that as Tuthmosis went on to become Egypt's greatest warrior pharaoh, he must have been in training with the army, but the historical record does not support this.

During Hatshepsut's reign, Tuthmosis III is not mentioned anywhere. He seemingly vanished from the face of the Earth. This enigmatic disappearance could have had a number of explanations. Perhaps the brilliance of Venus blotted out the Moon, or the Moon disappeared behind Venus, or the Moon simply disappeared below the horizon for many years. Whatever the reason, the Moon was not seen which is why Tuthmosis III was not mentioned.

Co-regency is a grey area and there is much controversy over certain partnerships. An example of one partnership which is wrongly attributed is that of Amenhotep III and Amenhotep IV. It is believed that Amenhotep IV (known as the heretic king) reigned alongside Amenhotep III before taking sole rule. It is assumed that Amenhotep IV was Amenhotep III's son because he took to the throne after Amenhotep III and adopted the same birth name. Amenhotep IV would have been fairly mature in years when he took the throne and he probably grew up as his father ruled Egypt. It is also likely that there was a period of co-rule before Amenhotep IV sat on the throne.

The problem with this assumed order of events is that Amenhotep IV is not mentioned once during Amenhotep III's reign. If the historical records are correct, this points to another enigmatic and sudden appearance of a royal figure. There are no images or statues of him during the reign of his supposed father, Amenhotep III. It seems that Amenhotep IV appeared from nowhere to take the throne.

The GKS explains such enigmas with ease. Amenhotep III and IV were both aspects of Mars, as were all pharaohs called Amenhotep. The transformation from III to IV occurred when Mars transformed its appearance or location. This did not warrant changing the birth name of Amenhotep but was enough to warrant different throne names. To the ancient Egyptians there was no Amenhotep III and IV – they were simply guises of Mars.

Scholars are responsible for giving pharaohs sequential names such as I, II, III, IV and not the Egyptians. Amenhotep IV did not suddenly appear from nowhere. This was a slight but noticeable change to Mars which was enough to warrant a different throne name and therefore there was no co-regency between Amenhotep III & IV. It is nonsense to assume the same body can co-rule with itself – Mars cannot co-rule with Mars. This principle can be used when considering the grey areas that surround co-regency. Any pharaohs with the same name are probably the same body and this body cannot co-rule with itself.

According to scholars, co-regency was first introduced in the 12th dynasty during the Middle Kingdom with the pharaohs Amenemhet (Mars) and Senusret (Moon). It is assumed it rose to prominence during the New Kingdom with many overlapping and shared roles during this period. However, I seriously question the appearance of co-rule during the Middle Kingdom and I suggest that the 12th dynasty has been misplaced and belongs in the New Kingdom with the rest of them. Why is this?

There are several reasons for my proposal and the first concerns co-regency itself. It is my belief that Mars and Venus reigned virtually unopposed until the New Kingdom.

I believe it was only when the Moon and Mercury entered the scene that the heavens began to dictate a shared throne. It was only when our four main bodies played havoc with Earth that they occasionally appeared similar in size. Prior to this, Mars reigned supreme in the foreground with Queen Venus in the background.

There are other reasons including the fine jewellery made during the 12th dynasty which indicates that this dynasty belongs to later times. The names involved are also revealing. For example, Amenemhet translates as 'Amun is at the head' (the god Amun is at the head). Amun rose to prominence during the New Kingdom and logically this descriptive name belongs to the same period; the name of Amun was used and coincided with Amun's dominance in the New Kingdom. I also identify Amenemhet with Mars and Senusret with the Moon. Although it is possible that the Moon took on lesser roles, it did not join the royal bloodline until the New Kingdom. This was when Venus /Hatshepsut, perhaps assisted by Mars, deposited the Moon in the vicinity of the Earth.

More research is needed in this area, but it makes sense to assume co-regency referred to two bodies which appeared roughly the same size. It is a grey area because scholars have failed to understand the minds of the Egyptians and cosmic chaos (cosmic chaos will always be a grey area). The Egyptians had no idea who would be king – there were no rules for kingship. How could there be? The gods dictated the throne of Egypt and occasionally this included a co-rule. This phenomenon of 'co-rule' is consistent with proposed cosmic chaos.

The gods and monarchy were of equal size

Images of the Egyptian monarchy adorn almost every temple, tomb and monument throughout Egypt. They are shown in a variety of scenes with an assortment of gods. In these images, the royal family are always depicted the same size as the gods whereas ordinary Egyptians or commoners are smaller as the following quote highlights:

'While the main register represents the sacred sphere in which the king and deities interact, the much smaller register below with two facing rows of bowing figures depicts the human world of which the king is also part. The smaller scale of the figures and their location in the lower register symbolises the subordinate position of humanity in relation to deities and the king within the cosmic hierarchy.'

(Robins, Art of Ancient Egypt, 2000, p 18 commenting on an illustration of a large fragment of limestone relief showing king Neuserra (5th dynasty) seated on a throne on a dais)

The monarch's size was not affected by the theme of the image. Whether an afterlife scene, offering scene, coronation or battle scene, royalty always commanded equal status to the gods. A classic example was Ramesses the Great depicted in the rock-cut Temple at Abu Simbel. The inner sanctuary contains four seated statues: Ra-Horakhty, Ptah, Amun and Ramesses. In this scene, Ramesses is exactly the same size as the gods.

Was this another bizarre Egyptian practice? No because the GKS maintains the monarchy of ancient Egypt were first and foremost guises of the planets Mars, Venus, Mercury and the Moon. Such imagery clearly reveals the divine status of our planetary kings and queens in respect to the numerous sky gods. It indicates that the astral monarchy, specifically the pharaohs, were truly gods amongst gods Which is why royalty were always portrayed the same size as gods. It is a very basic observation but one that is highly revealing and extremely important. Amun, Ptah, Osiris, Hathor, Isis and numerous others deities were all sky gods. As these four bodies inhabited the same vast arena they demanded equal representation which was reflected in the artwork. Unlike the sky gods, the monarchy was mortal in the sense that they lived and died as they moved back and forth to Earth. However, they were still gods among gods – sky gods as recorded in history.

How can humans be worshiped as gods?

Conventional wisdom states the royal family of ancient Egypt were mortal beings who believed they were gods and were worshiped as such. The pharaohs in particular were 'gods on Earth' or 'god-kings'. Familiar kings such as Ramesses, Tuthmosis, Akhenaten and Tutankhamun were considered human 'living gods.' This exalted status meant the kings were intermediaries between heaven and Earth, the receptacles of divine power and guardians of divine order (*ma'at*). Egypt was a pharaoh-centric society because divine wisdom was passed to the people through the pharaoh as the king was the 'perfect god'.

'The king was thus in some ways similar to, though not identical with, the gods, and one of his titles, netjer nefer, meant 'perfect god.'

(Clayton, 1994, p 6)

This divine status also extended to many of the queens. Hatshepsut, Nefertiti (wife of Akhenaten), Nefertari (wife of Ramesses) and the last queen of Egypt, the legendary Cleopatra, were considered 'living goddesses'. This practice was also displayed by the ancient kings of Mesopotamia, from Naram-Suen (approx. 2275 CC) through to the late Babylonian kings of the first millennium BC. Throughout the world, from China to the New World, we find this practice of mortals declaring themselves to be divine entities. Even in Roman times, the Roman Emperor Octavian considered himself 'son of the divine'. This habit of humans assuming divine status appears to be one of the most bizarre of ancient practices unless it is viewed from the perspective of the GKS.

How can a human be viewed as a god? If someone today declared themselves a god they would be an object of ridicule and humiliation. If they commissioned works of art to exonerate their exalted status it is likely they would be referred to a psychiatric hospital. Are we expected to believe that this was a normal practice in the ancient world? Most modern religions provide human intermediaries between god and humans such as priests and vicars, but they do not proclaim themselves as gods. However, in ancient Egypt, pharaohs regularly declared themselves gods in a practice that continued for 3,000 years. How did these rulers convince the population of Egypt that they were gods?

History reveals that ancient Egypt had many great kings. 'Ramesses the Great' and Tuthmosis III (the Napoleon of ancient Egypt) are credited with many epic battles. It was understandable that such kings were regarded as fearless warriors and mighty leaders, but to regard them as gods takes more than a leap of faith. Their mummified remains revealed they suffered from insect-born diseases such as malaria, trachoma (an eye disease), small pox, measles, tuberculosis, and cholera. In fact, Amenhotep III probably died from a tooth related disease such as an abscess.

This presents a dilemma. How do you convince the population of Egypt you are a god if you are struck down by tooth decay? The Egyptians believed that disease and death were caused by a god, a spirit, or some other supernatural force. Surely the pharaoh had the power to prevent disease and death with his supernatural powers. If the pharaohs were gods in name only, how were the masses convinced they were divine? Perhaps the pharaoh's divine status was implemented with an iron fist. Did the king proclaim he was a 'living god' or did priests enforce this policy? Would the Egyptian monarchy have risked the wrath of the gods by proclaiming themselves equal?

History suggests that the commoners were completely compliant and there is no evidence of discontent. However, it must have been challenging to convince the population that their pharaohs were gods and should be worshiped as such. Egyptian gods were believed to be mythical in nature and were invented to explain the workings of the cosmos. The Egyptian priests would therefore have needed much patience to explain the divine hierarchy to the people.

The further back in time we go, the more powerful the gods were. The doctrine of heaven was paramount and the gods dictated every aspect of ancient daily life. It was essential they were worshiped, placated and obeyed, so it is puzzling that mere mortals considered themselves of equal status. To declare oneself a god by adopting titles such as *netjer nefer* ('perfect god'), would surely have been regarded as blasphemy because it insulted the power of the almighty gods? This would have caused a rift between man and god.

Having established that the royal family were depicted the same size as the gods we will examine the intimate relationship that existed between Egyptian royalty and divine bodies. Much ancient artwork portrays the gods as physically touching royal figures. Gods are depicted holding hands with the monarchy as they led them to the afterlife, or caressing them by placing their arms around them. A prime example of an intimate scene is the 'god's wife embrace'. In the New Kingdom, the queens were considered to be married to the mysterious god Amun and it was believed the world would fall into chaos without this union. This belief was typically played out in scenes where the god Amun was seen caressing the queen by placing his arms around her and his foot between her legs.

Such glorious works of art reveal a direct and physical relationship between humans and gods, but we should also expect to see evidence of a noticeable division between them. For example, all humans including royalty should have been portrayed of equal size while the gods should have appeared larger. We may accept that humans and deities were of equal size in afterlife scenes where kings reached an exalted state at death and became equal to the gods. However, this does not explain everyday scenes where the gods were directly involved in the mortal world such as the 'gods wife embrace'. The majority of Egypt's deities were immortal gods of the heavens while their human subjects were earthbound. It is therefore impossible for humans to be equal to gods as they have no supernatural powers.

Humans were gods

There is only one way that kings and queens could be perceived as gods – if they really were gods, and I believe they were. The monarchs of ancient Egypt were 'living gods' and acted as intermediaries between heaven and Earth and as receptacles of divine powers. They were also guardians of divine order and 'gods amongst gods'. They were first and foremost guises of the planets Mars, Venus, Mercury and the Moon, which were represented on Earth by mortal doubles.

The kings and queens of Egypt did not declare themselves as gods, but the planets did! By their very location the planets were naturally regarded as divine kings and queens. There was no need to educate or cajole the population of Egypt into believing the monarchs were gods. They had only to look up to see the 'offspring of Re' reigning over Earth.

Inhabiting the same vast arena as sky gods Re, Amun and Hathor, the heavens revealed the monarchy were 'gods amongst gods'. There was no confusion as the Egyptians could physically see their god-kings such as Ramesses the Great (Mars) and his beautiful goddess wife Nefertari (Venus). The only difference between planetary gods and sky gods was the former were mortal, they lived and died to Earth as they moved back and forth whereas the 'sky' gods were eternal and remained for millennia.

Planetary kings and queens could never suffer the wrath of the gods by proclaiming themselves as equals. It was the sky gods that granted them divine status because it was they who dictated the throne of Egypt. The god-kings, accompanied by their divine consorts, were sent down from heaven by the gods to take dominion over Earth and the astral monarchy commanded 'divine' status.

Mortal kings and queens actually existed – we have their mummified remains as evidence. They were mortal 'doubles' and were chosen and believed to be at one with their astral counterparts. As a direct result of planetary bodies moving back and forth to Earth, all Egyptians developed the natural belief in an astral double. They believed they would join with their 'twin' at death to begin a life of eternity amongst the stars. However, our ancestors were mere puppets to a far higher order and played no part in celestial events apart from recording them for prosperity. They did this by carving and painting 'sacred' hieroglyphs and pictures on every tomb, temple wall and monument along the banks of the Nile. They provide a record of a time of cosmic chaos when hazy red orbs dominated the skies.

FOLLOWING THE DOCTRINE OF HEAVEN

Usurping

Some pharaohs adopted the odd practice of usurping certain monuments and statues. This occurred when a later king carved his name over a previous kings' statue or monument and took ownership of it. There are many examples of usurping including that of Ramesses the Great. During his reign countless monuments belonging to his predecessors were usurped and the name of Ramesses II is ubiquitous throughout Egypt. He is known amongst Egyptologists as the great usurper or the great chiseller. Wherever a wall or statue bore another king's name, Ramesses, in his extraordinary dedication to self-promotion, carved his name over it.

However, Ramesses was not immune from the practice of usurping. A later king by the name of Pinedjem (perhaps meaning Moon) usurped one of Ramesses II's statues and engraved his name on it. We know this statue once belonged to Ramesses because his cartouche is still visible beneath the base. This bizarre practice makes sense if we consider the GKS and to demonstrate this we will examine 'the great chiseller' Ramesses II.

Although Ramesses usurped many monuments in his 67-year reign, he also built more than any other pharaoh.

'... No other pharaoh constructed so many temples or erected so many colossal statues and obelisks.'

'... By the time he died, aged more than 90, he had set his stamp indelibly on the face of Egypt.'

(Clayton, 1994)

Among his works were the additions he made to the great temples at Karnak and Luxor, his mortuary temple in Thebes also known as the Ramesseum, the temple of Osiris at Abydos, and the completion of his father's mortuary temple at Gourna (Thebes). However, his most magnificent monument is the huge temple carved from the natural sandstone at Abu Simbel. Situated far to the south in Nubia, this huge structure took nearly 30 years to build and was called the 'Temple of Ramesses, beloved of Amun'.

Of interest here are the four enormous seated statues of the king which flank the entrance. They each stand over 18 metres high and are among the largest statues in Egypt. The Colossi of Memnon, two enormous statues dedicated to Amenhotep III at Thebes, are roughly the same size if we exclude the sphinx. The building achievements of Ramesses are on a Herculean scale and these colossal sculptures of the king are testament to this. Yet, despite constructing many gargantuan monuments, Ramesses the Great usurped many statues belonging to previous pharaohs such as Amenhotep III. Why did such a 'great' pharaoh feel the need to usurp other statues? Would a 'living god' need to search out previous pharaohs' statues, chisel out their 'sacred' names and replace them with his own? Would the great Ramesses undermine himself in such a way?

Self promotion is something Ramesses was extremely good at. However, usurping other pharaohs statues must be regarded as self-demeaning and counter-productive. What did the Egyptian population think of this? A glorious portrait of the god-king Amenhotep III would miraculously 'become' Ramesses II. Was Ramesses II really the 'king of kings' as recorded in history? Was it too costly for Ramesses to commission his own statues? He certainly had ample time to build his own monuments as one of Egypt's longest rulers. What were the criteria for usurping a statue? Was it necessary for the facial features to match or did this not matter as long as the statue was male?

Usurping monuments may have been acceptable, but statues were very personal as they were meant to be representations of the king. The ancient Egyptians believed that statues gave eternal life to the 'god kings' because they were embodied within them. As soon as the name of the pharaoh was added to a statue it became that pharaoh. Statues were symbols of divinity that were worshiped and revered during the life of the king and after their death and were sculptured in stone to last for eternity.

Why did pharaohs steal the identities of previous kings? Usurping undermined the very foundation of Egyptian religion because the pharaohs were chosen by the gods, and the gods dictated the throne. Only the pharaohs were allowed to come face to face with the gods, yet it was acceptable to steal another god-king's works. As Egypt's myriad of gods dictated every aspect of Egyptian life, are we expected to believe that Ramesses risked the wrath of the gods through petty pilfering?

Usurping makes sense is if we consider it alongside the GKS. The royal family of ancient Egypt were planets in chaos and every aspect of Egyptian art was connected to the celestial realm including the statues of the monarchy. Statues were symbolic representations of the divine planets above and the majority of them were meticulously sculptured and 'perfect of form' and bore little resemblance to their mummified remains. This is why there is relatively little difference between a statue sculptured at the beginning of pharonic Egypt and one sculptured 3,000 years later. Most people can identify an ancient Egyptian statue because they were personifications of astral bodies.

The Egyptians saw nothing wrong with the practice of usurping statues and monuments. It was common practice because they were merely renaming an idealised representation of a celestial body. It is the same principle as the renaming of the planets as they moved back and forth to Earth. They did it in reverence to the current reigning king who was the current aspect of Mars.

To understand this further we will examine Ramesses II and his apparent usurping of Amenhotep III's statues. Although a few decades separated them, both kings were guises of Mars. Mars ruled the heavens as Amenhotep ('Amun is pleased') during a prosperous period when many monuments and statues were erected in honour of this aspect of Mars.

In the following years Egypt then went through a traumatic period known as the Amarna period (birth of Mercury) and re-emerged stronger than ever. This eventually led to Ramesses II taking the throne, one of the greatest pharaohs Egypt has known. Mars as Ramesses maintained divine order (ma'at) in the heavens for a very prosperous 67 years and many great monuments and temples were built in his honour. It also prompted the Egyptians in their worship of Mars to rename many statues and monuments in the Great name of Ramesses.

It can not be stated with any certainty that only statues and monuments associated with Mars were usurped by kings that were also associated with Mars. It is possible that statues that once belonged to Mars were usurped by kings who were guises of the Moon or Mercury. In fact, this is quite possible when we consider that all kings ruled as the falcon god Horus. All kings were the embodiment of Horus when reigning over Earth which allowed for the usurping of virtually anything associated with the pharaohs.

Usurping is a term used by Egyptologists to explain the commandeering of artefacts. However, I believe this is the wrong term and prefer to use the term 'renaming'. The word 'usurping' implies a sense of seizing something whereas it was actually the process of renaming a symbolic representation. It was the practice of changing a monument from the previous king's name to the name of the reigning planet-king in accordance with the doctrine of heaven.

All Egyptians, from king to commoner, understood the practice of 'renaming'. A statue or monument which suddenly changed identity from Amenhotep to Ramesses was clearly understood. There was no need to educate the population of Egypt regarding this because the heavens revealed that the changes were in accordance with 'divine order.'

Hacking' out names

There were periods in pharonic Egypt which show evidence of 'hacking out'. This involved the removal of the name or image of a pharaoh (or deity as in the case of Amun in the Amarna period) in the belief that this person should never have existed. The removal or 'hacking out' of names was different to usurping which involved carving a new king's name over an existing king's name to produce a deeper relief.

The best known account of the 'removal' of a pharaohs 'memory' involved Queen Hatshepsut (Venus). This occurred when Hatshepsut's successor, Tuthmosis III (Moon), ordered the removal of any reference to Hatshepsut. During his reign, images of Hatshepsut were defaced and a number of Hatshepsut's cartouches were replaced by those of Tuthmosis III when the cartouches were re-carved.

Smiting pharaoh

The image below represents the god-king planet engaging in cosmic battles with the 'vile' space debris that threatened to bring the whole universe into chaos.

History teaches us that Egypt was a warring nation and a large army was big business. It wasn't required for defence as the Egyptians did not want peace; peace was not a virtue.

It was the role of the pharaoh to lead his army to conquer foreign lands and return home with the spoils of war.

Many battles were recorded for posterity on temple walls and some, such as Ramesses II and the battle of Kadesh, were repeated many times. The inscriptions provided details of the many pharaohs who fearlessly fought off and defeated the enemy, sometimes single-handedly. The battle accounts were accompanied by images of the pharaohs in the act of 'smiting the enemy'. The above illustrations are typical of the many recurring scenes which depicted the pharaoh with mace raised ready to vanquish the enemy. Such scenes echoed the mythical conflict between the gods Horus and Seth in the continuing battle of good against evil.

I was already a catastrophist when I made the incredible discoveries set out in the books of Velikovsky and Ackerman and their works convinced me that cosmic chaos occurred in historical times. However, my own discoveries centred on the battles of the pharaohs versus the battles of the planets. I could not understand how the battles of mortals took precedence over wars in the heavens. I reasoned that a by-product of planetary chaos was the production of colossal amounts of space debris. Since this debris has all but disappeared, it is reasonable to assume that the planets 'battled' up the debris and these cosmic battles should take precedence over any terrestrial conflicts. The battles of the pharaohs occurred at the same time as cosmic battles when the Egyptians inhabited the Nile Valley. This does not mean that battles in the heavens were ignored in favour of battles on Earth and it is therefore important to establish whether there are any written accounts of our 'warring' planets. Catastrophists believe that these events were recorded only in mythology, but it makes sense to assume the Egyptians recorded these cosmic disturbances.

The Egyptians did not ignore planetary battles and they were meticulously recorded in history. The warring planets were the warrior pharaohs! The battles of the pharaohs occurred when Mars, Mercury and the Moon (and occasionally Venus), in the guise of numerous pharaohs, fought and defeated the masses of space debris that once engulfed the solar system 4000 years ago. This was the same dust and debris that turned the Sun red for over three millennia.

I am not implying that the earthly Egyptians never engaged in warfare because evidence proved they did. In later times Egypt was ruled by foreigners such as Libyans, Assyrians, Babylonians, Greeks and Romans and therefore we must assume that some kind of conflict took place. How else could the Egyptians record and humanise cosmic conflicts unless they were based on actual events on Earth?

Distinguishing between human and planetary battles is very simple; the key is the sacred hieroglyphs or carvings. As hieroglyphs recorded cosmic events, they provide a record of the entire 3,000 year period of cosmic chaos and were therefore considered sacred. This included the perpetual battles undertaken by astral kings. From small border skirmishes to full-scale battles and sieges, they were recorded on temple walls via sacred inscriptions and scenes of 'smiting the enemy'. All hieroglyphs recorded battles and skirmishes in the heavens _ none of these battles occurred on Earth.

We will consider Mars as the main warrior planet in the guise of the pharaoh Ramesses. When records state that Ramesses marched out and fought a great battle in the north, this was actually Mars fighting vast armies of space debris in the northern skies. Similarly, accounts of Ramesses battling the enemy in the south referred to Mars vanquishing the enemy which clouded the southern skies. This reasoning applied to any location in the heavens _ if Mars encountered armies of debris directly above Egypt, this referred to Ramesses fending off the foreign invaders who were directly threatening Egypt's borders.

When considering the historical record, we need to apply an 'as above, so below' rule to identify exactly who the pharaohs were perceived to be fighting? As a result of cosmic chaos, all ancient cultures associated themselves with their own particular portion of the sky, usually directly above them, and the many astral bodies which inhabited it. Many of Egypt's contemporaries lived north and south of the ecliptic. This was either side of the path which the Sun and reigning planets occupied in the form of large rogue moons, orbiting rocks and large armies of asteroids which arched across the heavens. Some ancient cultures identified with the four main bodies and considered them to be their 'divine' royal family and named them accordingly.

If Mars/Ramesses was observed smiting the enemy above a particular town or city outside of Egypt's borders, this was perceived as Mars/Ramesses battling that particular nation. The records show that Ramesses led many military campaigns against the Hittites who were located in the north-east. This was actually Mars accompanied by a vast army of boulders as it crashed headlong into clouds of 'foreign' cometary bodies above the land of the Hittites. In other words, Mars/Ramesses vanquished the astral Hittites, thus giving the impression that it was waging war against that particular nation.

The above scenario applied to any pharaoh in any location. For example, many pharaohs carried out military expeditions against the Nubians in the south. This was actually one of the main planetary bodies as it waged war against the evil 'Nubian' space debris in the southern skies directly above the land of the Nubians. The planet returned home before marching out to fight the Hittites in the northern skies (Hittites translates as 'stones that hit'). Most god-kings were fearless warrior pharaohs because they were guises of planets at war with space debris.

We can use this model to explain battle sieges which occurred when a planetary body appeared almost stationary above a foreign land for months at a time. For example, to secure victory, Tuthmosis III laid siege to the fortified town of Megiddo for seven months which would have been impossible due to the lack of resources in ancient times. I therefore believe this refers to the Moon in the guise of Tuthmosis as it appeared almost stationary for seven months above the city of Megiddo which was in the north.

Why bother to march out and battle at all?

The Egyptians regarded Egypt as the greatest land on Earth and the envy of its neighbours. The annual flooding of the Nile allowed for a surplus of crops which meant the population did not have to concentrate solely on agrarian activities. Egypt had a large priesthood and a building programme for the construction of great monuments and trade between Egypt and its neighbours was extremely lucrative. The Nile abundance enabled the Egyptians to establish a standing army. The extent of Egypt's wealth meant that in later times it was known as the 'bread-basket of Rome' as it literally fed Rome. As well as an abundance of food, Egypt had its own gold mines at Wadi Hammamat which was located halfway between Qusier and Gift (ancient Coptos). Egypt was totally self-sufficient and whatever it lacked it could trade for and it is therefore puzzling that Egypt needed to go to war. Relations with its neighbours were amicable, so what were Egyptians risking life and limb for?

Warfare in ancient times was a gruelling affair. Armies were away from home for months on end as they crossed some of the most inhospitable terrains on Earth. According to historical records, Ramesses II, in his quest to vanquish the Hittites at Kadesh, led an army of 20,000 soldiers east across the blistering Sinai desert and north into Syro-Palestine on a route taken by kings before and after Ramesses. Although the army consisted of a few charioteers, the majority were foot soldiers who set the pace and it took several months of relentless marching to reach Kadesh. Yet why did they risk life and limb when they enjoyed a comfortable life in Egypt?

It would have been a logistical nightmare to keep 20,000 men clean, fed and clothed and free from disease. Supplying them with water would have required divine intervention, particularly when marching across the scorching Sinai desert. What happened as they travelled further away from their supply route in Egypt? What happened to the horses that led the chariots? Thinking back to the Egyptian attire, how could an army of 20,000 soldiers march across blistering deserts wearing nothing more than a loincloth?

Egypt is surrounded by deserts. To the Egyptians, the deserts were associated with Seth, the god of evil. Yet a vast army ventured across some of the most inhospitable places on Earth. What was the point of spending months on end marching across arid deserts and hostile lands if neighbouring nations were neither hostile nor aggressive?

Perhaps there were periods when the Nile was not abundant, when life was harsh and crops failed leading to death and starvation. Would this have prompted the Egyptians to form massive armies to attack their neighbours? The evidence does not support this view. Some of Egypt's most famous battles, such as those attributed to Ramesses and Tuthmosis, occurred during times of great prosperity. If death and starvation prompted the Egyptians to march out, how could they have supplied their armies with sufficient food and other resources to support a military campaign?

When considering Egyptian warfare, we must consider the power vacuum that would have occurred while the army was away. The pharaoh *was* Egypt. He was the pinnacle of Egyptian society and the religious and political leader _ the gods were worshipped through him. Therefore how was Egypt controlled or defended while the pharaoh was leading legions of men to war? What prevented Egypt's enemies in the south (the Nubians) from taking advantage of the situation?

It might seem logical to assume the Egyptians were consumed with a desire to rule the known world, but this is not true. If they yearned for world domination, they adopted a very poor strategy. The Egyptians did not believe in colonialism and never left behind a controlling army, fort or garrison in any of their conquered lands. They marched out, fought the enemy, pillaged the land and then marched back home. These appear to be ridiculous tactics.

Egypt's Napoleon, Tuthmosis III, extended Egypt's borders further than any other pharaoh. He led numerous military campaigns against the Nubians in the south, but it was his 17 campaigns against the Syrians in the north that are of particular interest. These were not sporadic campaigns that occurred once every few years but were annual campaigns. Tuthmosis marched out with 20,000 men and headed north across the scorching Sinai desert. He defeated the Syrians and returned home, only to repeat this action annually for 17 years. As he defeated the enemy for the first time, he failed to set up a colony or leave behind a controlling army which would have saved time, trouble and lives. If we consider the blistering Sinai desert, how many Egyptians would have died before they reached the battlefield?

The campaigns of Tuthmosis highlight a number of factual concerns. The enemy would have recognised the regular pattern of attack which occurred every year for 17 years. This would have enabled them to prepare by setting traps for the Egyptians. We must also consider any underlying reasons for the attacks. What did the enemy possess that the Egyptians lacked? What was the purpose of routing and plundering the enemy only to return year after year in a predictable manner, thereby giving their enemies plenty of warning?

LACK OF ARCHAEOLOGICAL EVIDENCE

The afterlife

In an attempt to explain why the Egyptians did not leave behind a controlling garrison in foreign lands, scholars have suggested they were obsessed with death and the afterlife. They point out that the Egyptians were resurrectionists who believed they would go to the 'next world' when they died. It was therefore essential that the body of the deceased was mummified and buried on Egyptian soil. For this reason the Egyptians always returned home to guarantee their place in the 'next world'. It was against their religion to be buried on foreign soil and they would not have risked dying in a foreign land.

As plausible as it may seem, this reasoning is flawed. If the Egyptians were concerned about losing their place in the 'next-world', they would not have tempted fate by leaving Egypt in the first place. What would have persuaded thousands of Egyptian soldiers to risk life and limb, their place in the next world and the prospect of immortality?

Archaeological evidence

There is very little, if any, archaeological evidence to support any battles fought by Egyptian kings. Although we know the exact location of many of their conflicts, these fighting pharaohs failed to leave behind any evidence that they were ever there. We would expect to find the remains of swords, arrow heads, battles axes, broken chariots, armour, battle-scarred human remains or mass graves.

However, there is a distinct lack of archaeological evidence and no data to support the existence of ancient battlefields.

We will consider Ramesses II and the Battle of Kadesh. History states that Ramesses marched into Syro-Palestine and fearlessly fought 40,000 Hittites for several years. Detailed maps exist which show the exact location of Kadesh near the Orontes River in Syria. They include diagrams, complete with arrows, which show how the battle was played out. Modern photographs of Kadesh can be found at http://touregypt.net/featurestories/kadesh.htm. However, despite an abundance of information, it seems the Battle of Kadesh existed in sacred words only as there is no archaeological evidence to prove it took place. Ramesses II's army of 20,000 soldiers plus 40,000 Hittites totalled 60,000 men. Yet it seems they left nothing behind as there are no battle implements or corpses which exist from the battle of Kadesh.

History suggests that Egypt was a warring nation which engaged in hundreds of battles over a 3,000 year period. However, the archaeological evidence does not support this. There is overwhelming evidence to support the Egyptian obsession with the afterlife and archaeologists are still discovering lost tombs, artefacts and mummified bodies in the sands of Egypt. Yet there is no evidence to support Egypt's other obsession _ that of war. The lack of archaeological evidence is very important and provides overwhelming support for the GKS. We will consider this in the light of the lack of human remains.

'We do not know where most soldiers were buried, especially those who died away from Egypt...'

(Partridge, 2002, p 126)

Throughout 3,000 years of pharaonic Egypt, there were at least 170 pharaohs. If we attribute two battles to each pharaoh, this makes an approximate total of 340 battles. If each king had an army of only 5,000 men, this equates to around 1,700,000 soldiers over a 3,000 year period. If 10% of these men died in battle, this would have resulted in approximately 170,000 bodies. How could so many men have disappeared off the face of the Earth?

Tuthmosis III led 17 campaigns into Syria, and at the Battle of Megiddo his army consisted of approximately 20,000 troops. If we assume he conscripted the same amount for all 17 campaigns to the north, this would have equated to 340,000 men fighting 17 annual battles. If we calculate a loss of 10%, this makes a total of 34,000 dead soldiers. Tuthmosis III also led numerous military campaigns to the south into Nubia, although the exact total is not known. We can assume that around 50,000 men would have been casualties of war during the reign of Tuthmosis III. This was just one of approximately 170 pharaohs and it is therefore safe to assume that the above figures are a conservative estimate. So where are these fallen heroes?

Partridge attempted to explain the whereabouts of the fallen in his book 'Fighting Pharaohs'. He stated that the Egyptians soldiers were buried close to the battle field:

'On campaign, most soldiers who were killed in action were probably buried close to the place they died.'

(Partridge, 2002, p 126)

This may sound plausible, but where is the evidence? Perhaps the slain soldiers were taken back to Egypt and buried there because they believed they had to be buried on Egyptian soil. In fact, this would have been impossible. How could thousands of dead bodies have been transported over 400 miles back to Egypt? Having routed the enemy and plundered everything, are we to believe the Egyptians carried hundreds of corpses across blistering deserts so that they could be buried in Egypt?

We must consider the logistics involved including the art of preserving bodies for long periods. Was it possible to preserve thousands of dead soldiers until they reached Egypt where they would be mummified? Egypt's northern foes were at least a month's march away _ four weeks of carting decomposing bodies across rough terrain. This would have been a physically impossible task. Even if the army had managed to transport their dead comrades back to Egypt, there would have been severe problems with preservation. The resulting rotting corpses would have been in no state to be mummified or interned correctly. The Egyptians knew there was no prospect of an afterlife unless a body was in a 'complete' state prior to travelling to the 'next world'.

The transportation of bodies was impossible and the archaeological evidence does not exist to support it. The tombs of Egypt do not contain masses of battle-scarred soldiers. We must remember that the figures we have calculated do not include enemy bodies. If the Egyptian soldiers have not been found, what of their enemies?

According to the annals of ancient battles, the enemy were mostly annihilated and their numbers far outweighed those of the Egyptian victors. It is likely that the enemy dead totalled approximately three to four times more than the

170,000 Egyptians lost in battle. If we total the losses on both sides, the final figure would be over 500,000. Over half a million people were killed in action, yet there is no archaeological evidence to support this.

There are many books on the subject of ancient Egypt and many make reference to the warrior kings. Many TV documentaries have also shown the warrior pharaohs fearlessly leading their troops into battle. Yet not one programme or book ever transports the reader to the scene of these famous battles. It is not possible to locate the remains of the thousands of soldiers that died in battle.

There are numerous reliefs on temple walls depicting piles of enemy hands. This illustrates the Egyptian practice of cutting off the right hands of the enemy so that they could be piled up and counted. Yet archaeologists have yet to uncover the graves of thousands of corpses with dismembered hands. In some cases they also cut off the penises of the enemy and piled them up and it is hard to imagine such barbaric practices.

Answer _ the GKS

If we refer to the GKS we can explain the above enigmas. The earthly Egyptians did not perpetually march out to vanquish the enemy; they were not obsessed with carrying out military activities every year. It was the pharaonic planets who were the true warrior kings of ancient times. It was they who led vast armies of asteroids, comets and other junk headlong into clouds of opposing space debris. The god-king planets had the power to fight the forces of evil that threatened to bring the whole universe into chaos. Our earthly forebears played no part in such events.

I believe the Egyptians rarely left the safety of the Nile Valley. They may have carried out trading and mining expeditions such as trading in timber in the Lebanon or mining for turquoise in the Sinai. While carrying out expeditions, and in order to placate their astral kings and gods, the Egyptians erected boundary stele (stone carvings) or carved sacred inscriptions into the native rock which described the astral god king's great deeds. This was true of the mining expeditions in the Sinai which were represented by images of the 4th dynasty king Snefru in the act of 'smiting the enemy'. The inscriptions proclaimed: 'Snefru, smiter of barbarians'.

It is also possible that the Egyptians ventured out beyond Egypt's borders with the sole purpose of honouring the astral kings. They may have ventured as far as they could to erect stele which told of the king's great exploits in extending Egypt's borders. However, I do not believe that the Egyptians formed armies of up to 20,000 men to march across blistering deserts for months on end to battle an enemy 40,000 strong.

Explanation of the Afterlife

I propose the Egyptians rarely left Egypt because of their obsession with the afterlife. They believed it was imperative to be correctly mummified and buried on Egyptian soil to stand any chance of immortality. The Egyptians lived and died by this belief and it dictated every aspect of their lives. They firmly believed that when they died they would 'get up and go' to the next world. This world was similar to Earth but far superior and eternal. The Egyptians would never risk losing immortality by marching out for months across scorching deserts for no reason. To step outside Egypt was to step outside immortality.

From a human perspective, the logistical problems of keeping a vast army in shape would have been outstanding. It would have included feeding them, providing them with water, keeping disease at bay and preventing them from being scorched alive across blistering deserts. However, for the god-king planets these problems did not exist. If a red orb was seen charging across the heavens with thousands of boulders in its wake, it was perceived to be a war-mongering pharaoh leading his army into battle.

By inhabiting the above, the monarchy was not faced with logistical problems the way an earthly army would have been. There was no gruelling march across scorching desert lands, no searching for food, no water supply problems, no disease and no decomposing bodies.

Humanising celestial events such as battles transferred the problems that existed on Earth to the heavens and obstacles were conveniently overcome or brushed aside. Sky pharaohs led their armies, fought and beat their enemies and returned home unscathed.

If we place pharaohs in the heavens, we can understand how they were able to lead armies of 20,000 soldiers across scorching deserts. Planetary kings traversed the four corners of the Earth many times, battling the enemy in an attempt to clear the skies to bring about 'divine order'. According to the annals of history, this was an eternal struggle which lasted over three thousand years.

No Power Vacuum

As they stayed within the boundaries set by the Nile, there was no power vacuum as a result of military campaigns outside Egypt's borders. Opposing forces could not take advantage of voids left by absent pharaohs because this situation never existed. As a nation with deep religious convictions, Egypt never sent armies across blistering deserts to dice with death or miss out on immortality.

No Colonies

As they did not march out to battle, the earthly Egyptians did not establish colonies. This tactic was the sole responsibility of the sky kings. Having slain the enemy, they did not leave behind a controlling army, fort or garrison because it was physically impossible for sky kings to colonise the heavens. They ruled the heavens and soared like a falcon (Horus). Planets in chaos were always on the move and never stayed in one place long enough to 'colonise' that particular portion of the sky.

A god king could lay 'siege' to a foreign city (as in the case of Tuthmosis III in the guise of the Moon) by appearing almost stationary above a particular town or city for a few months. As planets in chaos, they eventually moved on and wherever the pharaoh went the infantry followed. They never left behind an occupying force which is why the Egyptians never believed in colonisation.

Lack of Evidence

The lack of archaeological evidence supports the GKS. The locations of many battles attributed to the pharaohs are known, and many were fought in the same location. Yet there is no archaeological evidence because all pharaonic battles occurred in the heavens and not on Earth. Anything recorded via 'sacred' hieroglyphs points to divine events above.

Direct archaeological evidence of the many battles fought by the pharaohs can be found on the surfaces of Mars, Mercury or the Moon as they bear the hallmarks of numerous conflicts. The Moon provides a silent record of a very recent violent past as its surface has been pulverised repeatedly and meteoritic impacts have shaped the surface we see today. Such features are the legacy of battles which occurred when the Moon was in the guise of Tuthmosis III, who was born of the lunar god Thoth and also known as Egypt's Napoleon. This was an apt title because the Moon, under the guise of Tuthmosis, was Egypt's greatest warrior king.

I would like to challenge Egyptologists and archaeologists to provide substantial archaeological evidence for any of the major pharonic battles that are supposed to have occurred in ancient times. I am not referring to a few broken bones, the occasional sword, a battle axe or even a few broken chariots. The Egyptians fought many battles over a 3,000 year period and therefore there should be an abundance of archaeological evidence including the bodies of tens of thousands of dead soldiers. I can provide evidence from the surfaces of Mars, Mercury and the Moon as these heavily cratered planets provide the real legacy of pharaonic battles.

This is a crucial point because if I am wrong, thousands of dead soldiers will be disinterred near Megiddo in Syro-

Palestine or another battle location. If concrete evidence is provided, my theory would fall apart and that would be the end of the GKS. I am prepared to take this risk because I am confident that my theory as presented in this book is accurate and entirely correct.

Pharaohs leading from the front

Amongst the many battle scenes adorning temples walls, you will invariably find references to the king leading the army from the front. This was principally true of some of the more famous New Kingdom pharaohs such as Tuthmosis III and Ramesses II. A typical example is as follows:

'The King himself led the way of the army, mighty at its head, like a flame of fire, the king who wrought with his sword. He went forth, none like him, slaying the barbarians, smiting Retenu, bringing their princes as living captives, their chariots, wrought with gold, bound to their horses.'

(A viceroy of Kush recording Tuthmosis' exploits)

Other references speak of kings, with little regard for their own safety, charging headlong into the enemy, slaying all before them. These 'sacred words' are supported by images that show the brave pharaoh driving his chariot behind fiery steeds as he fearlessly leads his troops into the fray. Other images show the king firing arrows as he charges ahead, or beating his enemies to death with a club.

These cannot be literal depictions of actual events on earth. The religious and political leader of the greatest nation of ancient times would not have risked his own life by leading his troops from the front. Such poor battle tactics would have resulted in the king being among the first to die. Yet the records show that many kings adopted such a foolhardy battle plan.

The fact is, armies are led from the rear and not from the front. Leading from the front is a ridiculous military tactic and no experienced commanding officer or head of state would be stupid enough to adopt such an approach which would lead to certain death. On the other hand, leading from the rear would allow a military leader to take account of the battle; it would allow him to make crucial strategic decisions; he could deploy his troops to gain advantage over the enemy and live to fight another day. Leading from the front meant almost certain defeat.

To clarify this point, transport yourself back 4,000 years and imagine you are a frontline soldier just about to face the might of the Egyptian army. As battle commences you notice the Egyptian army is being led by the pharaoh. He is easy to spot due to his distinctive battle attire which included an ornate war crown. He would also drive a war chariot made of 'fine gold and electrum' (as in the case of Tuthmosis III) and as such was clearly visible. Who would you aim for as your main target?

Obviously it would be the pharaoh, as would thousands of your comrades. By killing the pharaoh, Egypt would be no more. Enemy forces realised that the Egyptians revered their kings as 'gods on Earth' and if the king died, Egypt would fall. Remember that the Egyptians believed that without the pharaoh the whole world would fall into chaos.

Propaganda

Scholars have suggested that accounts of pharaohs leading from the front were merely propaganda. It was meant to portray the king as a superhuman and fearless warrior god-king who was untouchable by enemy forces. I do not agree with this theory. It does not seem reasonable to pick out impractical or impossible events and categorise them as 'propaganda' because it is convenient to do so. Consider the scenes painted on Tutankhamen's chest. The boy-king is shown in his chariot leading the troops into enemy forces. These scenes are reminiscent of those found on temple walls which are attributed to other pharaohs. However, because of the age of the king and the political situation at that time, Egyptologists doubt whether Tutankhamun took part in any battles. They believe these scenes were not actual events but were propaganda to promote the young king as equal to his warrior forefathers.

Although this reasoning may sound plausible, it is wrong to pick and chose which battles were real and which were not based purely on the volume of inscriptions and images. Scholars regard the battles of pharaohs such as Ramesses II as fact because they were recorded more regularly than Tutankhamun's solitary battle which they regard as propaganda. They also feel that, given the king's status, 'leading from the front' would have been an extremely unlikely battle tactic and this too was propaganda. I believe this shows a very poor understanding of our ancestors.

Planet Warriors

Earthly kings would never have used the impractical tactic of leading vast armies from the front. In fact, it was the planetary kings who led from the front and it had nothing to do with propaganda. It was a natural phenomenon whereby Mars, Mercury and the Moon repeatedly took on the basic attributes of a cometary body _ a head or nucleolus with trailing debris. The head of the comet represented the red-orbed pharaoh while the tens of thousands of boulders and space debris which trailed in its wake represented legions of foot soldiers. This was the pharaoh leading his army into battle with little regard for his own safety, slaying all before him as he charged headlong into swarms of enemy space debris. This was exactly as recorded in the numerous battle annuls and 'smiting the enemy' scenes which are found throughout Egypt.

Furthermore, to the ancients there was no such thing as propaganda. They used symbolic representation to present the way they perceived events above. If inscriptions recorded that the kings led from the front, that is exactly what they did. If records stated that a pharaoh led their army wearing bright blue crowns on a chariot of gold and electrum, that is what he did, albeit symbolically. For example, it is recorded that Ramesses II, having been ambushed, single-handily fought off the Hittites. Does it seem likely that Ramesses really did slaughter 40,000 enemy troops?

Mars as Ramesses did vanquish innumerable amounts of enemy troops in the form of enemy space debris. Similarly, if a scene recorded that the boy-king Tutankhamun battled enemy forces as depicted on his funerary chest, that is exactly what he did. This is because Tutankhamun was one of the many names given to Mars. Unlike human kings, planetary kings were not subjected to age restrictions or the political situation on Earth, but rather they dictated such things. Therefore it was the planetary kings that led from the front and not their earthly representatives. In fact, mortal kings rarely left the safety of Egypt's borders.

IDENTIFYING THE MONARCHY

No pharaoh ever lost a battle

We have established that Egypt was a warring nation. In fact, they were totally obsessed with war. Their pharaohs had little time for anything else and they indulged in regular campaigns over three hundred centuries. Yet, despite the regular combat and the permanent state of war, no pharaoh ever lost a battle. How could a nation have victory after victory, generation after generation, for an incredible 3,000 years!

I find it extraordinary that nobody has questioned the military success of the ancient Egyptians. Remaining undefeated for 3,000 years is not only improbable but impossible, particularly if pharaohs actually adopted the military tactic of leading from the front. If there were only 10 battles throughout the three millennia, a 100% success rate would be extremely unlikely. Yet we are referring to hundreds of battles which all resulted in success for the Egyptians.

The truth is, pharaohs were always victorious in battle because they were first and foremost guises of the planets Mars, Mercury and the Moon. The enemy space debris stood little chance against such fierce warriors as they charged headlong across the heavens. The evil god Seth could do his worst, but the good and just god Horus remained undefeated.

By identifying Egypt's kings with astral bodies, their incredible rate of success begins to make sense. For example, a low estimate of 340 battles in total throughout the 3,000 years equates to 340 campaigns undertaken and won by Mars, Mercury and the Moon. Figures which seemed impossible when attributed to human kings appear completely logical when applied to heavenly bodies. Egyptian battle annuls recorded the events of planetary bodies as they encountered masses of space debris, and the planets were victorious every time.

Mars, Mercury and the Moon remained undefeated for millennia. Mars is presently a speck of light and it no longer rules our skies as a dominant red orb. Nevertheless, it is still undefeated. Mercury is occasionally observed with the naked eye, and the Moon has lost its incandescent red orb appearance, but they too remain undefeated. Venus, as a serene queen, is now a magical speck of light. This is a very important point when discussing why Egyptian pharaohs never lost a battle. The main perpetrators of chaos who were responsible for the monarchy of ancient Egypt still exist today. They are continuing their fight against the forces of evil as they sweep up the remaining vestiges of space debris born from celestial chaos of 4,000 years ago.

In summary of the warrior pharaohs

We will now examine the image of the king 'smiting his enemy'. This archetypal image can be found in scenes from Egypt through to the fertile-crescent and Anatolia. Some refer to this scene as 'God with the Upraised Arm.' My interpretation of this iconic image is clear; it is a symbolic representation of either Mars, Mercury or the Moon in the act of battling and vacuuming up space debris. The king is always shown larger than the enemy and such scenes have nothing to do with human monarchs. It is an image that remained virtually unchanged for 3,000 years and the key is contained in the 'sacred carvings'. The sacred text and the sacred images all tell of a time when Mars, Venus, Mercury and the Moon dominated the skies.

The Cartouche

The cartouche meant 'Everything encircled by the Sun'. The pharaohs were given a unique combination of five titles and they were of the utmost importance as they were primarily names given to certain aspects of planetary bodies which ruled the skies 4,000 years ago. Before we examine these names, we will look at the cartouche, the oval shaped glyph that enclosed the king's birth name and the throne name.

The cartouche (pronounced kar-TOOSH) was essentially an elongated form of the *shen* hieroglyph in the shape of a circle or ring. It signified the concept of 'encircling protection' and is believed to be a diagram of the universe. By incorporating the king's title, it implied he was the ruler of everything 'encircled by the Sun' (Dictionary of Ancient Egypt Shaw & Nicolson). The oval cartouche is ubiquitous throughout Egypt and is easily recognisable. It can be found on the walls of the famous boy king Tutankhamun's tomb as well as almost every corner of the magnificently decorated walls of Amun's temple at Karnak. Certain pharaohs' sarcophagi and tombs were oval-shaped which embodied the encircling protection of the cartouche. Tuthmosis III (Moon), the 'Napoleon of ancient Egypt' was one such pharaoh.

Wherever we look we find corroboratory evidence for the GKS and this includes the cartouche. The cartouche is highly revealing in its meaning because it clearly implies that the pharaohs were rulers of the cosmos. In the conventional sense this points to mortal kings who thought they were rulers of the universe. We can add this to some of the other bizarre traits adopted by the kings including mortal kings who, as *sa-re*, believed they were directly related to the Sun god Re. There were also 'living gods' who declared themselves gods and intermediates between heaven and Earth as well as pharaohs who proclaimed they were rulers of the cosmos.

What of the divinity of mortals? Is it possible that they dared suggest they were on a par with the solar deity Re? Would they risk the wrath of one of the original creator deities? The Sun is the driving force behind all life on Earth as it encircles the heavens. From an earthly perspective, the Sun is the supreme ruler of the universe, and yet mere mortals believed they ruled the same arena as the Sun.

When we consider the GKS, the clear and distinct celestial overtones of the cartouche should be taken at face value. The cartouche represents a diagram of the universe and, as our planetary kings dominated the cosmos with the Sun, they were naturally perceived as rulers of everything 'encircled by the Sun'. The planetary kings and queens were named according to their attributes. A collection of 'sacred' hieroglyphs were bestowed according to the actions and appearance of the god-kings. As they encircled the heavens, these 'scared' symbols were enclosed within the oval shaped cartouche – in effect within a diagram of the sky.

It is no coincidence that the 'Napoleon of ancient Egypt', Tuthmosis III, had an oval shaped tomb and sarcophagus in the Valley of the Kings. The Moon in the guise of Tuthmosis III extended Egypt's borders further than any other Pharaoh as it covered vast areas of the sky. Tuthmosis/Moon maintained divine order by battling up space debris in the north, south, east and west.

Tuthmosis/Moon, once captured by the Earth, covered more of the sky than any other body. The Moon today covers a larger area of the sky than the Sun and it does so more frequently. Such wanderings were reflected in the tomb and sarcophagus of Tuthmosis as the oval shape represented a diagram of the sky.

The cartouche provides us with a simple way to extract the names of the astral monarchy from the sea of hieroglyphs covering every monument along the Nile. The cartouche primarily represented a name given to either Mars, Venus, Mercury or the Moon as well as other bodies that have since disappeared.

The names of sky gods such as Amun, Ptah, Hathor and Isis were never enclosed in the cartouche; the cartouche represented the ruling planets. Famous pharaohs such as Ramesses, Tutankhamun, Akhenaten, Tuthmosis and Seti as well as queens such as Nefertiti, Hatshepsut and Cleopatra were all represented with sacred symbols enclosed in the cartouche.

It was imperative to visually separate the monarchy from the universal deities. Unlike the immortal gods, royalty were mortal in the sense that they lived and died to Earth and changed identity many times. It was a completely normal practice to magically encircle their names with the cartouche to represent the sky.

We have established that the Egyptians never experienced a golden glaring Sun – they experienced a diminished Sun that granted visibility to the astral monarchy during the day. The monarchy's most basic trait was similar to that of the Sun – a red disk. This led to the very apt title '*sa-re'* (son of re). Therefore the cartouche should be regarded as the kings as they ruled 'everything encircled by a red Sun'.

Where was our Moon?

It is important to remember an important point regarding the Moon. The Moon is a recent addition to the solar system and this view is supported by the oval shaped cartouche. It covers more of the heavens than the Sun because of its 29 _ day monthly cycle and it covers it more frequently. It is closer to Earth than the Sun and it dominated the clear night skies of ancient Egypt, yet it was ignored by the ancient Egyptians. If the Sun and Moon haven't altered their paths across the heavens for millennia, the cartouche should refer to the kings as rulers of everything 'encircled by the Sun and the Moon'.

We have established that there was no mention of the Moon in the cartouche because the Moon wasn't a permanent companion of Earth until much later. The Moon had not yet settled down into the regular phases of today. I propose that the Moon only entered its monthly cycle towards the end of pharonic Egypt around 320 BC. This was the time when the lunar deity Thoth became the measurer of time and the seasons, as well as law and order. By the time the Moon had settled down into its regular cycle it was too late – pharonic Egypt had ended.

Names/Titles

Names today have little meaning but in ancient times they were important and highly significant. The Egyptians believed the name of a person was of paramount importance and it was regarded as a living part of each human being. A child had to be named immediately at birth in order for them to fully come into existence. These beliefs derived from the naming of planetary bodies as they descended from the firmament to reign over Earth.

The monarchy, in shedding their star-like attributes to become 'living gods', demanded representation and it was imperative that they were given names. A name chosen at random was unacceptable because, as gods amongst gods, they had to be worshiped as such. The Egyptians therefore gave their kings up to five names; a birth name (B); a throne name (T); a Horus name (H); a golden Horus name (G); a nebti name (N). These names, in particular the throne, birth and Horus names, were dictated by the actions, location and appearance of the planetary bodies. It makes perfect sense to name planetary god-kings according to their attributes and their names and titles had nothing whatsoever to do with their earthly counterparts.

We will examine and analyse the names of certain pharaohs using P. Clapton's book 'Chronicle of the Pharaohs'. The names I have included appear in the same sequential order as they appear in this book. The majority of names support the GKS and are clearly celestial in connotation. They are unequivocally names given to astral bodies ruling over Earth and many make sense only when attributed to astral bodies. It isn't always necessary to explain what planet is involved – the important point is that they are first and foremost names given to planetary bodies and not mortals. Scholars are mystified as to the true meaning of kings' names because they believe they belong to a world we do not understand. However, names in ancient times had deeply significant meanings.

Narmer (H)   *'The striking catfish'*

Is it logical to perceive this king as a striking catfish? Would it not make more sense to look to the heavens and imagine Mars as a large hazy red orb striking out with huge lightning bolts and tremendous volcanic eruptions?

Hor-aha (H)   *'The fighting hawk'*

The hawk is a bird of prey and this is a description of a planetary bird swooping down to vanquish the enemy in the guise of space debris. Mars, Mercury and the Moon were fighting hawks and this name was therefore associated with the hawk-headed god Horus.

Djer (H)   *'Horus who succours'*

Den (H)   *'Horus who strikes'*

As 'gods on earth', all pharaohs were the embodiment of the falcon headed god Horus. As upholders of 'divine order' (*ma'at*), they maintained a balance between order and chaos. This belief can be traced back to the Osiris myth and the contending of Horus and Seth (good and evil). Mars, in the guise of many pharonic kings, was regularly observed courtesy of the diminished red Sun. It fearlessly battled the evil space debris that filled the skies and threatened to bring the whole world into chaos. Mars was forever the god Horus that struck the enemy down. On many occasions Mars banished the enemy from the skies of Egypt in a perennial battle fought by numerous kings.

Qa'a (H)   *'His arm is raised'*

This was a strange name to bestow upon a mortal king. Was he deformed, or did he walk around with his arm raised at all times? Did the pharaoh agree to such a name? I believe the name referred to Mars when he was adorned with a cometary tail which was perceived to be a raised arm.

The planetary kings ruled the heavens and dictated events, and they held the power of life or death in their hands. It was vital that they were placated so epithets matching their actions were chosen.

Hotepsekhemwy (H)   *'Pleasing in powers'*

Astral in connotation – the astral monarchy held great powers.

Nynetjer (H)   *'Godlike'*

All celestial bodies were godlike due to their location whereas humans were not and never will be godlike. This is why all kings were Horus or gods on Earth.

Khasekhemwy (H) *'The two powerful ones appear'*

This enigmatic name was a statement rather than a name and the astral kings may have commanded it to be used. As Khasekhemwy was from the Old Kingdom, the name may have referred to Mars and Venus which appeared to be close together when they were actually at a distance. An early Moon of Mars or Earth may have appeared in front of Mars giving the impression that they were almost equal in size. Either way, this name belongs to heaven and not Earth.

Sanakhte (H) *'Strong protection'*

This name was clearly celestial.

Djoser (H) *'Divine of the body'*

By their very location, all celestial bodies were 'divine'. Mars, Venus, Mercury and the Moon, as well as some of their children, were divine children of the red Sun.

Sekhemkhet (H) *'Powerful in body'*

Clearly celestial in connotation, planets are powerful in body, not humans.

Huni (H) *'The smiter'*

Warrior planets 'smite' the enemy.

Snefru (B) *'He of Beauty'*

Mars loomed larger than the red Sun which dominated the skies and was an incredible, awe inspiring sight.

Khufu (B) *'Protected by Khnum'*

As Khnum was a mythical god, we may therefore assume that the king was protected by an imaginary deity. Alternatively this may refer to Khnum as a celestial phenomenon or sky god. Khnum was perceived to be shielding Mars, thus protecting the planetary god-king Khufu which may have represented Mars in the northern skies low on the horizon.

Khafre (Chephren) (Kha-f-re) *'Appearing like Re'*

It is believed that this king built a large pyramid at Giza, but what was the reasoning behind his title? Did Khafre take on the appearance of the Sun? Perhaps he was born with bright yellow skin which radiated heat and dazzled the nation? This is extremely unlikely, and it is difficult to make sense of this name unless it is considered in the context of the GKS.

This name is clearly a description of a planetary body as it appeared like the red Sun. It could have referred to Mars, the red god of war, which resembled the Sun of ancient times. Mars made an appearance during the day courtesy of a twilight world brought on by a diminished red-Sun. Perhaps Khafre/Mars was very close to the Sun, or appeared to be the same size which would have contributed to the apt name 'appearing like Re'.

It is interesting to note that a late king by the name of Darius also had the title '*Setut-re*' which translated as *'likeness of Re'*. This was obviously a reference to a planetary body which was reddish in colour in the likeness of the solar deity Re.

Sahure (?)   *'He who is close to Re'*

This describes a body traversing across the heavens with the Sun. It is a description of Mars appearing in front of or close to the Sun god Re. We know this was a diminished red Sun which granted visibility to many astral bodies and therefore Shepseskare/Mars was observed during the day close to Re.

The Moon today can occasionally be seen during the day, and sometimes it manoeuvres close to the Sun which periodically causes a solar eclipse. Approximately 4,000 years ago, at the height of chaos, the Moon appeared to track close to the Sun for many years. The Moon was clearly visible due to the diminished Sun and this gave the Moon one of its guises, that of the lunar deity Thoth. This god was given a secondary title worthy of his location in the heavens close to the Sun. The name *'he who is close to Re'* was therefore entirely appropriate.

Pepi I Throne name Mery-re   *'Beloved of Re'*

This name is similar to Sahure. Mars was in such close proximity to the Sun that it gave the impression it was being looked after by Re. The pharaohs were all *sa-re,* offspring of the Sun, and with the cartouche they were also rulers of 'everything encircled by the Sun'. In this astral location, astral bodies jumped aboard Re's solar bark of millions of years many times.

Amenemhet I (Amen-em-het)   *'Amun is at the head'*

Who was Amun and what does this name mean? Amun's sacred colour was blue which could have referred to a red Mars in chaos with blue at the northern tip, or a blue haze on one side of Mars. Perhaps Amun was at the head of this planetary king. Either way, the key to understanding this enigmatic title can be found amidst cosmic chaos and not at ground level.

Anather Birth name; Heka Khaswt Anather   *'Ruler of the desert lands'*

This may have referred to Mars as it appeared above the deserts. It may have been situated to the east or west of Egypt because Egypt is a vast desert dissected only by the Nile.

Tao I-II Throne name; Sa-nakht-en-re   *'Perpetuated like Re'*

Our perpetual red Sun is forever rising and setting, chaos permitting. This name may have referred to Mars as it emulated our nearest star by going though a similar cycle of rising and setting. These titles do not make sense when applied to mortal kings because humans could never have taken on this trait.

There were no titles such as 'perpetuated like the Moon' even though the Moon has a more frequent and regular cycle than the Sun. Its perpetual cycle had yet to begin as the Moon had yet to settle down into orbit around the Earth.

Apepi I and II. Throne name Au-ser-re   *'Great and powerful like Re'*

Khyan   Throne name Se-user-en-re   *'Powerful like Re'*

These were throne names given to the Hyksos.

The Hyksos are believed to be foreign rulers who conquered and reigned over Egypt for about 100 years. They belong to a tumultuous period of ancient Egypt which is devoid of historical records and Egyptologists have labelled it 'The Second Intermediate Period'. The currently accepted translation of the name Hyksos is 'foreign kings' although the original translation was 'shepherd kings'.

This relatively short epoch had nothing to do with events on Earth. As with everything in ancient history as recorded via sacred hieroglyphs, it was a time-ordered recording of chaotic events above.

Although the Hyksos were foreign rulers, they were not mortal invaders from foreign lands. The Hyksos were large Moon-sized bodies with swarms of smaller rocky bodies trailing behind them. They ruled the skies of Earth during an intense period of cosmic chaos – the dark age of approximately 1100 BC. The Hyksos were 'foreign' kings because they were unfamiliar to the Egyptians. The main perpetrators of chaos, Mars and Venus, were either not seen or were too far away at this time to be considered 'gods of Earth'.

The original translation of the name Hyksos as 'shepherd kings' is the likeliest translation. It pointed to large moon-sized bodies with smaller debris trailing behind them which deemed these monarchs as true astral 'shepherd kings'. They were literally astral bodies tending their flocks of space debris. Egyptologists have proposed the erroneous translation 'foreign rulers' because they are unfamiliar with cosmic chaos. They cannot envisage shepherds as conquerors and rulers of the great Egyptians. However, they were not earthly shepherds as they originated in the heavens. Archaeologists will never find physical evidence of the Hyksos on Earth. They were connected with cosmic chaos and events above _ their names were written with sacred hieroglyphs and enclosed in the magical cartouche.

An optical illusion caused the 'shepherd kings' to appear larger than the Sun. They dominated the sky and were viewed as kingly bodies with titles such as *'powerful like the Sun'* and *'great and powerful like Re'*. Regardless of whoever ruled the heavens, the gods had to be appeased. Whether good or evil, they had to be placated as they held the power of life or death in their hands. The shepherd kings came close to Earth and they took on the appearance of red orbs, similar to the ancient red Sun.

All astral bodies were 'shepherd kings' and the main perpetrators were Mars, Venus, Mercury and the Moon. They were shepherds to gigantic flocks of asteroids, comets, dust and gasses and they represented nobles, viziers, right hand men, concubines and rank and file personnel. The symbols of royalty, the shepherd's crook and flail, were held by the kings. The flail was used by shepherds to remove small flies from the sheep and the heavenly flail removed small fly-like debris.

Amose I (Ah-mose) *'The Moon is born'*

Could this have been a reference to the Moon as it went through its predictable cycles? Perhaps it was a reference to a phase of the Moon such as 'new Moon' or 'full Moon'. If the Moon goes through the same cycle several times a year, why was this particular moment singled out to give a mortal king an enigmatic name?

This name was a declaration and should be taken literally. It was bestowed at a time when the Moon was 'born' or gravitationally tied to the Earth for the first time. Amose was one of the many names given to the Moon as it was slowly captured in orbit around Earth for the first time.

Our Moon was recently born from Jupiter. The Moon and Venus, plus incalculable amounts of space debris, spent two millennia being randomly tossed about the cosmos. The Moon began life as an erratic and unpredictable body which eventually settled down and fell into the monthly cycle we recognize today. This preliminary capture began with Venus and Mars as they crossed the orbit of Earth to begin life Sun-side (orbiting between the Earth and the Sun). This caused the dark age of approximately 1100 BC which was a period of true chaos in the heavens.

Evil ruled the skies and 'divine order' was in complete disarray because there were no recognisable god-kings. The god Horus, under whose banner Mars would reign, was nowhere to be seen as weak and temporary foreign kings took to the skies. These were the Hyksos or shepherd kings who ruled Egypt for approximately 100 - 200 years.

Eventually divine order' was restored. This occurred with the capture of our Moon, which appeared at least 400 times larger than today. Its hazy presence dominated the heavens and, because of its size, it was regarded as pharaoh and 'ruler of everything encircled by the Sun'. The Moon in the guise of Amose was gravitationally locked or 'born' to Earth. Amose was a king sent down from heaven by the gods to vanquish the enemy from the skies and unite heaven and Earth.

Amose began the task of clearing the skies of foreign invaders – this was the Moon clearing the skies by cataclysmically vacuuming up masses of space debris including the Hyksos. This evil debris had threatened to bring the whole world into chaos. The bravery shown by Amose is recorded on temple walls with sacred hieroglyphs and shows the iconic image of the pharaoh in the act of smiting the enemy, a god-king with upraised arm.

Divine order was slowly restored and a strong and rightful astral god-king once again took control of Egypt. The expulsion of the Hyksos took many years and the Moon was therefore named many times over and Tuthmosis was the next name. Prior to this preliminary capture, the Moon was observed numerous times and given many names. When it was at a distance and roughly the same size as it appears today, it was called the lunar god Thoth – a vizier as well as the god of writing, magic and scribe to the gods.

The Moon may also have had close encounters with Earth prior to being captured. It moved close enough to Earth and appeared large enough to be deemed a 'god-king' on many occasions as location and attributes dictated how it was perceived. If it battled the debris as the largest body in the sky, it was a warrior pharaoh. If it appeared small as it moved through the cosmos, it was the god Thoth. The actions of the Moon were entirely consistent with it being slowly captured by Earth.

The timing of Amose provided a crucial synchronical point, a time reference when the Moon was tied to Earth for the first time. Although the Moon took hundreds of years to settle down into orbit around the Earth, it must have locked into the pull of the Earth at some point. I believe this happened during the dark age of approximately 1100 BC which coincided with the appearance of the god-king Amose.

Tuthmosis I *'born of the god Thoth'*

This was a warrior pharaoh from the New Kingdom commonly known as the 'Napoleon of ancient times'. How are we to understand this name? Thoth was the ibis-headed lunar deity and therefore a mortal king would have believed he was related to the Moon. Thoth's association with the Moon may have been tenuous or perhaps Thoth was a mythical character. If so, the pharaoh Tuthmosis would have been born of a mythical god. Egyptologists tend to believe that such names belong to a bizarre world which we don't understand but it is difficult to make sense of this name in a human sense. We will therefore use cosmic chaos as we take a closer look at this enigmatic title.

On many occasions the Moon appeared the same size as it does today and was regarded as the god Thoth. He was the patron of knowledge, secrets, writing, magic and 'Scribe of the Company of the Gods'. His epithets were consistent with the Moon magically appearing and disappearing as it was tossed about by larger bodies. As the Moon fell under the gravitational spell of Earth for the first time, it took on an erratic, elliptical obit around the Earth. The Moon appeared large when it was close to Earth and diminished in size as it moved away. When it appeared larger than the

Sun and other main planets, it was regarded as 'god on Earth' (Horus). As size was important to ancient Egyptians, the Moon was recognised as the god Thoth and was aptly named Tuthmosis – a pharaoh 'born of the god Thoth'.

On many occasions the Moon was observed in the dutiful role of upholding 'divine order' by battling up incalculable amounts of 'enemy' space debris. This was a distinctly male trait and evidence of these incredible battles can be found on its surface. Planetary scientists believe this happened billions of years ago but I propose it happened only a few thousand years ago. The Moon's greatest battles were fought under the guise of Tuthmosis III exactly as history reveals. Thoth also dealt with the vile enemy when it acted as judge and jury to space debris. Thoth weighed the hearts of the deceased, and if they had led a true and just life they were granted a life of eternity in the kingdom of heaven (kingdom of Osiris).

Amose (the Moon is born) and Kamose (the soul is born) appeared before Tuthmosis as facets of the Moon. Therefore, as predecessors of Tuthmosis, they should have been 'born of the god Thoth' but they were not. This is easily explained – they existed within a chaotic sky awash with cosmic chaos. As the Moon was slowly captured, it was barely seen through a thick haze of space debris, dust and gasses. This happened after the global dark age in the Second Intermediate Period of approximately 1100BC. Due to the close passage of Venus, the Moon was deposited around the Earth. When Kamose and Amose, as aspects of the Moon, began to vacuum up and expel the 'shepherd kings' (Hyksos), the heavens cleared to reveal that the Moon was in fact an incarnation of the god Thoth.

THE NEW KINGDOM

Throne names

There are numerous throne names that refer to Re and the soul. Typical examples include:

'Beautiful is the soul of Re'
'Powerful is the soul of Re.'
'Strong is the soul of Re'
'The soul of Re comes into being'
'Noble is the soul of Re'
'The soul of Re endureth'
'The soul of Re is powerful'
'Holy is the soul of Re'
'Great is the soul of Re'
'Vigorous is the soul of Re'
'Appearing like the souls of Re'

Some of these names are repeated many times for many monarchs. How do we explain them? We know that Re was the Sun, but what is meant by the term Re's soul? Was this a spiritual term or did it have a physical meaning? These titles had deeply significant meanings and were clearly understood because they were repeated many times. Yet why were they bestowed upon the pinnacle of Egyptian religion _ the pharaohs?

Egyptologists do not understand the meaning of these names and often refer to them as 'untranslatable'. However, it seems odd that names of paramount importance which belonged to the Egyptian royal family were not understood. The root of the problem lies with the word 'soul' or 'ka'.

The Ka

*'Almost untranslatable term used by the Egyptians to describe the creative life-force of each individual, whether human or divine. The Ka, represented by the hieroglyph consisting of a pair of arms, was considered to be the essential ingredient that differentiated a living person from a dead one, and is therefore sometimes translated as sustenance. It came into existence when an individual was born, subsequently serving as his or her **double** and sometimes being depicted in funerary art as a slightly smaller figure standing beside the living being. Sometimes the creator god Khnum was shown modelling the ka on a potter's wheel at the same time as he was forming the bodies of humanity.'*

(Shaw & Nicholson, 2002, p 146 - my bold emphasis)

It is possible to understand the true meaning of these throne names if we use the GKS. The Egyptians believed that when a person was born there were actually two people; a physical person and a 'double' or 'ka'. The 'ka' was an exact replica of the physical body much like a twin. The Egyptians also believed that when a person died they joined with their 'ka' to live a life of eternity among the eternal stars. I consider this belief to be very important. I believe that, as a result of cosmic chaos, the Egyptian 'ka' or double was believed to be a very real, physical astral body. It was a celestial body that joined with the physical body at death. The planets, as well as the innumerable asteroids and comets littering the heavens, were believed to be the 'doubles' (ka) of all people. Everybody had a physical double above and this led to a physical association with the heavens – in effect two Egypts.

Egyptologists have glossed over this belief because they are unaware of cosmic chaos. They have erroneously assumed that when Egyptians speak of the ka, they are referring to some kind of spirit and therefore translate the word 'ka' as 'soul.' This is completely wrong and very misleading. In fact the Egyptians regarded the ka as a real astral being and it should therefore be viewed as a physical 'double'.

We will now examine the throne names and apply their true meanings. The name 'beautiful is the soul of Re' or 'Neferkare' can be broken down into 'Nefer' meaning 'beautiful', 'ka' meaning 'soul' and 're' meaning 'the Sun'. If we substitute the very confusing word 'soul' (which is suggestive of a spiritual being) with the word 'double' which is the true meaning of the word 'ka' the name now reads 'powerful is the *double* of Re'. We must consider this in the context of the GKS, not forgetting that throne names were given mainly to Mars Venus, Mercury and the Moon each and every time they visited Earth. The true meaning now becomes perfectly clear and refers to a planetary body when it appeared as the double of the Sun. In other words, the red disk of the planet appeared *like* the red disk of the Sun!

The throne name 'Powerful is the double/soul of Re' simply translates as 'Mars is powerful like the Sun'. Remember that the Sun in ancient times appeared as a red disk and the main colour of the astral monarchs was also red. This distinctive feature, as well as the location, led to the kings being given the ubiquitous title 'son of Re' (son of the Sun). The red-disk 'double' characteristic was also recorded in many of the throne names.

What of 'Strong is the soul/double of Re'? As the 'soul/double of Re' came into being, pharonic Mars appeared in the image of the Sun. Two red orbs dominated the heavens which was a common sight in ancient times. There were many doubles of Re. However, unlike the immortal and perennial father of all, the red disks (the planet doubles) were mere mortals who lived and died as they moved back and forth to Earth.

If we consider 'Noble is the soul/double of Re', it implies that Mars was noble like his father the Sun. The name 'The soul/double of Re endureth' refers to Mars as he emulated the Sun by enduring the perennial fight against the forces of evil. Pharonic Mars battled to maintain 'divine order' (ma'at) and he thereby endured.

'The soul/double of Re is powerful' implies that Mars was powerful like the Sun. You will note I am occasionally using the word 'like' in place of double. This is because, although the meaning is the same, the sense of the word is clearer. *'Holy is the soul/double of Re'* translates as 'Mars is holy like the Sun'. The royal family was, by their very location, 'godlike' and they were divine intermediaries between heaven and Earth.

'Great is the soul/double of Re'. Mars was an awe inspiring sight and was great like the Sun. The astral monarchy were also great like Re.

'Vigorous is the soul/double of Re' means Mars was very active, a living breathing Mars, a vigorous Mars just like the very active and vigorous red Sun.

Although the above are self explanatory, there are a few throne names that refer to the double/soul that are not so clear. However, I will offer an interpretation.

'Appearing like the souls (doubles) of Re'

'Eternal like the souls (doubles) of Re'

'Eternal are the souls (doubles) of Re'

You will note these three names refer to the 'double' in the plural. I believe these names are collective references. The planets appeared as red orbs like the Sun many times and these names reflect this. They refer to Mars in its many god-king guises as it appeared eternally in the image of the Sun. As Mars moved back and forth to Earth it was given many different pharonic names but its most common appearance was that of a red disk like the Sun.

Another name was 'golden are the souls/doubles of Re' which was very rare. It may have been used only three times in Clayton's book although there were over 300 pharaohs. It may be a collective reference but this is not certain. It would be useful to re-evaluate all names and titles with the GKS in mind. This may shed light on the name because so far it has been translated without any reference to cosmic chaos and a red Sun. It is important for Egyptologists to consider the GKS if the true meaning is to be unveiled.

Queen Hatshepsut *'foremost of the noble women'*
Throne name 'Maat-ka-re' *'truth is the soul of Re'*.

I will first discuss Hatshepsut's throne name and then the birth name. Overwhelming support for my interpretation of the word ka/soul/double as referring to the monarchy taking on a similar appearance to the Sun comes to us via Hatshepsut's throne name. This reads '*Maatkarre* ma'at-ka-re' which conventionally translates as 'truth is the soul of Re' Ma'at is truth or divine order, ka is the soul/double and re is the Sun. This could be translated as 'truth is the double of Re' or 'truth is Hatshepsut like Re'. As most queens of ancient times were guises of Venus, it could be translated as 'truth is Venus like Re'. A breakdown of the name would be as follows: True/order/balance (ma'at) is the soul/double/Venus (ka) of Re. However, there is an alternative translation that completely supports my interpretation of this name, and indeed all names where the word 'soul' is mentioned as referring to entities in the image of the Sun.

In 2005, the Discovery Channel aired a documentary called 'Queens of the Nile'. Consisting of two parts, the first part was entitled 'Hatshepsut the Great' and discussed the life of a queen who would become king. It began with a few lines on Egypt and then superimposed Hatshepsut's cartouche over a picture of her temple at Deir El-Bahri. It then stated: 'Her (Hatshepsut) throne name was 'ma'atkare' meaning 'just and full of vitality like the Sun-god'.

There was no mention of Clayton's translation 'truth is the soul of Re' and no mention of an imaginary sprit associated with the solar deity Re. This clearly supports my interpretation of the word 'soul' as meaning 'double'. In this instance it refers to Queen Hatshepsut in the image of the Sun or 'just and full of vitality *like* the Sun'. Although it supports my interpretation, whoever used this alternative translation was unaware of my outrageous proposal that all names given to the monarchy were first and foremost names given to planetary bodies each time they visited Earth. They were also unaware that Hatshepsut's throne name 'maatkare' was a name given to Venus when she doubled up as a divine second Sun, one of the many daughters of the perennial Sun god Re. Nevertheless, the programme did state that Hatshepsut (whoever they believed her to be) had a name that described her as 'like the Sun'.

Although this may seem like overwhelming support for my interpretation of the word soul, there is a problem; The transcript of this programme has been altered and the line referring to Hatshepsut's throne name and the image of her cartouche has been cut out. The programme now begins with a few lines on Egypt but omits Hatshepsut's cartouche and the words 'Her throne name etc'. It took me several months to realise what had happened, but luckily I have a copy of the original programme. I now have two versions of 'Queen of the Nile' Part 1 and I can prove it has been altered since its first release. But why was it changed?

I believe that Egyptologists complained that this was not the currently accepted translation and that 'maatkare' should read 'truth is the soul of Re' as per Clayton's translation. To announce this fact at the start of the programme makes no sense as it does not refer to Hatshepsut per-se. It is merely a reference to her throne names (referring to the solar god Re) and this would not have had much bearing on the content of the documentary. I have contacted the producers of the programme to ask why the documentary has been altered but to date I have not received a reply.

We will use the alternative name 'just and full of vitality like the Sun' and place it alongside the GKS. We are all children of the Sun, but it is illogical to assume our ancient forebears named a mortal queen 'just and full of vitality like the Sun.' It was 'divine order' or the myriad of gods involved in cosmic chaos that dictated all. If a name was recorded with sacred hieroglyphs then it had real meaning and the throne name 'maatkare' was no exception. It is actually a clear description of Venus, the beautiful and passive (ma'at) queen which took on a similar appearance and behavioural trait to our red Sun. It is a perfect description of a planetary body in the image of the Sun. This name is not dissimilar to the name 'Khafre' or 'appearing like Re'.

It is possible to look directly at a diminished red Sun and in ancient times it was possible to observe a very active Sun. It was a Sun full of vitality; a just and righteous red-Sun; a 'ma'at' Sun. The newly formed Venus as Hatshepsut (foremost of the noble women) took on a similar trait. Its scolding hot molten surface was a hive of activity, a cauldron of boiling lava. This, from the perspective of Earth, gave Venus a living breathing red-disc characteristic similar to the Sun – a just and righteous trait.

Other epithets attributed to Hatshepsut included 'like a god she brings peace and prosperity to Egypt' and 'her beauty is unsurpassed.' These are both consistent with Venus at this time. Although its surface activity played an important part, the main association with Re was the colour red. It was a colour synonymous with the astral monarchs. The colour and location led to the belief that all royalty were 'offspring of Re' and Venus as Hatshepsut was no exception. Venus appeared as a red-disk similar to the red Sun. Two divine red orbs dominated the vault of heaven.

Corroboratory evidence for Venus /Hatshepsut appearing red can be found in the art surrounding Hatshepsut. Hatshepsut's temple at Deir el-Bahri is considered the finest of all Egyptian temples. Hatshepsut left a legacy of architectural and statutory elegance. Her temple, in the area of Thebes at modern Deir el-Bahri, stood as a beautiful monument to her reign. Called by the people *Djeser-djeseru,* 'sacred of sacreds', Hatshepsut's terraced and rock-cut temple is one of the most impressive monuments on the west bank. Of interest are the 24 monumental statues of the female king fronting the temple on the third terrace and, more specifically, the colour that once adorned Hatshepsut's face. Despite the ravages of time it is clear the face of the female queen was once painted bright red. Why carve a statue in ones likeness and then paint the face a bright red rather than the natural tan colour we associate with the population of Egypt today?

Hatshepsut's statues at Deir el-Bahri are painted a vivid red because it is a symbolic representation of the red queen Venus. Colour was of paramount importance to the Egyptians and the faces on Hatshepsut's statues were painted red because Venus appeared as a bright red orb. It is a direct representation of the Hatshepsut/Venus appearance at that time. Whenever the face of a monarch's statue is painted red it is because they appeared red. Ramesses the great was another example and many of his statues show signs of a vivid red colouring which represented red Mars as it was systematically torn apart.

At the heart of the temple of Karnak are two of the largest obelisks ever built in dedication to Hatshepsut and they are carved from red granite. There is also a red chapel dedicated to Hatshepsut (chapel rouge). Venus, like other planets, appeared in a variety of colours and guises due to its location, light refraction and other variables and these differences were represented in art. For example, if Venus appeared black for a good length of time, a black statute would be commissioned. If golden, then the artwork would also reflect this colour.

The name Hatshepsut translates as 'Foremost of the noble women'. I believe this refers to Venus as she declared herself king of Egypt. This was a time in Egyptian history when a woman took to the throne as a female pharaoh due to the size of the planet. Venus moved to the forefront, very close to Earth, close enough to loom larger than any other body in the heavens. As a result she was viewed as a king rather than a queen of Egypt. Her statue depicted her in the kingly regalia of a false beard and crown of Egypt. Her name reflected this honorary position as she was *'foremost of the noble women'*. We now know why she declared herself king – size and location dictated it.

Hatshepsut also incorporated the epithet 'She who embraces Amun' into her name. Amun was the 'king of the gods' and yet scholars cannot physically identify him with anything in the natural world. They have therefore demoted Amun to that of another solar deity. In subsequent books I will conclusively identify Amun, but for now Amun was a god of the heavens. Hatshepsut was not a mortal Queen who embraced an 'invisible' deity; this was one of the many names given to Venus as she appeared as a beautiful incandescent orb – 'foremost of the noble women' and 'just and full of vitality like Re'. Hatshepsut/Venus was also a 'queen' goddess who 'embraced' the sky god Amun.

It is an interesting point that Hatshepsut's mummy has never been found. The heavens dictated events on Earth and it must have been difficult to find an actual Earthly queen to represent Venus in what was a male dominated world. The fact she was Venus also explains her enigmatic and magical disappearance from the annals of history.

Amenhotep I-III (Amen-hotep) *'Amun is pleased'*

Amenhotep (all kings called Amenhotep)

This is Mars amidst the god of the heavens. Amun was the 'king of gods' and appeared pleased and so we have the name 'Amun is pleased'.

What of the name *'The dazzling sun-disk of all lands'*?

Perhaps it was a description of the Sun as it rose in the morning or a devotional title given to the Sun on a glorious sunny day? Both of these suggestions are incorrect. It is actually one of the names given to the pharaoh Amenhotep III (18th Dynasty). If we refer to the GKS this makes perfect sense. There is no doubt it was celestial in connotation and was clearly a descriptive name given to a planetary body dominating the heavens and appearing close to the image of the Sun. How could anybody on Earth be bestowed with such a name? Remember _ names in ancient Egypt were very important and had real meaning. There is only one possible way that someone could have the title 'the dazzling sun-disk of all lands' and that is if they were first and foremost names given to planetary bodies dominating the heavens. The mortal 'doubles', believed to be 'at one' with the above were mere puppets to this far higher order. Astral bodies dictated names and titles according to their attributes and location, not mortal kings. This 'dazzling' title was given to Mars as it slowly gave birth to its scolding hot iron core – a core that would become the planet Mercury.

The tidal forces exerted upon Mars by Earth and Venus were so tremendous that its working dynamo, its central spinning core, was slowly sucked out to become the planet Mercury. The Egyptians called this body the Aten which was a temporary name. As it slowly broke through the Martian crust (Valles Marineris), the core of Mars grew hotter than the surface of the Sun, as would Earth's core. This, coupled with the fact that the genesis of Mercury occurred in close proximity to Earth, caused the planet Mars to shine far greater than the red Sun. In fact, having been sucked out from Mars, Mercury (the Aten) blotted out the diminished Sun. Interestingly, as the Aten (Mercury) slowly exited Mars, it illuminated Mars so much that it became just as the Egyptians described it – *'The dazzling sun-disk of all lands'*.

It is unnecessary to try to twist or contort this descriptive title to make it fit into a bizarre world we do not understand – it is an appropriate descriptive name that *must* be taken at face value exactly as the Egyptians intended.

Amenhotep IV   Akhenaten

1st name **Amenhotep** *'Amun is pleased'* changed name to **Akhenaten** (Akh-en-aten) *'Servant of the Aten'*

What of Amenhotep IV and his name change to Akhenaten? Amenhotep IV ('Amun is pleased') was one and the same as Amenhotep III. All kings named Amenhotep were Mars. Starting with Amenhotep I through to Amenhotep IV, they were all names given to Mars as it slowly gave birth to Mercury. That is why we have the gradual and scant references to the 'Aten' as they built up to Amenhotep III (Mars) which was bestowed with the very befitting title 'the dazzling sun-disk of all lands'. The name-change from Amenhotep IV to Akhenaten (servant of the Aten) was a direct result of the birth of Mercury. The scalding hot Aten/Mercury separated from its parent body (Mars) to become a blinding, glaring Sun. It was a body with such powerful initial energy that it blotted out the solar deity Re and all other 'sky' gods. Sky gods such as Amun, Osiris, Isis and Hathor were completely lost in the glare streaming from Mercury. The Aten/Mercury became the one and only supreme deity, a 'dazzling sun-disk' in its own right.

Although the traditional 'sky gods' were blotted out, the divine royal couple and their entourage were not. Mars and Venus were clearly seen in this totally new order in the heavens. The blinding light emanating from the Aten/Mercury was seen to stream out and physically touch Mars and Venus. This was perceived as a glorious new deity – the Aten granted them life. This was particularly true of Mars which, having just given birth to Mercury, was 'touched' many times by Mercury's 'sunrays'. This incredible event played out in the many images which depicted Akhenaten as Mars being blessed by the life-giving rays of the Aten. As a direct representation of what was seen (a blinding light touching Mars), the rays of the Aten appeared to have hands at the end of them. This led to a situation whereby Akhenaten/Mars was seen as a 'servant of the Aten'. As the inscriptions reveal, the earthly Egyptians could only worship the Aten through Akhenaten/Mars. This trait was dutifully recorded in the name Akhenaten which translates as *'servant of the Aten'*.

This new order in the heavens meant that Amun and the rest of Egypt's pantheon of sky gods could no longer be worshiped or honoured because they were no longer seen due to the light from the Aten. The devotional name Amun-hotep which was given to Mars was changed to Akhenaten out of deference to the Aten. In the hierarchy of divine order it was the Aten that reigned supreme. Mars & Venus as Akhenaten and Nefertiti were next in line and were followed by infinite astral bodies which all bowed to the Aten. When Mercury cooled down, there was a return to the old order which was reflected in the subsequent name given to Mars – Tutankhamun (Tutankh-Amun).

Tutankhamun – First name **Tutankhaten** (tut-ankh-aten) 'living image of the Aten'. The name was changed to **Tutankhamun** (tut-ankh-Amun) 'living image of Amun'.

These are clear, descriptive names which do not make sense in our world. If the Aten was the Sun, how was it possible for somebody to believe they were the 'living image' of such a blinding body? The god Amun is also a mythological god which was invented in an attempt to explain the natural world. Yet how can one be the 'living image' of a god whose 'true form was unknown'?

Tutankhaten was Mars. It was initially a servant (Akhenaten) to the newly formed and dominant Mercury/Aten. Mars then took on an image similar to

Mercury, hence the name 'living image of the Aten'. What image was this? I believe Mercury began life as a glaring golden orb which rapidly cooled down to become a predominantly glowing red orb. The temples and tombs at Amarna clearly depict the Aten as a large *red* disk with emanating red 'sunrays' which steam downwards. Images such as this should be taken at face value. If the Aten was shown as a red disk it implied Mercury appeared as a red disk. Colour was of paramount importance and the Egyptians would never risk the wrath of the gods by painting them the wrong colour.

It is not important to know the exact 'living image' of Mars. It is more important to establish how the names given to the god-kings of ancient times are clearly celestial in nature. They describe the celestial bodies that once habited our skies some 4,000 years ago. This is a very simple and plausible explanation where none had previously existed. It was basically two celestial bodies which took on a similar appearance. Mars having being subservient to the Aten (Akhenaten) took on the appearance of Mercury and became the 'living image of the Aten' and was renamed accordingly.

The name change from Tutankh-aten to Tutankh-amun refers to the cooling of Mercury. This planet began life as a scalding hot body that released so much energy that it blotted out all of Egypt's traditional gods including the solar deity Re. A new religion was born as Mercury became the pre-eminent deity and was christened the Aten. However, after approximately 17 years, the Aten rapidly cooled down. It slowly moved away from Earth to become an incandescent reddish orb. As a result, its glaring light that had once flooded the Earth became greatly diminished; the pre-Mercurian (pre-Aten) world gradually returned.

The traditional Egyptian 'sky' gods that had initially been blotted out slowly come back into view. The solar deity Re once again took to the heavens and the old order slowly resumed. 'Sky gods' such as Amun, Hathor and Isis once again began to dominate. Even the belief in an afterlife was restored as the stars and the night sky (heaven), which had previously been blotted out, also come back into view. The new religion faded with Mercury's light and the old religion was restored. Mercury cooled down so much that it joined the royal bloodline to become a divine god-king.

One of the first names given to Mercury as a god-king was Seti. Due to a combination of light refraction and the fact that Mars appeared during the day (Sun-side), Mars took on a distinct bluish hue. As blue is the sacred colour of the god Amun, and as Mars appeared blue, the Egyptians renamed Mars 'Tutankh-amun' which meant 'living image of Amun'. The renaming of Mars was assisted by a return to the old order and the need to hastily honour the previous 'king of the gods', Amun. Whether Mars appeared in a variety of other colours is not important.

We will look once again at Tutankhamun and the meaning of his name. On the side of Tutankhamun's painted wooden chest in his tomb in the Valley of the Kings is a battle scene depicting the king in his chariot leading his troops and attacking a group of Nubians. The text complements the theme:

'Perfect god, likeness of Re, who appears over foreign lands like the rising of Re, who destroys this land of vile Kush, who shoots his arrows against the enemy.'

This is perfectly clear. The term 'perfect god' alludes to the body of Mars and the term 'likeness of Re' clearly describes Mars as a red orb like the red Sun. What does 'who appears over foreign lands like the rising of Re' mean? This is clearly describing Mars as the red orbed Tutankhamun rising like the red Sun over foreign lands. The phrase 'shoots his arrows' is probably electrical discharges between Mars and the evil space debris. In other words, it refers to lighting bolts blasting space debris to pieces. I would strongly argue that my definition of this text is the only definition that makes sense.

During the Amarna period, history reveals that the pharaoh Akhenaten was known by the Egyptians as the 'heretic' king. By referring to the GKS, this can be explained. Throughout the whole process of Mercury's birth the Egyptians were understandably very confused. They witnessed a god-king giving birth to a 'second sun' that later turned out to be another god-king.

Mars as Amenhotep gave birth to Mercury/Aten. The glaring light given off by Mercury dictated a totally new order in the heavens. As its light rays streamed down and touched it, Mars was perceived to worship the Aten. The Aten became the one and only supreme god. Mars was accordingly renamed as Akhenaten, 'servant of the Aten'. The Aten/Mercury cooled down, its light faded, the old order returned, the old gods returned.

UNDERSTANDING THE WILL OF THE GODS

It seems the Egyptians made a terrible mistake in interpreting the will of the gods. The solar deity Re and the pantheon of other gods did not leave _ they were there all along. How could the Egyptians be so foolish as to believe their traditional gods would ever desert them? Who was to blame for this sacrilegious and rebellious act? It was Mars in the guise of Akhenaten! Akhenaten/Mars dismissed all other gods in favour of the Aten/Mercury. Akhenaten/Mars bowed down and solely worshipped the Aten. And it was Mars/Akhenaten who attempted to change Egypt's religion from the well established and accepted polytheistic religion to a monotheistic one in his worship of the Aten. It was Mars as Akhenaten who inaugurated a religious revolution.

This act of heresy was swiftly dealt with – the ancient Egyptians dished out justice with a chisel _ wherever possible they hacked out the name of Akhenaten and the Aten. Every image and hieroglyph that referred to the Aten was destroyed with ruthless efficiency. Every reference to Akhenaten, Nefertiti and even their children was hacked out of existence. The entire royal family associated with this terrible mistake was torn from the pages of history. If Akhenaten was ever referred to again it was as a heretic.

Nefertiti '*The Beautiful one has come*' (wife of the 'heretic' pharaoh Akhenaten) (Nefer-titi)

We have established that names were of paramount importance to the Egyptians. Every child had to be named at birth otherwise they would not fully come into existence. Yet how can the name 'The beautiful one has come' be given to new born baby and future queen? It may be possible to understand the birth name 'the beautiful one is born' but 'the beautiful one has come' is difficult to understand. It is a statement name and is clearly indicative of a beautiful and mature queen arriving somewhere. It does not, as some believe, describe the birth of a new born queen because the word 'born' is not mentioned.

Egyptologists are baffled by Nefertiti's parentage because nothing is known of her background. Just as her name suggests, Nefertiti suddenly entered the scene from nowhere. This caused much speculation and it is not known if she was of royal blood or not. Some have suggested Nefertiti was probably a daughter of the army officer and pharaoh Ay (Aye). Others have speculated that Nefertiti was a foreign princess who was sent as a tribute to Egypt. She may have been the daughter of Queen Tiye, or a cousin of the heretic pharaoh Akhenaten. Many other explanations have also been suggested but they are highly speculative. Nefertiti's genealogy remains shrouded in mystery.

Scholars are also baffled as to how such a powerful and influential queen suddenly disappeared. This queen played a major role in the Amana period and her famous bust has become an icon for ancient Egypt. Yet no record survives to detail her death and to this day her departure remains an enigma. Her body has never been found and both her enigmatic appearance and disappearance has led to much controversy.

Many Egyptologists accept Nefertiti's disappearance as one of the many Egyptian enigmas. After all, the origins and deaths of many monarchs remain shrouded in mystery. Some scholars have suggested that Nefertiti did not vanish but changed her name a number of times culminating with the pharonic name Smenkhkare and a co-regency with Akhenaten. However there is little agreement other than acknowledging that Nefertiti vanished just as mysteriously as she appeared.

Nefertiti/Venus

The truth is, planets in chaos magically appear and disappear, not Earthly kings and queens. Nefertiti was just one of the many names given to Venus. The name 'the beautiful one has come' is merely a reference to Venus which suddenly appeared in the sky. It is a name that totally befits the appearance and behavioural traits of the beautiful and divine Venus.

Nefertiti's sudden appearance may have been due to Venus rising above the horizon after a few years of absence. Or perhaps Venus was initially blotted out by the light given off by the newly born Aten until it suddenly came into view as Mercury rapidly cooled down. It may have been a combination of both. Either way, if the Egyptians gave Venus the name 'the beautiful one has come' it should be interpreted literally.

Nefertiti is clearly Venus arriving in the skies above Egypt – the beautiful Venus occupied the same expanse as Mars in the guise of Akhenaten. Venus once again took up her dutiful role as the kings 'great wife'. The perennial and predominantly passive queen of all times appeared as a beautiful and supportive wife.

Nefertiti's sudden disappearance can also be explained. We cannot rule out the possibility that Venus dropped below the horizon which may be why Nefertiti vanished from history. However, it is more likely that it was a simple name change. Venus changed her location and attributes and warranted a name change. Although Venus was a great distance away, it was twice the size of Mars and therefore appeared to be the same size and commanded equal status.

Akhenaten/Mars and Nefertiti/Venus ruled the heavens as part of a co-regency and Venus was subsequently given the pharonic name Smenkhare. Venus and Mars were renamed many times over. It was sometimes a smooth transition but many times it was confusing and unclear. This is understandable because cosmic chaos is totally unpredictable.

The GKS has explained Nefertit's sudden emergence and disappearance, which by extension neatly explains the confusion surrounding her genealogy. Archaeologists will never find the answers in the sands of Egypt because Nefertiti was Venus suddenly arriving in the heavens above.

Seti *'He of the god Seth' (sometimes spelt Set) (Repetition of Births)*

Seth was the god of evil, darkness, and chaotic forces. He was fundamentally a destroyer and evil personified. Depicted with the body of a man and a head of a strange unidentified animal, Seth was detested throughout Egypt. He was also highly venerated. This distinctly odd trait was epitomised by some of the titles given to certain kings and the above is an example. Seti translates as 'he of the god Seth' which was a name adopted by a pharaoh in honour of Seth, the god of chaos. Not only did Seti honour Seth in this way, he also considered himself as the high priest of Seth. But Seti was not alone in venerating Seth. There were many other examples of pharaohs associating themselves with 'evil'.

An Old Kingdom king honoured the god Seth by changing his name from the Horus name Sekhemib to a Seth name Seth-Peribsen. Another example was the title given to the pharaoh Peribsen's consort which was 'she who raises Seth'. Sometimes the king was called Horus-Seth (Greenberg 1993a: 14). A later pharaoh had the name Setnakhte which meant 'victorious is Seth' or 'victorious is evil'.

Some pharaohs used Seth's violent nature to help with their war efforts. The famous pharaoh Ramesses the Great, in his campaign against the Hittites, split his army into four divisions and named them after the gods Amun, Re, Ptah and *Seth*. Ramesses also took on the attributes of Seth; this is clearly seen on the walls of the Ramesseum. The account of the Battle of Qadesh sees *'His majesty (Ramesses) was like Seth, great of strength, like Sekhmet (aspect of Hathor) in the moment of her rage'.* In a scene at Karnak, the god Seth can be seen teaching Tuthmosis III how to use the bow. The Hyksos also worshiped Seth.

It was the duty of the pharaoh to maintain divine order (*ma'at*). This involved the king as the embodiment of the god Horus, a good and just god battling to keep evil (Seth) at bay. This roll played out many times in the recurring myth dealing with the contending of Horus and Seth. A statue currently residing in the Cairo museum provides a perfect example of a pharaoh acting as an intermediary between good and evil (Horus and Seth). The king

Ramesses III is shown shoulder to shoulder between the gods Horus and Seth. How do we explain the king's close and personal association with such a detested and hated god? How do we explain a world where evil is venerated almost on a par with good?

Egyptologists are at a loss in trying to explain this bizarre practise but they have attempted to provide an explanation. They propose that Seth was a counterbalance to the 'good' side of the Egyptian universe, helping to keep everything in balance. Is it likely that a nation would use evil to convince the population to do good? There is only one conceivable way that Seth (evil) could possibly be venerated and held in high esteem and that is if the heavens were dominated by chaotic forces. Havoc above would reap havoc below. Everything bad was associated with Seth: winds, storms, chaos, darkness, war, conflict and confusion. This badness dominated the skies and caused untold destruction on Earth as the skies were awash with the forces of evil. Mayhem ruled the four corners of the cosmos and was largely attributed to the god-kings. This evil had to be appeased and the evil god Seth had to be venerated. Why?

Seth had to be appeased simply because this evil god dictated whether or nor the Egyptians lived or died. It dictated whether or not the crops would grow and whether livestock would perish. By blackening the skies and turning day into night, Seth also had the ability to prevent the solar deity Re (red-Sun) from rising. By venerating and placating Seth, the Egyptians gave themselves a chance to survive. The appeasement of Seth was vital and there was a very fine line between order and chaos. If Seth was placated, it would ward off its vengeful spirit. If the planetary kings were perceived to take on the attributes of evil Seth, they too had to be recognised and venerated. This was done in several ways such as incorporating Seth's name into the name of the planetary body.

I believe Seti, 'he of the god Seth', was the first pharonic name given to Mercury after it cooled down. Mercury was, initially a glaring sun-disk which rapidly cooled down to become an incandescent reddish orb similar in appearance to the original divine couple, Mars and Venus. It was only during Mercury's debut that this relatively small but powerful orb was in complete chaos. It was like a planetary fireball, a ball of fire meandering across the heavens. It appeared as a ball of scalding hot iron taking on the attributes of a cosmic snake as it trailed enormous amounts of gasses in its wake. This was a direct association with another of Egypt's evil gods – the serpent Apepi. The Egyptians believed this god battled the Sun god Re on a daily basis.

It mattered little what chaos Mercury caused – it was the largest and most prominent orb in the heavens and was perceived to be a divine king, a god-king in a state of Seth. As celestial kings had to be worshiped, the Egyptians took the attributes of this king and recorded them in his name to give 'he of the god Seth' and therefore Seti was born. Divine order may have been upset by the evil within Mercury, but even this evil aspect had to be worshiped.

I believe it is no coincidence Seti was one of the first pharonic names given to Mercury after it cooled down. This follows a normal sequence of events. Mercury, the core of Mars, is sucked out and its initial energy blots out all others gods as it remains suspended in the heavens. Assisted by Venus, Mercury breaks away from the tidal force of Earth and, with Venus, begins its journey to its current location as the first rock from the Sun – a journey that would take at least 700 years and see Mercury, Mars, Venus and the Moon 'dance' with Earth many times. This journey saw Mercury renamed many times.

The explanations given so far may not be entirely accurate in every respect and there are still areas that need further research. However, my proposed ancient world of cosmic chaos, where there was a real threat of impending doom and a fine line between order and chaos and good and evil, is based on historical evidence. Alternatively, scholars point to a bizarre world where people venerated evil? This was a world where human kings divided and ruled by venerating the detested god of evil and where they incorporated their own name with that of the evil god Seth? Which account sounds more plausible?

Repetition of births (repeater-of-births)

Seti also had the additional title *whm mswt* meaning 'repetition-of births' (repeater of births) as did a later high priest of Amun called Herihor. An earlier pharaoh called Amenemhet (12th Dynasty, Mars) had a very similar title *Wehem-mesut* which meant 'he who repeats births'. It is important to note that both titles have the same meaning.

Like many titles and epithets given to the kings, Egyptologists are at a loss to explain the true meaning of this name. Some suggest it implied the beginning of a new line or a new era (Clayton's Chronicle of the Pharaohs, 142). Some have suggested it refers to the monthly rebirth of the Moon but if this was true, all kings would have been given this title. Most Egyptologists favour a renaissance or a rebirth which implied they would make Egypt great again. Are we really expected to believe the Egyptians, with their sacred inscriptions, did not possess the ability to say exactly what they meant? If the Egyptians were alluding to some kind of 'renaissance' as Egyptologists believe, then we would expect to see titles like 'a rebirth of Egypt's greatness' or 'Egypt will arise anew'. We would not expect to see titles which alluded to a 'repetition of births' as this does not imply an inauguration of Egypt's greatness.

All pharaohs had the title '*sa-re*' meaning son of Re and therefore Egyptologists and I agree that this title clearly states that pharaohs were 'offspring of the Sun'. However, I believe that the pharaohs were physically related to the Sun because they were first and foremost guises of planetary bodies inhabiting the same arena as the Sun. Therefore, it is impossible to take the name 'repetition of births' literally.

This title clearly states that the king repeats his birth. This is gleaned from the phrase 'repetition of births' or in the case of Amenemhet, 'he who repeats births'. We can break it down into 'repeater' or 'repetition' which means 'to repeat' followed by 'births' in the plural. There is no mention of the Moon, or a new era, or a renaissance, or an inauguration of Egypt's greatness. There is simply a reference to the king being born many times, a king 'repeating his births'.

It is easy to understand why Egyptologists struggle with this meaning because it makes no sense. The Egyptians lived in a bizarre world of weird animal-headed gods and strange enigmatic beliefs, but a king being reborn many times is difficult to accept. However, if we consider this in the light of the GKS, this title becomes self-explanatory.

Seti, 'he of the god Seth' was the first pharonic name given to Mercury. The god of chaos was venerated within the name Seti because Mercury was in a state of chaos, a planetary body meandering across the heavens wreaking havoc. I believe this chaotic state took Mercury/Seti below the horizon repeatedly, only to reappear many times. This was perceived to be Mercury/Seti as it died and dropped below the horizon to be reborn as it rose again in a cycle of death and rebirth – a king 'repeating his births' or 'he who repeats births'.

The Egyptians believed that when the Sun set in the west each night, it physically died and was reborn anew each morning in the east. The same belief must be applied to the god-king planets. If they dropped below the horizon for a period of time they would temporarily die as the Sun and when they reappeared they were reborn. When the planet Mercury, in the guise of the god-king Seti, repeatedly disappeared and reappeared, this was seen as a 'repetition of births' or the king 'repeating his births'.

It is possible that Mercury/Seti may have taken on an erratic orbit in and around Earth. Seti adopted a similar path across the skies to that of the rising and setting Sun. Seti/Mercury was therefore given the title 'repetition of births'. Herihor (high priest of Amun), who was probably associated with the Moon because of his close connection with the lunar deity Thoth, had the same title. As the Moon was slowly captured in orbit around the Earth, it 'repeated its birth' many times before settling down into the very regular and predictable cycle we recognise today.

Seti/Mercury's 'repetition of births' may refer to Seti/Mercury moving back and forth between heaven and Earth, living and dying to Earth. We will never know for certain because there are so many permutations to cosmic chaos. However, the title 'repetition of births' or 'he who repeats births' refers to a planetary body repeating its births in the heavens. It has nothing to do with human kings, a renaissance or otherwise. The title 'sa-re' (son of Sun) or 'repetition of births' should be taken literally.

Ramesses (Ra-messes) *'Re has fashioned him'*
Throne name User-maat-re Setep-en-re (The justice of Re is powerful, Chosen of Re)

This is a statement and honorary name. I identify all pharaohs called Ramesses, of which there were at least 11, with the planet Mars for a number of reasons. History shows that Ramesses the Great (Ramesses II) had at least 150 children and he even married two of his daughters. To simplify the calculation we will assume the ratio was 50% sons and 50% daughters.

It is not important to know the exact number of wives or children that the human pharaoh Ramesses possessed. It may seem far-fetched to think he had many children and took at least two of his daughters in marriage. The fact is, this pharaoh was credited with so many children because Ramesses was one of the many names given to Mars, and Mars gave birth to many children. These 'children' were the enormous chunks of debris that were blasted out into space as Mars was slowly and systematically torn apart by the tidal forces of larger planetary bodies. We recognise them as asteroids and comets, but to the Egyptians they were real beings. As they were born from the body of Mars, what else could they be apart from children of Mars? I believe that the rockier asteroids were perceived as male whereas the cometary bodies were female due to the beautiful, almost peacock-like tails that streamed out from the comets.

The Olympus Mons and Valles Marineris on Mars produced a constant source of space debris and, with many thousands of volcanic vents, they gave birth to many hundreds of divine children. To support this assumption we can look to a title given to many of Ramesses' children which was 'King's Son of His Body'. The meaning of this title is very clear. The children of Ramesses/Mars were 'of his body'. Enormous great chucks of Mars blasted out into space as Mars convulsed in close proximity to Earth.

Many children congregated around Mars – some ventured off alone while others died (before Ramesses) as they moved away from Earth or disappeared below the horizon. Some came close to Earth and loomed large enough to be viewed as the pharaoh Merneptah. History reveals that Ramesses married as least two of his daughters. These were two moon-sized cometary bodies, or queens, acting as consorts to Ramesses/Mars. The space debris produced by Mars was clearly observed. It was large enough and lived long enough to warrant being recorded in sacred cartouches.

Having identified Ramesses as Mars, we will examine his birth name 'Re has fashioned him'. We could view this name as an extension of the title 'son of Re' or in other words Re (the Sun) has fashioned him (Mars/Ramesses). This family tie derived from location and colour. Mars was a vivid red colour like the Sun and inhabited the same area as the Sun which led to the name 'the Sun (Re) has created him'. However, I believe there is more to this name.

I believe Ramesses/Mars followed the same basic path as the Sun many times and occasionally appeared fixed on the horizon (Horus Harakty = the king in the horizon). This location caused the Sun to rise behind Mars and its location and living colour gave rise to the name 'Re has created him'. Mars was a large red-disk which appeared fixed on the horizon as a living, breathing god-king. Some surface activity was faintly visible because Mars was in turmoil. The red Sun was 'full of vitality' and slowly rose behind Mars which led to the name 're has fashioned him'.

It could be argued that the Sun rising behind Mars should be viewed as Mars fashioning the Sun. However, the Egyptians were fully aware of Re and believed he was the perennial father to all and one of the original creator deities. Re was always in the background creating many monarchs, and he also remained in place, chaos permitting, long after many monarchs had made the perilous journey to heaven. Re is still with us today, the very same Sun god that traversed the heavens 4,000 years ago.

There were eleven pharaohs who shared the birth name Ramesses, although their throne names and titles varied. Ramesses was Mars as it moved back and forth to Earth. When it came close to Earth, Mars settled in the same location and had the same appearance as on previous occasions and this was the form referred to by the name 'Re has fashioned him'.

If Mars (or any other planetary body) was locked in a particular location and appeared in the same basic form every day, it is likely it would be given one name only. This was impossible because all planets involved in cosmic chaos were constantly changing appearance, location and behavioural traits which is why there are so many different names and titles for the monarchy. If the solar system had not changed in the last 5,000 years, there would be just one Ramesses and one aspect of Mars which would easily be recognised.

Nefertari *'the most beautiful'* **(**Nefer-tari)

Nefertari was the wife of Ramesses the Great and is not to be confused with Nefertiti the legendary wife of the 'heretic' pharaoh Akhenaten.

Inscriptions stated that 'she was a beauty beyond compare' and described her as his beloved wife, 'the one for whom the Sun shines'. She was also referred to as Nefertari Merit-en-Mut, meaning 'the Lovely One, Beloved of Mut'. Other titles described her as 'appeasing the gods', 'beautiful face' and 'pretty with two feathers'. Scholars may believe these were references to an earthly queen's physical appearance, but this was not the case.

As Nefer means beautiful and the name Nefertari means 'the most beautiful', this was clearly a description of the planet Venus. This name, along with Nefertari's other titles, were physical descriptions of the beautiful and divine queen Venus as she dominated the heavens. This name is very similar to the name Nefertiti which was given to the 'heretic' pharaoh Akhenaten's wife. This translates as 'the beautiful one is come' and also described the very beautiful

Venus. It described a period in history when Venus suddenly emerged in the skies above.
Nefertari/Venus appeared in the sky during the day courtesy of the diminished red Sun and was undoubtedly a magnificent sight. What higher accolade could a planetary queen be given other than titles and epithets alluding to her beauty? Her titles included 'she was a beauty beyond compare', 'the one for whom the Sun shines' and 'the lovely one'. If Venus were to visit Earth again, she would probably be adorned with similar names. Venus was a major Roman goddess principally associated with love and beauty. Nefertari/Venus was also associated with love and beauty and there are many poems dedicated to her.

'Appeasing the gods'

As Venus was in such a divine location, it no doubt appeased the many sky gods that made up the Egyptian pantheon. These gods were granted life as a result of cosmic chaos, and they were no longer visible because comic chaos had recently settled down.

'Beautiful face'

Did this title imply that there was something wrong with the body of Nefertari or is this simply a reference to the beautiful face of Venus? As a radiant and very passive red orb, the beautiful-faced Venus accompanied the fearless warrior pharaoh Mars/Ramesses in his dutiful act of vanquishing Egypt's enemy _ space debris.

'Pretty with two feathers'

Without going into too much detail, the two feathers (sometimes called plumes) were two enormous cometary tails emanating from Venus. The scalding hot Venus emitted incalculable amounts of material and the solar wind manifested this debris into two great plumes – in other words this is Velikovsky's illusive 'comet Venus'. Of course, we could consider an alternative _ that it was an Earthly queen adorning two feathers for a few days as some kind of fashion statement. Would this have been worthy of the descriptive title 'pretty with two feathers'?

Nefertiti (Venus), the wife of Akhenaten (the Moon), was an enigmatic queen. Her origins are shrouded in mystery and according to history she appeared from nowhere. She reigned with Akhenaten for a few years and then suddenly disappeared.

There are similar mysteries surrounding Nefertari's background. As with Nefertiti, this divine queen seemingly appeared from nowhere. Regarding Nefertari's death, her recently restored tomb in the Valley of the Queens is considered to be one of the most beautiful tombs in Egypt. It records Nefertari's journey to the afterlife but her origins are still unknown.

Nothing is known of Nefertari's background. As with Nefertiti, the name Nefertari was one of the many names given to the beautiful planet Venus. Venus/Nefertari either made a very sudden appearance in the heavens or changed location and attributes to such an extent that the Egyptians gave her a different name. Pharonic Egypt records many enigmatic appearances and disappearances and, if we consider the GKS, it becomes clear that we are observing the movements of the planets in chaos.

Psusennes I   Birth name + (epithet)

Pa-seba-kha-en-niut-mery-Amun)

'The star that appears in the city (Thebes), beloved of Amun'

Psusennes – this is possibly Mars (or Mercury) taking on the appearance of an enormous star.

Psusennes II

Birth name *'Image of the transformations of Re'*

This is a very descriptive title. It describes a planetary body (Mars or Mercury) which appeared like the red Sun or appeared in the image of the living, breathing red Sun.

Alexander the Great

Beloved of Amun, chosen by Re

Name changes

On many occasions the names given to pharaohs were changed. Here are a number of examples:

Mentohotep III's vizier/governor of the south was also called Amenemhet and it seems highly probable that he and Amenemhet I are one and the same (Clayton, Chronicle of the Pharaohs, 1994, p 77). This is simply two aspects of Mars – therefore Mars altered its appearance enough to warrant a name change.

Akhenaten of the New Kingdom changed his name from Amenhotep III to Akhenaten – this represents the changing facets of Mars.

The Second Dynasty pharaoh Seth-Peribsen changed his name from the good 'Horus' name Sekhemib to the evil 'Seth' name Peribsen. Horus was the embodiment of kingship while Seth was the god of chaos. We can find a plausible explanation using the GKS – this was a planet-god transforming from the relatively stable appearance of 'Horus' to the chaotic appearance of 'Seth'. It is possible that the Horus appearance was Mars appearing in the night sky, rising and setting with the advent of night. Due to planetary chaos, and an encounter with Venus, Mars took on an erratic movement and comet manifestation. The mortal kings merely had to obey the divine doctrine by honouring the celestial deity and renaming themselves accordingly.

It was no coincidence that Seth-Peribsen's successor, a pharaoh called Khasekhemwy, incorporated the names of the gods Horus and Seth with his name. The current interpretation is that this was a religious diplomat who was trying to mollify two religious factions on Earth, but this is totally incorrect as it clearly represented Mars in partial chaos.

Only planet-gods were associated with gods of chaos and were worshiped by mortals. There were numerous references to the battles between good and evil in the form of Horus and Seth – this did not point to mortal kings. Human pharaohs did not declare themselves evil as in the case of Seth-Peribsen or part evil and part good in the case of Khasekhemwy. The entire scenario only makes sense if it is viewed as the will of the planet-gods.

Nefertiti (Venus) – It is believed that Nefertiti disappeared, but another possibility is that she simply changed her name to Smenkhkara (Glory Ancient Egypt 3 p 47). However, this was another example of a god-like celestial body changing its attributes and it is more plausible to assume Venus transformed to become Smenkhkara..

The mummies of Ramesses VII and VIII have never been found. However, the enigmas surrounding these kings can be explained. They were mortal representatives who added slight variations to their titles and therefore they took on new identities. Hence there were no mummies and, in the case of Ramesses VIII, no tomb.

The above name changes are well known to Egyptologists. However, if we consider the GKS, it is likely that there were many more name changes which we are totally unaware of.

THE TWO EGYPTIAN LANDS OF HEAVEN AND EARTH

Egypt – The Two lands & Unification

The 'two lands' is the most misunderstood aspect of ancient Egypt.

Throughout pharonic Egypt we find infinite references to the 'two lands'. History reveals that they were of tremendous importance to the Egyptians and much of the symbolism of ancient Egypt referred to the union of the Two Lands.

Original creator gods such as Atum and the solar god Re (or Ra) were referred to as 'lord of the two lands'. Re, as the Sun god, also had the very apt epithet 'illuminator of the two lands'. In the New Kingdom, Amun as 'the king of the gods' also had the title 'lord of the two lands'. Amun was typically depicted wearing a flat topped crown with two tall plumes; it is believed they were symbolic of the two lands.

The 'two lands' were frequently mentioned in connection with the 'universal gods' or 'sky gods'. The record also reveals they were of paramount importance to the royal family, notably the god-kings. The god-kings were bestowed with the title *neb tawy* meaning 'lord of the two lands'. It was the role of the pharaoh to maintain 'divine order' (*ma'at*) by uniting the 'two lands'. Other similar connections revealed the kings as 'unifying the two lands' or 'ruling the two lands'. Another title was 'the king of the dualities'.

Tuthmosis III

'The Good God, Lord of the Two Lands, King of Upper and Lower Egypt, Menkheperre, Son of Re, Thutmosis, given life eternally.'

(Davies, 1987, p 45)

In the New Kingdom, the 'gods-wives of Amun' were depicted wearing a double plumed crown similar to that of Amun. Again this was a symbolic representation of the two lands. To show how important the 'two lands' were to the ancient Egyptians, I have enclosed a number of references extracted from various sources, in particular from the Book of the Dead, a collection of spells to assist the deceased to the afterlife.

'Hail to you, king of kings, lord of lords, ruler of rulers, who took possession of the two lands.'

(Faulkner, Book of the Dead, p 27)

'...he shall not be turned from any gate of the west, but shall be ushered in with the kings of Upper Egypt and the kings of Lower Egypt.'

(Faulkner, Book of the Dead, p 34)

'Who is the Dragoman of the two lands? He is Thoth.'

(Faulkner, Book of the Dead, p 33)

'Turn your face to the west that you may illuminate the two lands with fine gold.'

(Faulkner, Book of the Dead, p 40)

Hail to you, Horakhty, Khepri the self created! How beautiful is your shinning forth from the horizon when you illuminate the two lands with your rays!'

(Faulkner, Book of the Dead, p 41)

'O lord of terror who is at the head of the two lands'

(Faulkner, Book of the Dead, p 49)

'...who make the two lands content...'

'Controller of the two lands'

'Lady of the two lands'

'Ruler of the two lands'

Cleopatra: *'Hail Cleopatra, daughter of Re, mistress of the 'two lands.'*

These expressions and more can be found repeated many times throughout Egypt. They clearly reveal the two lands to be of the utmost importance to the ancient Egyptians. But what does this mean? What or where are the two lands? Why were they so important to the Egyptians? Why was it important for the kings to unite the two lands?

The conventional belief – the only explanation you will find in your history books

The term 'two lands' which characterises dynastic Egypt is believed to be derived from two kingdoms, one inhabiting the north and the other the south. They were separated, not by a natural geological feature such as the Nile which dissects Egypt from south to north, but by an imaginary east-west line which was drawn roughly in the area of modern Cairo. The north, where the Nile fanned out and where there were several mouths into the Mediterranean, was known as Lower Egypt. The south was called Upper Egypt and stretched as far as Elephantine (modern Aswan). The 'two lands' were divided into Upper and Lower Egypt and this division was 75/25 % in favour of southern Egypt (Lower).

The two kingdoms, Upper and Lower Egypt, were united under one king at around 3200 BC, but each had their own regalia. Lower Egypt was represented with the low red crown (*deshret*) and its symbols were the papyrus plant and the cobra goddess Wajet of Buto. Upper Egypt was represented by the tall white crown (*hedjet*), the flowering lotus and the Vulture goddess Nekhbet of Nekheb. The combined Red and White crowns became the *shmty* (double crown) and were symbolic of Upper and Lower Egypt. This symbolism of the two lands remained for three millennia, the duration of pharonic Egypt.

In layman's terms, the orthodox belief dictates that the 'two lands' were, and still are, the north and south of Egypt. These lands were not separated by a great river, valley or mountain range but by an 'imaginary' line or border which was approximately in the area of Cairo. Is this correct? I believe it is not. I propose this is a misunderstanding regarding the identification of the 'two lands'. As a result, the very foundation on which pharonic Egypt was built, that of unification, has also been grossly misunderstood. Before I give the true location of the 'two lands' and by extension 'unification' as understood by the Egyptians, I will first analyse the orthodox stance. As I do so, it will become apparent that there is something drastically wrong.

Problems with the original unification of the two lands

How can two kingdoms unite if they don't exist? Common sense dictates that for unification to occur we first need two cultures or kingdoms with substantial or opposing differences. It is also common sense to assume that these opposing kingdoms must have developed over many years. In other words, early man formed small settlements which amalgamated into larger units. They become two 'opposing' kingdoms that eventually united, possibly through warfare or diplomacy. In the case of Egypt, it is believed that warfare united the two kingdoms. However, scholars cannot find the 'development stage' and it therefore seems that pharonic Egypt suddenly appeared 'fully formed' out of thin air.

'Prior to that date [3100 BC], prehistoric people had roamed the river swamps and the high desert gebal, but why, suddenly, should Egyptian civilization erupt almost like the lotus flower from the primeval waters in one of the old creation legends, and where did it come from? The full answers to these questions have yet to be found.'

(Clayton, 1994, p 15)

It is evident that Egyptologists are struggling to explain the birth of the sudden 'united' pharonic Egypt. However no archaeological evidence exists to prove the existence of two early kingdoms that were sufficiently developed enough to unite into one kingdom. There is no evidence that two early pre-Egyptian kingdoms occupied the two lands even though the art associated with the two kingdoms clearly indicated they must have existed. This art included the regalia associated with Upper and Lower Egypt which took many years to develop and become established.

We will first examine the white crown of Upper Egypt (North) and the red crown of Lower Egypt (South). These were pharonic crowns worn by Egyptian kings to show their authority over their respective kingdoms. This society evolved from hunter-gatherers into a people ruled by kings wearing distinctive crowns. This regalia suggests a development stage lasting at least a few hundreds years. It is therefore evident that unification of the two lands as per the conventional belief is unlikely.

The Nile, a great natural divide ignored!

Egypt is defined by the Nile and the deserts which flank it. The Nile flows from the south to north and it dissects Egypt into two great land masses. The Egyptians believed in a land of the living to the east and a land of the dead to the west. This belief, which was dictated by the solar god Re, rose in the east each morning and died in the west in the evening. It was a natural geological divide which was the lifeblood of the Egyptians and without it there was no Egypt. It was deified in the form of the god Hapy. The Nile therefore provided two distinctive and very natural land masses in the east and west. However, the currently accepted view is that the 'two lands' were north and south. Are we therefore to ignore the large natural divide in favour of an imaginary line drawn somewhere near Cairo?

The conventional idea of the two lands actually led to the creation of four lands. This is because the two kingdoms of north-south Nile were split into two halves which produced four lands. Upper Egypt comprised land to the east and west of the Nile and Lower Egypt was also divided into east and west. This geological divide would have posed many problems to the two illusive kingdoms that were believed to have existed prior to unification. How did the inhabitants of the east communicate with their western comrades?

In ancient Egypt, people travelled on foot or on the back of an animal such as a donkey. As there were no bridges, the Nile was navigated by boats which were scarce in ancient times. Therefore communication between members of the same kingdom would have been slow and difficult. It would have been easier to communicate with the enemy from the opposing kingdom as they were on the other side of an invisible line drawn down the middle of the desert.

Each kingdom would have had two borders to defend; one on the east bank and one on the west bank of the Nile. It would have been difficult to defend two invisible borders and it would have been a logistical nightmare. How would the east side know if the west side had been attacked? If unification was brought about by the kingdom of the south (Upper) attacking and defeating the kingdom of the north (Lower), would this have been a coordinated attack? Did the army of the south advance northwards simultaneously either side of the Nile, or did they advance down the eastern side and across the river to defeat the west? Did the invisible border dissect the Nile on both sides exactly? There were no natural geological features separating the so-called two lands, so how did each kingdom know when they had crossed the line? Are we to believe that both sides defended the same invisible border line both sides of the Nile? This scenario sounds strategically impractical and confusing.

The south was arid and in certain areas the deserts reached the waters edge where life was extremely harsh. This was in stark contrast to the north. Here, the Nile fanned out into tributaries and marshes and life in the delta region was abundant. This was exemplified by the annual flood which swept down from the south, flooding the plains of the north to leave behind a rich deposit of fertile silt. In later times, this land was capable of sustaining two successive crops every year. While survival in the south was precarious and life was inhospitable, the north sustained life easily which enabled humans, livestock and crops to benefit from the life-supporting vast plains and marshes.

Does this seem logical? If there were two 'primitive' kingdoms, wouldn't they have coexisted and developed either side of the Nile valley? Both would have been able to take advantage of the richer and more fertile agricultural lands of the north and the marshy delta region. Survival in the north would have been easy compared to the difficulties of the south. With such a natural arrangement they could have lived peacefully side by side for many centuries. They would also have realised that an attack from across the Nile was less likely than an attack across the land.

It is believed that King Menes, a great king of Upper Egypt, conquered the north thereby unifying Egypt into one nation. However, I propose that the northern kingdom would have developed at a greater rate than the south and would have been far stronger. If an opposing kingdom had existed in the south, the kingdom of the north would have quashed any threat of rebellion.

Let us assume that the 'two lands' were south and north as outlined above. Let us also assume that the kingdom of Upper Egypt (south) conquered the kingdom of Lower Egypt (north) and united the 'two lands' into one nation. How do we explain the absence of ceremonial monuments? The Egyptians built great monuments to commemorate a variety of events. However, there is nothing to celebrate the unification of the two lands. Are we to believe the very foundation of Egypt existed in words only?

Unification of the 'two lands' was the genesis of the world's greatest civilization and was celebrated by the Egyptians. References to the two lands, two kingdoms, the dualities, and Upper and Lower Egypt were carved on every tomb and temple wall. As the pinnacles of Egyptian religion, the god-kings were considered unifiers of the two lands and as a result were given the ubiquitous title 'lord of the two lands' (*neb tawy*). Ra (the Sun god) and Amun (the king of the gods) maintained this title. Life in ancient Egypt revolved around unification of the two lands, so why didn't this prompt the construction of any sort of monument. The infinite references and titles lasted for over 3,000 years, yet there are no obelisks, monuments, temples or tombs to commemorate these events. It is now becoming apparent why Egyptologists had to invent an invisible line!

Symbolism associated with the two lands maintained

Long after the first unification, the 'two lands' continued to be referred to with their own respective symbols and they continued to be referenced as the 'two lands'. However, the invisible border that separated the two had gone, so why did they not refer to a united Egypt with one set of symbols?

Unification is believed to have occurred when the kingdom of Upper Egypt conquered Lower Egypt. It is quite possible that this actually occurred. However, having defeated the enemy, the victors decided to keep and maintain the defeated kingdom's symbolic representations including the kingly red crown, the papyrus plant and the cobra goddess. Wouldn't the victors have immediately imposed their own representations on the defeated kingdom, causing the old symbolism to disappear without trace? Why did they continue to use the individual symbols of both lands? Surely this would have damaged any hope of unification as because it fragmented the Egyptian empire?

The maintaining of separate symbolism can be seen within the kingly crowns. The double-crown (*shmty*) was formed by a combination of the red and white crown. The tall, conical, white crown fitted inside the red crown and this double crown represented dominion over the 'two lands' and a unified Egypt. The pharaohs can be seen wearing the double crown in a variety of scenes such as the iconic 'smiting the enemy' scenes and 'offering' scenes.

There were many scenes which depicted either the red or white crown, for example:

Tuthmosis III (Moon) wearing the red crown (Clayton, 1994, p 108)

Ramesses III (c.1182 cc) (Mars) wearing the white crown (illustration Clayton, 1994, p 160)

Akhenaten (Mars) wearing the Red crown (Clayton, 1994, p 124)
Tutankhamun (Mars) wearing the red crown of Lower Egypt? (Clayton, 1994, p 133)

Sneferu of the 4th Dynasty is often depicted wearing just the white crown.

The triads of King Menkaure provided examples of the solitary wearing of the white crown.
If the 'two lands' were unified and the double crown represented dominion over Upper and Lower Egypt, the kings would have worn the double-crown rather than the red or white crown. Why did the pharaohs choose to dissect Egypt in this way when it was vital for all god-kings to portray themselves as rulers of a united Egypt with authority over both Upper and Lower Egypt?

We would expect Egyptian art to portray kings wearing the *shmty* (double crown) as this represented divine strength and absolute power over the two regions. The title *neb tawy* (lord of the two lands) would have been particularly apt in battle scenes as a mark of authority. Instead, these 'living gods on Earth' chose to demean themselves by appearing in a red or white crown.

Although ninety percent of the population of ancient Egypt could not read hieroglyphs, they recognised and understood the 'vanquishing the enemy' scenes. They also understood the meaning of the different crowns including the red, white and double crowns. Therefore, what did the average Egyptian make of scenes depicting the pharaohs battling the enemy wearing either the red or white crown? Did they view their divine leader as the god-king of both lands? If so, he would certainly have worn the double crown.

If a king was depicted wearing the double crown, he was visually presenting himself as the divine king of Upper and Lower Egypt – Horus, god on Earth. If a king wore either the red or white crown, he was in effect demeaning his authority over the two lands and was declaring himself king of either the north or south of Egypt. In fact, Egyptian kings continued to wear either the red or white crown throughout the 3,000-year duration of pharonic Egypt. The pharaohs listed above ruled approximately 2,000 years after unification, yet they chose to be portrayed wearing either the red or white crown.

It is an incredible coincidence that the two crowns fitted together. The red crown was shaped like a chair with a coil protruding from the middle. The white crown was tall, bulbous and conical. Together they formed the double crown or *shmty*. What would have happened if the two crowns had not fitted together? Would it have prompted the invention of a new crown to represent the two lands? It is interesting to note that not a single crown has ever been found.

Traditional reasons

It could be argued that the symbols associated with the two lands were maintained for traditional reasons. This would have been a celebration of the first unification, a time when a divine king from the south advanced and conquered the north, thus uniting Egypt into one nation. We would therefore expect to find evidence of ceremonial markers such as a series of obelisks along the illusive 'invisible' dividing line. Are we to believe that not one of the many pharaohs wanted to commemorate the two lands?

Why did the Egyptians retain titles such as 'lord of the two lands' even after unification? Their titles should have referred to a unified land, for example 'king of Egypt' or 'lord of the land of Egypt'. The constant references to 'two lands' indicates that they were unified but still maintained a high level of independence.

We must also consider the 'reunification' of the two lands. Around 2100BC, approximately 1,000 years after the first unification, Egypt entered a dark age. This was a period Egyptologists labelled the First Intermediate Period which lasted for 150 years. It was a time of chaos and scholars have little or no information about this era. It was brought under control by a succession of princes from Upper Egypt at Thebes. This led to the reunification of Egypt and the start of the Middle Kingdom. The king credited with this reunification was the 4th king of the 11th Dynasty, Mentuhotep I. This was eloquently attested to by the series of titles he adopted – 'He who gives heart to the Two Lands,' followed by 'Lord of the White Crown' (Upper Egypt), and finally 'Uniter of the Two Lands'.

This situation was similar to that which existed prior to the first unification. It was a time of opposing factions occupying land north and south of an imaginary line near Cairo. It is unlikely that the Egyptians remembered where this 'invisible border' was or that they reverted back to two opposing kingdoms either side of this illusive 'line'.

Considering the lack of markers, how would the Egyptians have known if they were in Upper or Lower Egypt? Did each kingdom go back to its previous position either side of the invisible line that cut across the Nile? During reunification, did Montuhotep advance from south to north on both sides of the Nile, or did he conquer the lower east side before moving to the lower west side? As reunification took place after 150 years of turmoil, it is surprising that they not celebrate the event with a geological marker? This was a great feat, yet no festival or commemorative structure marked the event.

Throughout the phases of turmoil, the separate symbolism of the red and white crowns continued and there were no crowns representing a united Egypt. Did rival factions form an allegiance and adopt the symbolism associated with the two lands? Perhaps those who moved south adopted the white crown and those who moved north adopted the red crown.

Hieroglyph for the two lands

In the illustration above, the two symbols represent the hieroglyph for the 'two lands'. They took the form of two separate pancakes or rectangular shaped glyphs one above the other. This glyph appears on many wall reliefs and features in many titles as outlined previously. Two such titles are 'Protector of the two lands is Re' and 'Lord of the two lands is Re'. This glyph also featured in the common title given to the god-kings, 'Lord of the two lands' (*neb tawy*). It is significant that this hieroglyph always appears as above, one land above the other. As two separate icons comprise this glyph, it is obvious that they are symbolic of two lands.

Egypt is a desert split into two very natural east-west lands. Yet this enormous geological divide was apparently ignored in favour of a transparent line drawn across the Nile somewhere near Cairo. It appears this imaginary north/south divide was represented by two separate 'pancake' shaped glyphs which is a complicated way of representing the two lands. Why should two separate icons represent an invisible geological north/south divide? Where is the Nile – the lifeblood of the Egyptians? If the 'pancakes' represented the north and south of Egypt, shouldn't they be dissected in two to show the Nile? The Egyptians relied on the Nile for their existence, yet they chose to ignore this fact by omitting the Nile from the symbol of the two lands. It would make more sense if the two 'pancakes' represented the two 'natural' lands of the east and west, but scholars believe the two lands, Upper and Lower Egypt, were the north and south of Egypt.

The hieroglyph for the sky was represented by an easily recognisable symbol – a broad rectangle with the two lower corners pulled down to form two small points. However, the hieroglyph for the two lands was not easily understood. It would have made more sense had it been an oval or circle shaped hieroglyph representing Egypt with a broad line down the middle representing the Nile. This could then have been dissected with a perpendicular line to show the north/south divide – basically an oval shape dissected by a cross.

There is something drastically wrong with the orthodox belief that Upper and Lower Egypt were north and south of an imaginary line running across Egypt.

Deshret & Kemet

The Egyptians made many references to the black and red land. One such reference was:

'I am Horus, lord of the black land and of the red land.'
(Faulkner, Book of the Dead, Spell 138)

The red land – deshret

The Egyptians referred to the desert as *deshret* meaning 'red land'. This seems logical as Egypt is a vast desert dissected by the Nile and the sands regularly take on a reddish hue. This is particularly true at times when the red Sun reddens the desert even further.

Egypt, the black land – kemet?

The currently accepted definition of 'kemet' is that it represents Egypt and refers to 'black land'. It is believed to be a reference to the black fertile Nile silt which was spread across the land annually due to the inundation or annual flood. I believe this is incorrect. It would be understandable if Egypt was described as 'a fertile strip of emerald green' or 'greenery in a sea of sand'. However, it does not make sense to refer to Egypt as 'black land'.

The inundation, or annual flood, apparently turned the Nile Valley black for approximately two to three months of the year. It is believed this was due to the fertile silt which was deposited either side of the Nile. During this period, the Egyptians utilised this phenomena to plant their crops which were necessary for survival. This led to ten months of abundant plant growth when both crops and the natural flora blossomed and literally turned Egypt into a mass of 'abundant' green. This was the very 'green' which allowed the Egyptians to survive! It therefore seems odd that the Egyptians ignored nearly ten months of a predominately green landscape in favour of a short 'black' period of approximately two months.

If you watch any documentary or read any book on ancient Egypt during and after the inundation, you will find it difficult to find anything resembling a 'black land'. Even during the flood, there was an abundance of flourishing flora and greenery and it therefore seems extremely unlikely that the Egyptians would have called their land 'black'. They were able to provide an accurate description of the reddish coloured deserts, but when describing Egypt they gave a very confusing and inaccurate account.

We could ask the same questions as those asked in relation to Upper and Lower Egypt. If Egypt was the black land and the surrounding deserts were the red land, why was the Nile not mentioned? It dissects both the black and red land into two distinct land masses, east and west. This would have produced two black lands and two red lands, yet the majority of references to these lands were in the singular. If the black and red lands were added to the north-south imaginary divide, there would have been six or eight lands. This would lead to an incredibly complicated situation when Egypt was basically a red land divided by a fertile green strip.

Egyptologists rarely describe Egypt as the 'black land' and only refer to it as such when they are explaining how the ancient Egyptians described their land. Eminent Egyptologist, Bob Brier, has appeared on many TV documentaries and has written many books. He has produced audio tapes of his lectures which describe the inundation as follows:

'.... now let me describe inundation for you as the Egyptians saw it.....First, the Nile turned **red**, now it turned **red** because it was carrying with it the top soil, the rich **red** soil, from Ethiopia, northward. So first it turns **red**, then it turns **green**, that's the slower moving vegetation coming from the south, the top soil moves quickly, its small, suspended in the water, the vegetation floating on the top....turns **green**....then it rises 30 feet.

There is no mention of *black* fertile silt following inundation. Bob Brier described the land just as the majority of Egyptologists believed it to be which was exactly how the Egyptians saw it. During inundation, the River Nile turned red which turned the flood plains a similar rich colour – it certainly did not turn the area black.

Two lands –Two Egypt's
One up – one down
One heaven – one Earth
One red – one black (at night)
Two parallel worlds living side by side
As above – so below

It is relatively simple to understand the minds of our ancient forebears. The so-called 'two lands' were not an earthly geological north/south divide dissected by an imaginary line or border. Upper and Lower Egypt were the two lands of heaven and Earth. Furthermore, 'unification' of the two lands, the very foundation on which the

Egyptian empire was built, referred to the celestial god-kings traversing between the two lands.

To the Egyptians, there were two great land masses – one up, one down, the Upper and Lower Egypt or the 'two lands'. Lower Egypt was Earth represented by the red land which was home to mortals. Upper Egypt was heaven represented by the black land which was home to the divine Egyptians or stars. This led to two Egypt's coexisting side by side, 'as above, so below'. The two worlds were inextricably linked by god-kings and an enigmatic array of deities who inhabited the vast space between.

We will examine this area in more detail, particularly in relation to Upper Egypt, to understand the radical new proposal of the 'dualities' as understood by the Egyptians. We will look at each area separately before unifying them with the 'god-kings'. This will initially involve little reference to planetary chaos and the intermediary location of the astral royal family and their entourage. This is because the concept of the 'two Egypts' can be understood without celestial chaos. However, we will draw on cosmic chaos and unify the 'two lands' when certain areas have been clarified.

Lower Egypt = Earth (the red land)

All ancient cultures believed the Earth (Lower Egypt) was a fixed flat firmament (pancake-shaped like the land glyph) at the centre of the universe with the Sun travelling around it. The Sun also appeared to travel across and underneath the flat Earth. All Egyptian myths and beliefs pointed to a flat Earth with the solar deity Re traversing the heavens in a solar barque. As it set in the west, Re battled the demons of the underworld (under the flat Earth) and appeared victorious as it rose in the east the following morning.

The universal belief in a flat Earth can be supported by a Babylonian clay tablet from around 700 BC which resides in the British Museum. This shows a map of the world as a flat disk surrounded by the oceans (Ref. Gods, demons and symbols of ancient Mesopotamia p 53, Black & Green). This clay tablet clearly reveals the beliefs of all ancient cultures which was that the Sun revolved around a flat Earth. It was not until 1543 that Nicolas Copernicus, in his *De Revolutionibus*, proposed that the Earth travelled around the Sun and therefore the Earth was not the centre of the universe. It also became apparent at this time that the Earth was spherical, although the conviction that the Earth was flat was natural and understandable for ancient peoples.

Egypt is a vast red desert dissected only by the Nile valley and the occasional oasis. The English word desert derives from the Egyptian word *deshret* which is the name given to the red crown of Lower Egypt. This is no accident; the kingly red crown was invented as a direct result of the vast red desert land of Egypt. Therefore we can state that:

Lower Egypt = our flat Earth = the red land.

THE REAL FIRMAMENT ABOVE

Upper Egypt = the next world = the black land = a mirror Egyptian world or parallel world

While Lower Egypt as Earth requires little explanation, Upper Egypt as a land above requires more attention. The key to understanding Upper Egypt is the afterlife and the next world. This is because Upper Egypt was a mirror image which existed above as the 'next world'.

The Egyptians were resurrectionists; they believed that when they died they would be reborn as a star in the 'kingdom of Osiris'.

'They were reborn in god's land as a 'star/god,' in the kingdom of Osiris.'
(Faulkncr, Book of the Dead, p 11)

It was the goal of every Egyptian to become a divine star or an *akh*. The word *akh* actually translates as 'effective one' or 'powerful one'. Once a person had successfully journeyed to the 'next world' they were resurrected as an *akh* and many tombs had rows of akhs/stars painted on the ceiling. As an akh, you could affect the daily lives of your family here on Earth. The Egyptians looked up at the stars in the night sky and believed they were viewing *akhs*, the spirits of their ancestors that had passed before. The *akh* is the fully resurrected and glorified form of the deceased in the 'next world' or in 'the field of reeds'.

The ancient Egyptians viewed the next world as a continuation of this one, a very real place where they could literally get up and go. Because Egypt was mainly agrarian, they believed the next world was a place where they would spend their time farming. Tomb walls show scenes of ordinary people farming in the fields of the next world. Many tomb paintings and papyri typically depicted the deceased wearing white loincloths or full length white attire; they were depicted carrying out activities such as hacking up the Earth, pulling flax, reaping grain and ploughing or reaping the fields.

It is believed that the main objective of ancient Egyptians was to prepare for death. As they considered the next world to be the same as this world (only better), they ensured a variety of Earthly possessions were buried with them. For example, the funerary items buried with the mortal boy king Tutankhamun included a gold gilded wood chariot, gold daggers, sandals, a board game, a gold perfume box and food items such as mummified duck, dried beef, wheat, barley and wine. A total of 3,500 items were recovered and all were considered useful in the next world.

Many burials included ushabtis ('answerer') which were little statuettes or mummiform. These statuettes assisted the deceased and spared them from the corvee labour in the afterlife. This form of labour enabled the deceased to produce his or her food (Shaw & Nicholson, 2002, p 266). Some of the deceased were buried with 365 ushabtis, one for each day of the year. As there were a large number of ushabtis, they were managed by an 'overseer' ushabtis who kept control with a whip. He kept an eye on the 'ordinary' ushabtis and made sure they kept in line. There were many ushabtis buried with Tutankhamun.

In order to attain a life in the 'elysian fields' and become an *akh*, the body of the deceased had to be mummified. The sole reason for mummification was to preserve the body so that the deceased could spend eternity in the next life. The Egyptians believed if you were not physically preserved in this world you would not exist in the next world. You would not be resurrected as a star (akh) or remain for eternity. If the deceased had a limb missing in this life, an artificial one was made and attached to the mummified body to enable the deceased to walk again in the afterlife. The tombs of the dead were considered 'houses of eternity' because they enabled the deceased to rise anew each morning with the Sun. This is an important point to remember when considering the beliefs of ancient Egypt.

It was possible to take away a person's eternal life by destroying their mummified remains because this would end their life in the next world. They also believed that there was no hell, only heaven or non-existence. At death you cither journeyed to the next world to be resurrected as an *akh* to live a life of bliss, or you were eaten by Ammut, the devourer of the dead. Your future prospects depended on whether or not you had led a good and just life here on Earth. To obtain a life of bliss and become a star/akh in the next world involved a hazardous journey fraught with incredible dangers and demons in the form of planetary chaos. To assist the deceased through these dangers, magical spells (from the Book of the Dead) accompanied the dead; they were typically written on the coffins of the dead or on papyri and placed inside the coffins.

The next world was known by a variety of terms such as the kingdom of Osiris, field of reeds, elysian fields, paradise, or heaven. Scholars believe it was a fictitious place which existed in the mythological world of the Egyptians; a made-up place created in minds of the Egyptians to explain what happened to them after death. I disagree with this reasoning. I believe the 'next world' was a 'mirror image' world which existed directly above the Earth in the form of Upper Egypt. Ancient Egyptians believed it was a real place, a divine land they could physically see and point to especially at night. It was a paradise that spanned the expanse of the cosmos and literally canopied the four corners of the Earth. It was a land that the Egyptians travelled to in a journey fraught with dangers and where they were reborn to live a life of eternity.

Of course, there is no land above. We know, after 4,000 years of science, that the stars shine against the backdrop of space. However, the Egyptians did not possess this scientific information and their outlook was childlike. It is this naivety which led the Egyptians (and indeed all ancient cultures) to believe that existing within the blackness of space was a real, physical landmass. They were not referring to planetary bodies such as Mars or Venus. The land of Upper Egypt existed beyond the sky and covered the vast expanse of space.

'And God made the firmament, and divided the waters which were under the firmament from the waters which were above the firmament: and it was so.'

(Gen 1:7 KJV)

The word 'firmament' refers to a fixed, immoveable landmass above. Upper Egypt was simply the backdrop of space and the starry sky gave the illusion of a fixed black land or firmament. It was a land that was completely immoveable just as the Earth was. The solar deity Re, the stars and the god-kings were busy traversing the heavens, but the world above was eternal and steadfast. It was a rigid cosmic land that literally canopied the four corners of the flat Earth. It was held up by four cosmic posts symbolised by the Egyptian Djed pillar.

This was the next world, the 'black land' (*kemet*) and Upper Egypt. This was the divine land that the Egyptians believed they would journey to and where they would be reborn as a star (*akh*) to live a life of eternal bliss. This was the duel world that the Egyptians were obsessed with and which they portrayed on hundreds of tombs walls. It is vital that we examine this dual world if we are to understand our ancient forebears.

We are prevented from seeing this second land by our modern day outlook and 4,000 years of science. When we look to the heavens on a clear night, we are aware that the trillions of stars are similar to our own Sun. We realise that space is a vast expanse which is forever expanding. Ancient cultures had no knowledge of the physics of the universe. To them, the blackness of space was not infinite, for everything had a beginning and an end. The end of their mortal world was the land of Upper Egypt – a mirror image of Earth that canopied the four corners of Lower Egypt.

We know this was an illusion, but it is important to remember that ancient cultures had no knowledge of science and it was logical for them to view the universe in this way. On a clear night when the sky is clear, you can observe billions of stars of varying degrees of brightness. Apart from the polar stars which appear fixed, you will notice the stars moving slowly and peacefully across the heavens. They appear to move in unison with the backdrop of space due to the spin of the Earth. To ancient cultures, these stars were divine beings, real people who were the descendents of those living on Earth. These divine beings moved 'upon' space as if they were slowly moving upon land – this was the black land of Upper Egypt.

This so-called *kemet* or black land has nothing to do with Egypt during inundation and this assumption is totally inaccurate. Rich red alluvial silt cutting through vast areas of red desert does not warrant calling Egypt the black land. Inundation lasted approximately two months of each year, and it makes no sense to assume the Egyptians would have ignored the colour of the land for the other ten months. Kemet is simply a name given to the land above as it appeared during the night.

Scholars have assumed that all references to 'black land' were referring to land on Earth. Yet their own teachings explain that the Egyptians lived by 'divine order'. Every aspect of Egyptian life was linked to the gods and the heaven above. It is not necessary to twist or contort enigmatic references to fit unrealistic notions concerning the Egyptians. It is obvious that these ancient people were referring to a 'black land' in the sky.

Colour was of paramount importance to the Egyptians and a prime example was the red Sun. This applied to the two lands. Egypt was a red land dissected by the Nile. It was further reddened by the red Sun and this is why Egypt was referred to many times as the red land and Lower Egypt. The land above appears black as darkness falls which is why it was referred to as the black land. It was also above and was therefore referred to as Upper Egypt. It is difficult to understand why Egyptologists have failed to grasp this fact. Support for my identification of Upper and Lower Egypt as the black and red land representing heaven and Earth can be found in the 'Book of the Dead':

'I am Horus, lord of the black land and of the red land.'

(Faulkner, Book of the Dead, Spell 138)

This spell points to two separate 'universal' lands. It should be understood literally, i.e. the god Horus was the lord of the black land of heaven and the red land of Earth. It makes no sense in the conventional sense unless the two distinctive red desert lands skirting either side of the Nile were merged together. How would we explain the black land running through the middle of the red land? It would make more sense if the red land was in the plural, i.e. 'I am Horus, lord of the black land and the red lands'. However, both lands are referred to in the singular as two separate and distinctive lands.

We must remember that the pharaohs were the embodiment of the god Horus. We can therefore substitute the god Horus with a god-king planet such as Ramesses. The spell would therefore read: 'I am Ramesses, lord of the black land and of the red land'. Given the astral and intermediate location of the kings, this spell makes perfect sense. Another example from the 'Book of the Dead' is:

'The black land and the red land are at peace.'

(ibid Spell 183)

Again this spell points to two totally separate land masses. It does not lend itself towards a black muddy strip of land dissecting an enormous red land. If the red land was at peace, the black land would also be at peace and vice versa. It therefore seems odd to separate them in this way? Why not simply state Egypt was at peace? Are we to believe there were times when Egypt as the black land was in turmoil when the red land was at peace? As the deserts flanked Egypt on both sides, this was impossible. Any climatic event affected both the Nile valley and the deserts because they were one and the same.

There were many times when the two lands of heaven and Earth were in turmoil, times of chaos in Upper and Lower Egypt. After such traumatic events, chaos eventually subsided and peace prevailed as the black and red lands were at peace once again. It is possible that the Egyptians perceived the black land of Upper Egypt to be in turmoil at a time when the red land was at peace. This would have been due to events in the cosmos occurring at a great distance from the Earth. However, I do not believe that the red land was seen to be in turmoil when the black land was at peace because any close hand events which were observable in the sky were perceived as occurring in the two lands of Upper and Lower Egypt.

Hieroglyphs

We have examined the hieroglyph for the two lands _ the pancakes shaped glyphs, one above the other. The two separate, rectangular glyphs represented the two physical and separate lands of heaven and Earth, Upper and Lower Egypt. The fact that one pancake appeared above the other provided support for this. The sky hieroglyph was a slightly larger rectangle with the two lower corners pulled down to form two small points. It was a simple representation of the sky and this is something we can easily recognise as the 'two lands' hieroglyph represented the two lands of heaven and Earth.

Stars = transposed Egyptians

The black land, which existed long before the ancient Egyptians came into existence, is still with us in all its divine glory. One only has to venture outside on a clear night to observe Upper Egypt as viewed by our ancestors. In fact, the ancient Egyptians are still with us. I am referring to the transposed Egyptians who, after undertaking a journey fraught with danger, were reborn in Upper Egypt. They are now living an eternal life in the heavens undertaking similar chores to those they did on Earth. They exist as the stars in the night sky in the form of the divine Egyptians inhabiting Upper Egypt, the duel world above.

The Egyptian belief in a rebirth as a star (*akh*) in the 'next world' is an extremely important concept. It was meant to be understood literally and a thorough understanding of it will help us appreciate the thoughts and convictions of the Egyptians. They believed they would eventually become stars, and they physically pointed to the location of the 'next world' which was the blackboard of space. This was perceived as a vast expanse of land and the stars which inhabited this parallel world were believed to be divine Egyptians.

We may find this hard to accept. After all, we are living in the 21st century and we know what a star is and the distances involved. We realise that each star is just a tiny part of a huge galaxy, but we need to remember our ancestors were not privy to this information. They viewed stars as transposed entities of themselves, real superior beings.

Ancient cultures were not aware of the incalculable size of the cosmos and the infinity of space. To them, the stars were not divine Egyptians suspended in the infinity of space, but they were real people, the 'powerful ones'. These 'effective ones' lived an eternal life in a very real and physical land above. We can glean much information about this world from the glorious afterlife scenes of this great civilisation. They reveal a world bustling with life, a very active duel world coexisting alongside our Earthly world.

It may seem bizarre to perceive the stars as living entities, people working the fields and harvesting crops etc. Stars are by their very nature passive and serene, almost motionless as they watch over us. They appear to be peacefully residing in the heavens in a deep sleep. In fact, at night the stars were perceived to be sleeping just as the Egyptians were sleeping. With no electricity or artificial light, the Sun dictated the day to day life of ancient Egyptians. The twinkling white stars could have represented the divine Egyptians wrapped in white linen sheets, reminding us of the god Osiris and mummification. With the advent of day, heaven and Earth exploded into life with the rising Sun.

The solar deity Re – two lands, one *red* Sun

When referring to the 'black land' (kemet), I proposed it was a reference to Upper Egypt at night. This is because the *kemet* wasn't always black, but was only black at night. During the day, Upper Egypt was bathed in Re's sunlight _ this was the same sunlight that shone on Lower Egypt. One red Sun inextricably linked the two parallel worlds.

The red Sun traversed the heavens somewhere between the 'two lands' of heaven and Earth. This was an intermediate location inhabited by the monarchy and an array of sky gods including Hathor, Isis and others. As such, Upper Egypt was subjected to the same daily cycle as Earth. The time of day and cycle of life was dictated by the Sun traversing both lands.

Dawn on Earth was dawn above, daytime on Earth was daytime above, dusk on Earth was dusk above and night was night in both lands. The Sun was the perennial life-supporting orb which shone on the two kingdoms of Upper and Lower Egypt. Evidence for the two worlds is contained within Re's epithets and they are repeated many times and lasted for the duration of pharonic Egypt.

'Illuminator of the two lands'

This title should be taken literally. The solar god Re illuminated the two lands of heaven and Earth as it traversed the heavens in a solar barque lasting millions of years. The red Sun bathed Upper and Lower Egypt in light as it rose and set each day. The red Sun's energy was diminished but, apart from times of intense chaos, nothing prevented Re's light from shining through. While conventional wisdom states that the Sun god Re illuminated two indefinable lands somewhere on Earth, I propose that the Sun illuminated the two separate lands of heaven and Earth.

'Lord of the two lands is Re.' (a title also given to the pharaohs)

Current understanding points to Re as the lord of two imaginary lands dissected by an imaginary line drawn roughly through the area of Cairo. However, this makes no sense if we take into account the natural geological divide of the Nile. I believe this title is easily understood if we consider Re in an intermediate location between the two lands as this would deem him as the perpetual 'lord of the two lands'.

'Powerful is Re protector of the two lands.'

As a result of cosmic chaos, there were a number of dark ages throughout history. These were periods of turmoil where day turned to night and the Sun was not seen for many centuries. Egyptologists have labelled these phases intermediate periods. Although the world was typically shrouded in darkness, Re eventually shined through. As the perennial star, Re banished the enemies of Upper and Lower Egypt and once again revealed himself in the heavens above. This gradual emergence following times of turmoil led to the belief that Re was the 'protector of both lands', and this solar deity still protects the two lands today. He remains the illuminator of the two lands of heaven and Earth and the perennial 'lord' of Upper and Lower Egypt. There are many similar 'two land' epithets, titles and phrases which confirm this as the true meaning.

Bringing the stars to life

Having examined the land above, we will now turn our attention to its divine inhabitants, the stars. We have established that the divine Egyptians were sleeping during the night, residing peacefully in the land above. As Re dawned in the east, both lands burst into life. On Earth, Egyptians awoke to begin their daily chores of working the fields and constructing great monuments for the astral kings.

It is important to note that the Egyptians above also woke up with the Sun to begin their daily activities. They carried out the same chores as they had on Earth. They dressed, travelled, worked, ate and drank, returned home, sang and danced, and finally retired to bed. Life was the same above as it was below. The one difference was that the Egyptians above were divine and their lives were eternal, just like the Sun god Re.

From the perspective of Earth, the land of Upper Egypt and its inhabitants the stars were rarely observed during the day. This was due to the powerful light from the Sun which shone without glare. Any activity in the distant land was 'virtually' invisible. However, for the Egyptians on Earth, Upper Egypt was always there. It never physically disappeared but was immoveable, a mirror image world that burst into life with the advent of day, just as it did on Earth. These glorious afterlife scenes can be found on tomb walls throughout Egypt.

How did celestial chaos affect these two worlds? The vast space between the two lands was a hive of commotion during the day due to the activity of the god-kings and their entourage. It is possible that Upper Egypt and its inhabitants came into view during daylight hours due to darkened skies and a diminished red Sun. However, it is likely that the distant land above was rarely seen during the day and it could only be seen as night spread over the land. To clarify this point, we will examine the cycle of the Sun as it rose and set over the two lands of Upper and Lower Egypt.

Night: Both lands were in darkness. The solar deity Re was battling the demons of the underworld beneath the flat Earth. The stars (akhs) were peacefully sleeping in the land above after a hard day's toil. Similar events occurred on the Earth as the nation slept peacefully in white linen blankets.

Day and Dawn: Re reigned triumphant over his enemies as a glimmer of light was observed on the eastern horizon. As day slowly dawned, heaven and Earth were flooded with light. Both lands came to life and their inhabitants began their daily chores such as fishing, hunting, ploughing the fields and erecting great monuments.

Sunset: The red Sun traversed the heavens and continued to illuminate both lands until it set in the west. Re's light was slowly extinguished and both lands fell into darkness. Earth was silent as daily activities ceased and people began to settle down for the night. Upper Egypt, or the black land (kemet) came into view as its divine inhabitants settled down for the night. Darkness granted visibility to the divine and they appeared as stars peacefully residing in the land above. As night fell, Re battled the demons of the underworld in the form of cosmic chaos. As a new day dawned, the cycle began again. This was the duel world

(Upper Egypt) as it coexisted side by side with Earth as part of an 'as above, so below' world.

To describe Upper Egypt as the 'next world' or afterlife is slightly misleading for this implies something 'following on' or 'coming after'. This may have been so for the recently departed who undertook a hazardous journey to be reborn in the land of eternity. However, it was actually a world existing side by side with this world – a divine Egypt synchronically tied with the mortal Egyptians on Earth as part of a duel world. The Egyptians called it Upper Egypt and with Earth it was know as the second of the 'two lands'.

Similarity with today

There are similarities between ancient and modern beliefs. However, whereas modern heaven is a place of mystery, heaven in ancient times was a place where life continued for eternity. All ancient cultures viewed it as the blackboard of space which gave the illusion of land and stars were always perceived as transposed human entities.

We have established that the 'field of reeds' or the 'next world' was Upper Egypt which was a real land directly above the Earth. It is understandable that the Egyptians were obsessed with their preparation for death and the afterlife. They could look up to see their ultimate destination where their long-dead relatives were watching over them. Every aspect of Egyptian religion and the afterlife therefore makes sense.

Contact with 'home'

The Egyptians built false doors inside many tombs and mortuary temples. They were rectangular imitation doorways made of stone or wood which first appeared during the Old Kingdom. The doors would serve as a link between the living and the recently departed. The Egyptians communicated with their loved ones by leaving offerings and notes of papyrus in recessed niches. It was believed they could actually talk to the deceased via these false doors as they were a portal to the real world above. They were used to open up a direct communication with the stars, the divine people residing in the black land above. If they wished to talk directly to the stars, they visited a false door and left offerings and messages for their loved ones. They also conversed with their relatives and asked for advice in their daily lives.

Egyptologists have discovered false doors incorporated into the figure of the deceased stepping out of the door. This was the *ka* or spiritual double of the deceased. This clearly reveals the belief that the deceased were resurrected as real people in the world above. It is likely that the stars in the night sky were perceived as the divine who communicated with those on Earth.

Today, many people visit a tombstone or symbolic marker to 'talk' to their departed loved ones who peacefully reside in their particular heaven. The Egyptian tradition of using a false door is much the same. However, heaven today is not a physical place whereas 4,000 years ago it was a real abode. More importantly, with the use of the false door, heaven could be contacted. Friends and relatives could literally talk to their loved ones via this virtual portal.

The belief in a real land above explains why so much time was spent in preparation for death? The ancient Egyptians believed that the traditional ritual of preserving the deceased through mummification enabled the deceased to exist in the next world. We can therefore understand why funerary items were buried with the deceased. The Egyptians were obsessed with what happened to them at death and they looked forward to gaining immortality as an 'effective one' or 'powerful one'. As an akh they had the power to directly influence their friends and relatives on Earth.

THE UNIFICATION OF HEAVEN AND EARTH

Unification

It could be argued that the kings unified the two lands by their astral location. Any large body which took up an intermediate position between heaven and Earth provided a stepping stone to the next world, thus bonding them together. However, unification was the foundation upon which Egypt was built and was primarily concerned with planetary bodies moving back and forth to Earth. Planetary bodies provided a direct link between Upper and Lower Egypt by traversing between the two and I believe this was the true meaning of unification. The process of unification involved a variety of deities and sky gods such as Isis, Hathor and Osiris played major parts in nurturing and transporting the kings back and forth to Earth.

The First Unification

To keep things simple I will use Mars as the original king. There existed two kingdoms prior to the birth of chaos _ the kingdom of Upper Egypt and Lower Egypt, heaven and Earth or the two lands. Both lands were at peace as chaos had not yet begun. The planets that existed at that time appeared as they do today, as bright stars slowly traversing the heavens. The Egyptians perceived them as divine beings inhabiting a distant black land (*kemet*) along with trillions of other divine entities. There was no Moon and no 'gods-on-Earth' and the largest orb in the sky was the Sun. There was no celestial body close enough to Earth to act as an intermediary between the two lands. In other words no large astral bodies were close enough to Earth to provide a stepping stone to the next world. The solar deity Re could never unify the two lands in the true sense because it never moved back and forth to Earth. In short, unification was a concept which was unknown to all ancient cultures.

Planetary chaos changed everything. Jupiter, one of the brightest stars, was hit by a galactic interloper and planetary chaos began. Initially this involved the birth of Venus, which caused unimaginable amounts of debris including our Moon. Shortly after its birth, Venus collided with Mars and kicked it out of its orbit. Mars, Venus and tons of debris slowly migrated towards Earth as Mars magnified in size and lost its star-like attributes.

Mars appeared as a hazy reddish orb in the heavens above Earth. It became a living, breathing 'god on Earth,' the first of many god-kings – Horus of the heavens. Mars was a god that came down from heaven to Earth to unite the two lands for the first time. Mars, as heir and offspring of the red Sun, reigned for a period of time and paralleled the historical record before it eventually died. The dying process involved Mars slowly moving away from Earth. It lost its 'living breathing' red orb appearance and took on the attributes of a gigantic star as it became wrapped in the blackness of the night. Mars then journeyed to Upper Egypt and eventually became an akh as it rejoined the divine in the land above. Mars, Venus, and later the Moon and Mercury repeated this journey many times over for an incredible 3,000 years.

By travelling between the two lands, Mars provided a direct link to the next world – to Upper Egypt and the afterlife. This is the true meaning of unification. There is no need to invent 'imaginary' kingdoms or borders on Earth. We should not demote the Egyptian world to a bizarre world we don't understand. Unification points to planetary kings as they linked heaven and Earth by physically traversing between the two lands.

We can now understand why everything revolved around the king and why they were the pinnacle of Egyptian society. The kings were the receptacles of supernatural and divine power, intermediates between the mortal and the divine. Any large celestial body traversing between heaven and Earth was always going to be perceived as a stepping stone to the world above. Every single epithet bestowed upon the kings can be attributed to their astral location and the unification of the two lands was no exception. This occurred when the planets in chaos journeyed between the two lands of heaven and Earth. This was a real physical bonding between the mortal and the divine by means of a gigantic celestial body. Armed with the true meaning of unification, we can now give definitive answers to the many enigmas surrounding it.

We looked at the orthodox belief which stated that Egypt formed when two kingdoms, Upper and Lower Egypt, united under one king around 3200 BC. However, the historical evidence, including Egyptian art, clearly suggests that two early kingdoms must have existed because each had their own symbolism. This included the red and white kingly crowns as well as the papyrus and the lotus plants associated with Upper and Lower Egypt. It would have taken many years of development to reach this stage, but the archaeological evidence does not support this. It seems that pharonic Egypt magically appeared fully formed as a united kingdom.

The reason for this is now apparent. Archaeologists will never find evidence of two pre-Egyptian kingdoms because they never existed. They will only find evidence of one early emerging Egyptian kingdom. This was a simple culture that inhabited Lower Egypt, the red land of Earth. It was a small populace born into a world of planetary chaos. However, another kingdom did exist, and still exists today, but not on Earth. It was Upper Egypt or the land above, and this kingdom was united with Lower Egypt by means of planetary kings who descended from heaven to Earth. The early Egyptians celebrated this occasion by inventing symbolic representations for both heaven and Earth. The red crown, the cobra and the papyrus represented Lower Egypt and Earth while the white crown, the vulture and the lotus plant represented Upper Egypt and heaven.

The origin of these particular symbols is complex, but it is no coincidence that the red crown represented Lower Egypt (red land) and the white crown represented Upper Egypt (white stars). The sudden emergence of such symbolism was the results of the first time that heaven and Earth were bonded by means of planetary kings. Prior to this there was little if anything to inspire or prompt the Egyptians into creating such symbolism. The astral gods enlightened them at the same time as they were emerging in the Nile valley. By observing the god-king-planets journeying back and forth to heaven, the Egyptians developed the natural belief that they too could be resurrected above. The god-kings taught them how to become resurrected as 'all powerful ones' in the divine land above. Given such incredible events, the two lands had to be placated by means of regalia, symbolic representations and 'sacred' hieroglyphs which lasted over 3,000 years.

Why maintain the symbolism of the two lands if they were supposedly unified?

Another enigma surrounding unification concerns the symbolism of the two lands which remained for 3,000 years. After the north and south were unified into one kingdom, why did they maintain separate symbolism? Upper and Lower Egyptian regalia remained throughout periods of reunification; these were times when warrior pharaohs apparently battled to reunite the two lands. Why didn't they simply represent one united land with a single set of symbols?

The fact is, the symbolism remained throughout the pharonic period for the same reasons outlined above. Upper and Lower Egypt were not terrestrial lands dissected in two by an imaginary line, but were two permanent and totally separate lands – heaven and Earth. As a result they demanded separate representation. Even though the two lands were unified by means of wandering planets, they could never be totally moulded into one land mass. Throughout periods of turmoil when 'divine order' was being turned upside down, the two Egypts remained fixed and immovable. It wasn't just a matter of rubbing out an imaginary border on a map. The two lands were always separate with one above the other as they appeared in the hieroglyph. This is why each maintained its own symbolism for over 3,000 years.

Unification wasn't easy. In fact it was a perennial battle that continued for 3,000 years. As previously discussed, these were the battles of the warrior planet-kings, and in particular Mars, and later the Moon and Mercury. Mars attempted to maintain 'divine order' (*ma'at*) by hoovering up incomprehensible amounts of debris littering the cosmos. By doing this, Mars united the two lands and acted as a conduit between the mortal and the divine.

This explains yet another enigma surrounding unification. If unification involved a kingdom from the south (Upper) advancing and defeating a kingdom from the north (Lower), why did the conquering army maintain the defeated kingdom's symbolism? If unification was the result of a battle on Earth, the conquering army would have banished the symbolism of the enemy in favour of its own. Yet this did not happen and the symbolism of the north remained for 3,000 years despite unification.

The reason for this can be explained by cosmic chaos. It was the planets, particularly Mars, which battled to unify heaven and Earth and not their mortal doubles. Mars fearlessly fought the space debris that threatened to bring the whole world into chaos. Despite the fact that Mars was always victorious (no pharaoh ever lost a battle), no kingdom ever imposed their symbolism on another. The god-kings were uniting heaven and Earth and not two imaginary lands on Earth, and these two universal lands required separate representation.

The first unification is believed to have occurred when a king of Upper Egypt conquered Lower Egypt. We are told that his name was Menes, although the name is of little importance. What is important it is that it was a king from Upper Egypt that conquered Lower Egypt. This happened when a god-king planet came down from heaven to unify the two lands for the first time just as recorded by history.

Reunification

Several kings were credited with the 'reunification' of Egypt. This is clarified by transferring history to the heavens. Reunification is merely a warrior 'god-king' making a victorious appearance after a period of turmoil. This saw Earth bonded with heaven and the route to the next world, Upper Egypt, was once again reopened.

We will consider Mentuhotep as a facet of Mars to explain his role in the reunification of heaven and Earth. This was a time of planetary chaos and global disturbances, when the skies and the divine land of Upper Egypt were in chaos and ruled by foreign rulers in the form of followers of Seth. However, help was at hand in the form of the god-king Montuhotep (Mars). A cosmic battle ensued and slowly the heavens began to clear to reveal the warrior king Montuhotep. This warrior king was observed 'smiting the enemy' and clearing the skies by sweeping up space debris to unite the two lands and bring about 'divine order' (*ma'at*). The subsequent reunifications occurred as this process was repeated again and again. These periods of turmoil could prove to be useful in sorting out the true chorology of ancient Egypt because it should be possible to tie them in with geological evidence of global disturbances.

Lord of the two lands

If the two lands were united into one, why did they maintain the title *neb-tawy* or 'lord of the two lands'? Why refer to the 'two lands' in the plural? Was Egypt united or not? Why not use a title which referred to a united country? If the two lands were based on Earth, it would simply involve crossing out an imaginary border.

Heaven and Earth could never be joined as one great land mass but they could be bonded together by divine planets as they traversed between the two lands. They could communicate via the false doors built in many tombs and temples but they could never be one. This is why the two lands were always referred to in the plural. Whether referred to as Upper and Lower Egypt, the two lands, the dualities or the red and black land, they pointed to two totally separate land masses.

The crowns of Upper and Lower Egypt

From left to right, the white crown (*Hedjet*) the red crown (*deshret*) and the double crown (*shmty*).

The red crown represented Lower Egypt and the white crown represented Upper Egypt and together they formed a double crown. I believe the red crown was invented as a symbolic representation of Earth (red Earth) while the white crown was invented to represent Upper Egypt. The white crown was influenced by early observations of Venus as it meandered across the heavens, taking on the attributes of a gigantic comet. Its shape and colour represented a cometary body or the early comet Venus before it visited Earth.

On the many battle scenes which adorn temple walls, the pharaohs are depicted in the iconic image of 'smiting the enemy' wearing a variety of headgear. Sometimes they wore white, sometimes red, and at other times they wore the double crown. It would have made sense to represent dominion over the two lands by wearing the double crown at all times. However, the Egyptians had a childlike outlook on the cosmos and the two lands of heaven and Earth. The backdrop of space gave the illusion of a fixed land and the astral kings occupied the flat Earth below – together they formed the two lands.

If a king was observed battling the enemy (space debris) low on the horizon, he was perceived to be physically close to Earth, closer to the red land than the black land. As a result, any celebratory relief depicted the king in the act of 'smiting the enemy' wearing the red crown. Similarly, if a king was observed vanquishing the enemy high in the sky, he was perceived to be closer to the black land than the red land. As a result any relief depicted the king adorning the white crown of Upper Egypt. Any king observed sweeping up the enemy somewhere in-between the horizon and the zenith was perceived to be somewhere in between the two lands – this location warranted the wearing of the double crown. I believe this is the basic principle behind the wearing of the red, white or double crown.

Of course the whole thing was an illusion. Any king that appeared low on the horizon was not physically closer to Earth than when he was high in the sky. It simply appeared that way because of the belief that the Earth was flat, immovable and at the centre of the universe. Heaven was a physical land above that canopied Earth. Any celestial body directly above was perceived to be closer to heaven than a body that appeared low on the horizon.

It is clear why, despite unification, the kings were continually shown wearing the red and white crown and not the double crown at all times. When worn by the kings in a variety of different scenes, the crowns commemorated the king's location in relation to the two lands. It was no coincidence that the red and white crown fitted together to form the double crown as the whole thing was pre-planned. The Egyptians fashioned the white crown after the image that began the whole process of unification – that of the comet Venus. The red crown was invented to represent the red land of Earth. As it was a king from Upper Egypt that united with Lower Egypt, the red crown was purposely designed to accommodate the white crown which formed the double crown. The double crown, as well as symbolising the location, was also symbolic of a king entering the vicinity of Earth, i.e. the white crown fitted inside the red crown.

No monuments – the sema tawef

History reveals that, apart from religion, the unification of the two lands formed the very foundation upon which the Egyptian society was formed. It was of paramount importance and yet it wasn't important enough to warrant the building of a celebratory marker or monument. How do we explain this? The reason is that it was impossible to build a monument between heaven and Earth? How could the Egyptians physically mark a location in space? This is why Egyptologists have erroneously invented an invisible line somewhere near Cairo.

The Egyptians did celebrate the two lands; they referenced them with 'scared' images and inscriptions on every tomb, temple and monument throughout Egypt. The pharaohs were bestowed with many 'sacred' titles alluding to the two lands. All these titles and epithets celebrated the bonding of the two Egypt's of heaven and Earth as follows:

'Lord of the two lands' (neb-tawy)
'King of Upper and Lower Egypt'
'Maker of peace in the two lands' (Intef I through to III)
'Uniter of the two lands' (Metuhotep)
'Binder of the two lands'
'He who gave heart to the two lands'

The art symbolically celebrated unification as seen in the *sema-tawef* motif.

Sema-tawef – a celebration of unification of the two lands

This motif consisted of the lotus (water lily) and the papyrus reed which served as emblems for Upper and Lower Egypt respectively. When joined together, these two plants formed the *Sema-tawef* motif which was symbolic of the union of Upper and Lower Egypt.

This is the *sema-tawef* motif below the king's throne. The papyrus and the lotus are entwined.

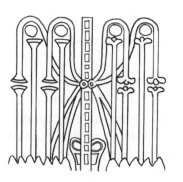 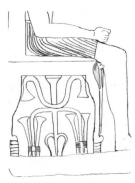

The *sema-tawef* motif was shown throughout Egypt in tombs and temples. However it was most commonly found below the thrones of the seated kings as in the illustration above. The colossal Ka-statues of Ramesses II which guarded the entrance to the colonnade in the temple at Luxor depicted the sema-tawef on the side of Ramesses II's throne. Other examples included Tutankhamun – the gold inlaid throne of this king depicted the seated king with his wife Ankhesenpaaten as Venus. They appeared entwined with the sema-tawef which was clearly seen below the throne. (Illustration Chronicles of the Pharaohs, Clayton, p 129 or the Cairo museum) There are many more examples which include:

King Neuserra (5th dynasty) (illustration Robbins, The Art of Ancient Egypt, 2000, p 18)

Khafra (4th dynasty) Head of a seated statue – on both side of the seat the *sema tawy* motif is carved (ibid 51)

King Nedhepetra Montuhotep – side of the throne (ibid 89)

The colossal quartzite statues of King Amenhotep III – the side of the thrones decorated with the motif (ibid 130)

Akhenaten (ibid 155)

Seti I (ibid 174)

Setting aside the reasons as to why the lotus and the papyrus plants were chosen to represent Upper and Lower Egypt, the meaning of the *sema-tawef* in such a location below the king's throne is obvious. It denoted the union of Upper and Lower Egypt by means of a god-king-planet.

The kings unified heaven and Earth by moving back and forth. What better way to commemorate this than to use the two emblems associated with the two lands? They were entwined and incorporated into the king's throne. The *Sema Tawef* is highly significant and reveals much about the astral kings that dominated our skies some 4,000 years ago. The seated position of the king was also highly revealing. It symbolically highlighted that Mars appeared almost stationary in the heavens at this time. King Mars literally presided over and united the two lands as he sat upon a cosmic throne. The king took a rare and well-earned break from beating up the enemy. These facts do not disagree with history but merely transfer 'sacred' images to a real world of cosmic chaos.

It is no coincidence that the Sumerians had the phrase DUR.AN.KI which translates as 'bond heaven and Earth'. This was a reference to when the gods came down from heaven to Earth to bond the two together and was a result of planetary chaos.

Osiris, Asar (a star)

The process of living and dying to Earth, that of being transported back and forth between the two lands, involved a variety of gods and goddesses, some of which have been briefly mentioned (Hathor – Isis). We will now discuss the primary god of death and resurrection – Osiris.

Osiris: background

'One of the most important deities of ancient Egypt, whose principal association was with death, resurrection and fertility. He is usually depicted as a mummy whose hands project through his wrappings to hold the royal insignia of crook and flail. He wears the distinctive atef crown, consisting of the tall 'white crown' flanked by two plumes, sometimes shown with the horns of the ram. His flesh was sometimes shown as white, like the mummy wrappings, black to signify the fertile Nile alluvium, or green in allusion to resurrection. Osiris was one of the earliest Egyptian gods, probably originally regarded as a chthonic fertility-god overseeing the growth of crops, with some connection to the inundation as source of alluvium.

His main southern cult centre was at Abydos, which was said to be the burial place of his head. In the new Kingdom (1550-1069 BC cc), the tomb of the 1st dynasty ruler Djer (c. 3,000 BC) was claimed to be his burial place, and the site became a centre of pilgrimage. As well as a chapel for Osiris in the temple of Seti I (1294-1279 BC) there was also the so called 'Osireion', the masonry of which was intended to resemble a temple of the old kingdom (2686-2181 BC), although it was the work of Merenptah (1213-1203 BC.) ……

… The combination of his fertility and funerary aspects naturally transformed Osiris into the Quintessential god of resurrection. By at least the 5th dynasty (2494-2345 BC),

the dead king was identified with Osiris while the living king was equated with his son, Horus.

With the so called 'democratisation of the afterlife' that took place…it appears to have become possible for any deceased person to be resurrected in the guise of Osiris.

…in order to gain eternal life, it was essential for the mummified body to imitate the appearance of Osiris as closely as possible.'

(Shaw & Nicholson, 2002, p 215)

Who was Osiris in the context of the GKS? Egyptologists believe he was another mythological figure created by the ancient Egyptians as they attempted to conceptualise their place in the universe; in other words, the Egyptians decided to invent yet another fictitious character to help their understanding of the cosmos. Catastrophists on the other hand have tried to identify him with various bodies such as Jupiter, Mars, Venus, and the Moon as well as bright stars such as the dog star, Sirius. Although Osiris was associated with all these bodies, none come close to the true identification of Osiris. I will therefore extract Osiris from the mythological world and give him true physical presence as understood by the ancient Egyptians.

To understand and identify Osiris we need look no further than the God King Scenario. We have established that the god-kings were living red orbs (Horus) when reigning over Earth and gigantic stars as they moved away from Earth. It was the process of becoming a star where we will find the true identification of Osiris. The god Osiris was basically a star attribute. He was embodied in the whiteness that surrounded planetary bodies as they moved away from

Earth. He was the white 'star-like' haze that shrouded the kings as they journeyed to the next world.

As the planetary kings died they became gigantic stars and this was perceived as the god Osiris cocooning the kings and transporting them to Upper Egypt. It was the god of the dead protecting the deceased as they made their final journey to be resurrected in the firmament of heaven. The birth of the kings to Earth was primarily attributed to the nurturing goddesses Hathor and Isis. This occurred when the kings appeared as 'living gods' in the form of active red orbs within the haze surrounding Earth's equatorial regions. Osiris appeared as the planets retreated and became wrapped in 'stardust'. His primary role was that of transporting the deceased to a life of eternity as recorded by history.

Although Mars is a planet, when observed with the unaided eye it looks like a bright star moving slowly through the cosmos. Mars is in 'Osirian' form meaning it is being looked after by the god Osiris in the land above. If Mars were to move closer to Earth, it would shed its star-like quality to reveal a hazy red surface. In a sense, Mars has come alive to Earth. If we reversed the process so that Mars moved back out to space, it would become immersed in the attributes of a star and would take on the image of Osiris. If we did this with the Moon, the results would be the same. The Moon has clear black and white surface features but, if it moved away from Earth and out into space, it would slowly lose its features and become a star. The Moon would therefore 'become' Osiris. Egyptian mythology spoke of Osiris entering the Moon which is hardly surprising given the whitish colour of the Moon.

Any celestial body which took on the appearance of a star was associated with Osiris regardless of size or colour. From the astral kings and their entourage of moons, asteroids and comets to the billions of stars inhabiting the backdrop of space – if they appeared white and 'star-like' they were connected to Osiris the god of the afterlife. This included the Sun which, under certain atmospheric conditions including chaos, occasionally appeared white which resulted in a connection with Osiris. Bear in mind that it is possible for the Sun to appear white, for example on a foggy day. All astral bodies were real individual beings with their own personalities. When they took on the attributes of a star they were all perceived to be shrouded, looked after, or in the company of Osiris.

Osiris could be described as a transparent deity. It was not attributable to any one particular body or star, but at the same time it was attributable to all. It was a powerful god and was associated with every object in the sky which took on the attributes of a star. This is why it was difficult to understand or correctly identify Osiris. Scholars have either placed him in a make-believe world or have identified him with one particular object which has led to some confusion.

White Crown

When depicted in human form, Osiris always wore the white crown of Upper Egypt and never the red or double-crown (*shmty*).

We have examined unification and the fact that the kings did not show dominion over the 'two lands' by wearing the double-crown. We must now ask a similar question regarding Osiris: As the god of the dead '*par excellence*' he did not wear the unified double-crown but was only ever portrayed wearing the white crown. If we accept conventional wisdom, the white crown was worn to represent southern Egypt, but how could this be?

The afterlife was at the foundation of Egyptian religion. Most of what is known about ancient Egypt points to their obsession with the 'next world'. Yet the great god of the afterlife, Osiris, chose to wear the white crown symbolising Upper Egypt alone. Why divide Egypt in this way? If Osiris was the god of the afterlife for all, why not give him a crown representative of the whole of Egypt?

The fact that Osiris wore the white crown of Upper Egypt speaks volumes. It is very deliberate and precise in its meaning and informs us that Osiris presided over the land above as this was his kingdom. This belief was born from observations of planetary bodies as they transformed into stars while traversing out towards the blackness of space. It was a belief born from the trillions of divine stars which inhabited the *kemet*. This provided a direct link between the colour and symbolic meaning of the Upper Egyptian crown.

The white crown represented the white stars and Upper Egypt. Osiris may have occasionally visited Lower Egypt (Earth) in the form of a gigantic planet which took on the attributes of a star. In fact mythology speaks of Osiris as the first king of Egypt. However, the domain of Osiris was the land above which is why Osiris was shown wearing the white crown. This not only assists in our identification of Osiris, but it corroborates my definition of the 'two lands' as representing heaven and Earth.

All Egyptians wanted to be associated with Osiris when they died. This belief was so strong that Egyptians added his name to their own to form names such as 'Tutankhamun Osiris' or 'Ramesses Osiris'. Astral bodies became Osirians as they traversed to the land above and the inhabitants of the land above were viewed as real people wrapped in Osiris. Once they attained a life of bliss, the stars became 'all powerful ones' and were associated with Osiris. The land above was the domain of Osiris, particularly during the night, and the twinkling white stars were inextricably linked to this god.

OUR ANCIENT FOREBEARS ARE WITH US

Osiris as a hieroglyph

The most common hieroglyph for Osiris was the eye and the throne and there is a certain amount of dispute over the exact meaning of these glyphs.

The throne represented Osiris as the king of the afterlife and it symbolised the authority he exerted over the deceased as he transported them in the form of stars to the 'next world'. It symbolised the dominion of Osiris over Upper Egypt as this land came into view at night. It also symbolised Osiris as king of the 'all powerful ones' as he wrapped them up for the night in white linen.

The eye glyph associated with Osiris symbolised the divine inhabitants of the above _ the 'single-eyed' stars watching over us. The stars were perceived as real people as they slept during the night. They twinkled as if reaching out to us as singular points of light or 'eyes'. Osiris therefore adopted the 'eye' glyph and one of his aliases was 'Asar' meaning 'many eyed'. This is no coincidence as Osiris was the king of the *many-eyed* starry night.

Another hieroglyph associated with Osiris' is the *djed pillar* or *tet*. The association of Osiris with this particular glyph is unmistakable. The four horizontal layers at the top of the *djed pillar* are symbolic of the four corners of the Earth – the four cosmic pillars that hold up the 'land above'. This provides another connection between Osiris and the land above.

The Egyptians mummified the deceased in the image of Osiris. It was a slow and meticulous procedure which involved preserving the body before wrapping it in *white* linen. This strange practice is completely understandable when we consider the divine land above. The Egyptians preserved the body to enable the deceased to literally 'get up and go' in this very real world.

The use of *white* linen bandages can also be explained. It clearly represented the colour of the planets as they moved away from Earth. White also represented the divine stars. Colour was of paramount importance to the Egyptians and white stars and planetary bodies were represented exactly as they appeared and this was represented by wrapping white linen around the deceased. Direct observations of events above led to and dictated all beliefs and practices on Earth whether symbolically or otherwise.

While the use of white linen explains the colour connection with astral bodies and the stars, it doesn't explain why the Egyptians used long lengths of bandages to wrap the deceased. How did this practice come about? Why did they not use one large blanket or a few smaller sheets of white linen? The explanation involves the planets in chaos and the spinning of the original Horus king, Mars.

We have established that Mars was systematically torn apart 4,000 years ago which created tons of debris, dust and gasses which were blasted out into space. Mars also spun on its axis once every 24 hours in virtually the same pattern as Earth. It resembled a spiralling galaxy or slow motion Catherine wheel – a central core or body spinning and ejecting material. I believe this image was seen many times due to chaos and as Mars moved away from Earth, streams of white dust and gasses spiralled from its body. Mars, complete with spiralling debris, was perceived as a deceased king being mummified. The spiralling material which encircled Mars resembled white linen bandages as they slowly wrapped around the red planet. Mars therefore transformed into Osiris as it was dressed in white linen.

From the perspective of Earth, the Egyptians believed they were watching a god-king being mummified as he began his journey to the next world. In ancient Egypt, the entire process from death to burial took seventy days, fifteen of which were spent bandaging the body. I believe this time period was dictated by the actual time it took for Mars to move away from Earth to become a star, although this is merely a theory.

Mars was 'mummified' numerous times which set a precedent that lasted for 3,000 years. I believe the other main planetary bodies played no real part in the development of mummification. This is because the perennial queen Venus barely spins at all and is almost stationary. When Venus accompanied Mars for the first time, it did not produce debris in a spiral form as Mars did. It is likely that Venus was surrounded by tons of dust and gasses but, as it didn't spin, it did not take on the attributes of a spiralling galaxy. The other two main perpetrators,

Mercury and the Moon, were late editions to 'chaos' and therefore played no part in the origins of mummification.

Anubis

Who was responsible for mummification and who wrapped the bandages around the astral monarchy? Whose role was it to assist in the process of becoming an Osirian star? Who assisted Osiris in looking after the stars as they peacefully resided in the kemet? This role fell to the blackness of the night or, as the Egyptians perceived it, the god Anubis.

Anubis (Inpew, Yinepu, Anpu) was an ancient Egyptian god of the underworld who guided and protected the spirits of the dead. The worship of Anubis was an ancient one and probably predated the worship of Osiris. In the pyramid texts of Unas, his role was clear. He was associated with the Eye of Horus and was regarded as the guide of the dead in the afterlife, showing them the way to Osiris. The text stated: 'Unas standeth with the Spirits, get thee onwards, Anubis, into Amenti, onwards, onwards to Osiris'.

(http://www.touregypt.net/featurestories/anubis.htm)

Anubis was generally depicted as a black jackal-headed man or a black jackal. Unlike a real jackal, the head of Anubis was black which represented his position as a god of the dead. He was rarely shown fully-human, but was depicted as such in the Temple of Abydos of Ramesses II. There is a beautiful statue of him as a full jackal in the tomb of Tutankhamun   (ibid)

Anubis, yet another mythical figure brought to life

The Egyptians believed in a real world above canopying the flat Earth. It was a world inextricably linked to our world via the red Sun and the god-kings. It was bathed in light with no glare during the day and shrouded in darkness at night. A vast expanse of space existed between these two lands which came under the authority of many gods including Isis.

During the day, the chief god was the solar god Re. As master of the universe and the 'illuminator of the two lands', this was his domain. At night, as Re set in the west to battle the demons of the underworld (chaos), both lands became shrouded in darkness. I believe this 'blackness', the black space between Upper and Lower Egypt, was deified as the god Anubis. Anubis was basically the vast expanse of the night sky.

This identification makes sense in the context of the God King Scenario because Mars was a spiralling body wrapped by the night sky or Anubis. It was the role of the jackal god to wrap the kings in lengths of white linen bandages. Mars did not wrap himself in linen as this was the role of whatever entity surrounded Mars. At night, this was the blackness above which was Anubis. As Mars took on the traits of a spiralling galaxy, it was merely spinning off debris. From the perspective of the Egyptians, the god-king was transformed into Osiris by the god Anubis as he wrapped linen around the body. Anubis, as the blackness of above, assisted the god Osiris as he transformed the body of Mars into a star.

In many funerary paintings, Anubis was shown supervising the ritual 'weighing of the heart' which was the dreaded final reckoning of the dead. This decided whether or not a person could enter the kingdom of Osiris. As Anubis was located between the two lands, such scenes are self-explanatory. The recently deceased became Osiris and had to physically pass through Anubis. This position was reflected in an attribute of Anubis which was the 'opener of ways'. This was consistent with the 'blackness' above as it opened up the way to the 'next world'.

Upper Egypt was a duel world, but light from the Sun deemed it invisible during the day. At night, although shrouded in darkness, it opened its doors by becoming visible. The divine inhabitants, the descendents of those that had passed before, were also granted visibility as Anubis opened up the way to the blackness above.

Evidence that Anubis was in fact the 'blackness' above is found in the colouring of Anubis. Certain breeds of jackals do have a thin blackish line on their backs but they are typically a brownish colour, not black. It is also true that black-headed jackals do not exist, and yet Anubis commonly appeared as a black-headed jackal.

The 'Anubis black' was obviously chosen to represent the blackness of the night; the dark mass existing between the two lands. It clearly reveals that the 'blackness' surrounding the spinning Mars was embodied in the god Anubis. According to one of his epithets, Anubis was the god of mummification which was consistent with physical observations of astral bodies being wrapped in bandages by the blackness of space. Once again, colour was of paramount importance and there was a direct correlation between what was seen and what was painted.

As a god of the dead, Anubis was also the god of embalming. This was a special process where all moisture was removed from the body to leave a dried form that would not easily decay. This process typically turned the body a pitch black which linked to the colour of Anubis. Black was also the colour of fertility and was linked to death and rebirth in the afterlife. As Anubis controlled such a vast expanse of sky and guided many people in the afterlife, he was helped by 'men of Anubis' who assisted in the mummification process.

Why a Jackal?

There is a definite connection between Anubis, darkness and embalming. However, why was a jackal, which was a type of dog, used to represent the god of embalming and guide of the dead? Jackals are nocturnal animals and were often observed prowling around cemeteries at night. They were attracted to rotting flesh and their high sense of smell drew them to Egypt's cemeteries. It is highly unlikely that they actually reached the dead due to obstacles such as shifting sands, solid coffins and acres of linen wrapped around each body. I believe the Egyptians observed jackals prowling around graveyards and made a direct link between the animal and the dead. Jackals were therefore perceived as presiding over and protecting the deceased.

The trait of watching over the dead is played out in the epithet 'lord of the sacred land'. This referred to Anubis in the form of the night sky as he took care of the stars as they peacefully resided in the *kemet*. This was the nocturnal god Anubis who looked after and presided over the transposed Egyptians in the 'next world'. Among the beautiful treasures in Tutankhamun's tomb were two recumbent canine forms of Anubis which were placed there to protect the dead king in the afterlife. This was understandable and pointed to the blackboard of space which was the night sky deified as Anubis as it protected Tutankhamun (Mars) in the next world.

A god-king becoming a star

Abydos was the ancient cult centre of the god Osiris. Many pharaohs wanted to be buried at this site, or at least be present in spirit via a mortuary temple in their honour. The largest temple constructed by Seti I and dedicated to Osiris was the Osireion. It was here that the incredible process of a planet-king transforming into a star (Osiris) was written down.

We earlier identified Seti with the newly formed Mercury due to the Seth-state or evil state of this body shortly after its birth form Mars. The reliefs on the wall of the Osireion depict Seti in separate phases making his way to the afterlife. I propose this was Mercury becoming a star.

1. *First Anubis, the jackal headed deity, handed Seti a crook and a fan, the insignia of the god of the dead.*

This is symbolic of Mercury heading out into the blackness of the night; Mercury first passed through the god Anubis before beginning his journey towards the divine land, Upper Egypt.

2. He was given the sign of life by Thoth.

As mentioned many times, the Moon, because of its slow capture by the Earth, took on many names and roles, one of which was the god Thoth. Thoth was a facet of the Moon which also acted as an intermediary to the next world above. In a sense, Thoth gave Seti his blessing to begin his journey to the second land.

3.*The scene depicted Seti, still with a red face, but with his lower half mummified.*

This was Mercury as it was slowly wrapped in white linen. It is likely it took on the trait of a spiralling galaxy as it was slowly transformed into a star. Although the transmutation took its course, Seti's red face revealed he was still partially based in the mortal world. Although a white haze slowly shrouded Mercury, its red hue was still visible to the naked eye.

4. *Seti was shown as both pharaoh and priest at the same time.*

This curious behaviour has baffled many, but a celestial answer reveals that this was the god-king Seti/Mercury as he transformed himself, hence he was both pharaoh and priest. There may not have been any other celestial bodies close enough to perform this ritual although there are many variations to this.

5. He made a sacrifice complete with incense to celebrate his own death ritual. Finally, Re-Harakhte performed the last stage of the process.

This was symbolic of the 'god of the horizon', *Re-Harakhte,* as he performed the 'last rites' as Seti/Mercury joined the divine realm above.

This is clear support for the God King Scenario. It explains how the planets in chaos lived and died, and is yet another aspect of Egyptian mythology that can be attributed to real events above. The Egyptians were literally providing evidence of the processes involved as planets moved to and from Earth to become red orbs as they reigned over earth and stars in their journey to the above.

There are many variations of this. There were many different ways of attaining a life in the 'next would'. It was believed that some spent a life of eternity with the Sun god Re and the variations depended on what was occurring above. This involved much symbolism as the scenes above were transferred to tombs and temple walls.

How the 'double concept' between humans and astral bodies worked.

The God King Scenario maintains that the monarchy of ancient Egypt were first and foremost guises of planetary bodies. They were represented on earth via mortal doubles, people who believed they were at one with astral bodies.

Yet, how did mortals bond with astral bodies? To answer this, we need to look to the 'sacred' inscriptions where the entire 'double' concept is written down for us.

The physical body, the ka, ba and akh

The Egyptians believed each individual person was made up of many parts; the physical body, the ka, the ba, the akh, the name and the shadow. With a childlike outlook on the cosmos, it is easy to understand why the Egyptians believed that the shadows we cast have a spiritual existence. Our shadow is always with us and to a certain extent it appears to watch over us and protect us eternally. It was also reasonable for this ancient culture to believe a person's name was vital regarding the afterlife. They believed that simply mentioning the name of the deceased brought that person to life. However, of greater importance was the *ba, ka akh* and the physical body. If we consider these we will understand how humans were 'paired' with astral bodies.

Scholars do not understand the *ka*, *ba* and *akh,* or anything connected to the 'soul'. They cannot grasp how and why the Egyptians came to the belief that each person consisted of so many 'spiritual' parts. They are also at a loss to explain the true purpose and role of each part or 'soul'. They assume the entire spiritual concept is yet another aspect of a totally bewildering world.

'The precise meaning of ka, ba, ach (akh), `shm (sekhem) and so on is no longer clear to us. Well-meaning scholars try again and again and again to force the Egyptian idea of the soul into our traditional categories without enabling us to understand even a little of it any better.'

(Poortman, 1978)

I will offer a very simple and plausible explanation for the roles of the ba, ka and akh based solely on the convictions of the ancient Egyptians and the real world of celestial chaos.

Physical body

The physical body was very important. As resurrectionists, the Egyptians believed they would simply 'get up and go' in the next world'. It was therefore necessary to keep a person's earthly form intact which is why the Egyptians mummified the dead.

The 'ka'

The ka was the physical 'double' – it came into existence the moment a person was born. On many occasions the creator-god Khnum was shown modelling the ka on a potter's wheel at the same time as he was forming the body of a human.

In funerary art, a persons 'double' or ka was sometimes depicted as a slightly smaller figure standing behind the living being. When an individual died, the ka continued to live and as such required the same sustenance as the living person required in life. For this reason it was provided with genuine food offerings, or with representations of food depicted on the wall of the tomb. While not physically eating the food offerings, the ka was thought to absorb their preserving life force.

Many tombs and temples had false doors and these were west-orientated and served as a link between the living and the dead. Offerings were typically made to the ka before the false doors. After death, the ka was 'at rest' whilst the body was prepared and mummified. The ka was then reactivated so that the spiritual transformation of rebirth in the 'next world' could take place. The deceased then travelled to join their ka and by doing so, the link to the next-world through their tomb was established. The ka was represented as a hieroglyph consisting of a pair of arms pointing upwards. It was believed the two outstretched arms magically warded off evil forces. An interesting point to note is that the Egyptians believed that animals, plants, water and even stones had their own ka.

Giving physical identity to the 'ka'

As discussed, 4,000 years ago the whole solar system was engulfed in space debris; the skies of Earth were dominated by kingly planets and littered with incalculable amounts of asteroids and comets of various shapes and sizes. The Egyptians regarded the planets, stars, asteroids, comets and debris as real beings. They were not lumps of rock or dirty snowballs (asteroids and comets) as we know them, but real living, breathing individuals. They were also perceived to be physical 'doubles' of people living on Earth – they were the kas of the Egyptians.

Herein lies the key to understanding the Egyptian idea of the 'soul' and the entire 'double' concept. From the Egyptian perspective, a ka was not an individual being living a separate life in another world or dimension; it was not a spiritual part of a human as with our understanding of 'soul'. It was a real astral 'twin' or stellar 'double' living a parallel existence, totally 'at one' with humans.

The behavioural traits of these bodies dictated their roles and how they were perceived and this was drawn from the natural world. For example, rocky bodies orbiting around the monarchy were viewed as members of the royal court, fan bearers, scribes, overseers, concubines or right-hand men. The legions of rocks trailing behind Mars were the rank and file soldiers of the king. They sometimes acted as intermediaries or 'stepping stones' to the kings and gods, and any 'shaven headed' moons that orbited Earth were seen as the 'all powerful' priests of Egypt. The skies of earth were teeming with masses of cometary bodies and all were paired with or perceived to be the kas of humans. This included the enemy forces – the swarms of debris that smashed into the kings were 'doubles' of the enemy on Earth.

The following is taken from Queen Hatshepsut's mortuary temple at Deir el-Bahri. It is a request from Amun to Khnum for the creation of Hatshepsut and her *ka*.

'Amen-Ra called for Khnum, the creator, the fashioner of the bodies of men.'

'Fashion for me the body of my daughter and the body of her ka,' said Amen-Ra, 'A great queen shall I make of her, and honour and power shall be worthy of her dignity and glory.'

'O Amen-Ra,' answered Khnum, 'It shall be done as you have said. The beauty of your daughter shall surpass that of the gods and shall be worthy of her dignity and glory.'

*'So Khnum fashioned the body of Amen-Ra's daughter and the body of her ka, the two forms **exactly alike** and more beautiful than the daughters of men. He fashioned them of clay with the air of his potter's wheel and Heqet, goddess of birth, knelt by his side holding the sign of life towards the clay that the bodies of Hatshepsut and her ka might be filled with the breath of life.'* (My bold emphasis)

This is a perfect example of the god Khnum simultaneously creating two exact forms of the same person; the god Khnum fashioned two identical Hatshepsut's – one human and the other her ka or celestial 'double'. In this particular case it was a guise of the planet Venus (the majority of queens were guises of Venus). In other words this was a guise of Venus plus a mortal representative.

It was not possible for Egyptians to identify every double because size was the determining factor. Mortal kings, queens, courtiers, priests and other dignitaries could make a connection easily due to their association with the dominating planets, moons and other large bodies. However, commoners were associated with asteroids and comets and, because of their relatively small size, it was difficult to identify their respective kas. Nevertheless, all Egyptians vehemently believed in a 'double' above due to a belief brought about by cosmic chaos and a sky crowded with infinite bodies. The ka would occupy an intermediate or transitional space between the 'two lands' in the same intermediate location as the ruling kings.

Although existing above, a 'double' occupied a totally separate location to the divine stars. Stars dwelt in Upper Egypt which was the divine firmament whereas 'doubles' occupied an intermediate or transitional location somewhere between the 'two lands'. This, from the perspective of Earth, was roughly the same location as the ruling planets, the Sun and many of Egypt's enigmatic 'sky gods'. In effect, this was three basic locations and all of them were perceived to be inhabited by real beings. Lower Egypt or Earth was home to humans, an intermediate region was occupied by human 'doubles', and Upper Egypt or the 'land above' was home to the complete and eternal form of humans, the 'all powerful' stars. In simple terms there were two lands, one up one down, and an intermediate space in-between.

Although further research is required, I believe that by occupying the intermediate space, all Egyptian 'doubles' were involved with pharaoh's court. They took on roles such as viziers, overseers, fan bearers and foot soldiers and did not undertake agrarian tasks such as farming. Unlike Upper and Lower Egypt which were fixed lands where ploughing, sowing, reaping and harvesting took place, the intermediate space was not a firmament. It resembled a magical 'transitional' space; a world where pharaohs rode chariots of gold and electrum and where cosmic battles were fought. It was a place of activity where evil was an ever-present threat.

Life in the intermediate space was precarious and restless for all kas and this was in total contrast to the lifestyle of the divine Egyptians who had reached 'heaven' and who enjoyed a peaceful existence. Here ordinary Egyptians enjoyed more leisurely activities such as hunting and farming. This was recorded in the glorious afterlife scenes painted on the tomb walls of the ordinary Egyptians. Of course, royalty were an exception and upon 'rebirth' in the 'elysian fields', the pharaohs could take on any form they chose.

Despite the possibility of taking on slightly different roles, humans and their 'doubles' coexisted simultaneously; one existed on Earth and the other inhabited the transition world above. However, at death a person united with their ka to journey to the land above.

The 'ba'

The ba was considered to be an individual's distinctive manifestation similar to our concept of personality. It comprised all non-physical attributes which made a human unique. It was the entire deceased person with its own identity and was not separate from the body. In Ptolemaic and Roman times it was said of the deceased: 'May his ba live before Osiris.' The ba was depicted as a human headed bird (the head of the deceased) with human arms and the ba-bird could assume whatever shape it wished.

Having identified the ka, the ba is self explanatory. It was necessary for the deceased to journey from their tomb to unite with their ka if they were to be transformed into an akh (star). As the physical body could not do this, it was the job of the individual's ba to do this. After death, the ba-bird collected the deceased's personality from the mummified remains and took it to be reunited with the deceased's physical astral 'twin'. Only after this union, when a person was 'complete', was it possible for them to be reborn as an 'effective one' in the 'next world', the 'black land' of space.

Although this point was not entirely clear, it is possible that the process of transferring one's 'manifestation' took time, with the ba flitting between the mummified remains and the ka to ensure every aspect of its humanity was transferred to its 'double' above. It was therefore helpful for the perfectly persevered body to lie in state in its tomb. This gave the ba-bird plenty of time to relocate every aspect of the deceased person's personality as it carried out its duty. This time-span was probably adopted from observations of Mars as it was slowly wrapped in white linen as it moved away from Earth.

The bird form was chosen because of its ability to navigate land, sea, air and space, although the Egyptians were unaware that space was devoid of air. They believed that conditions above were similar to those on Earth, particularly in relation to Upper Egypt which was exactly the same as Earth, only better. The Egyptians believed all astral bodies were living kas. After death, it made sense to use the ba-bird as a manifestation of oneself to provide a direct link to ones ka.

Once the ba and ka were united and the astral 'twin' was 'complete', a final journey to the 'next world' was undertaken. This was a journey fraught with dangers as the body travelled from a chaotic intermediate location to the relative tranquillity of heaven. Chaos posed an ever-present threat in the transitional location and Egyptians therefore needed assistance. Magical funerary spells and amulets were used to help guarantee a safe passage. Known as the 'Book of the Dead,' spells were written on papyri and placed in coffins or were put in magical amulets and wrapped in mummy bandages. Much time and resources were spent assisting the dead to the 'next world' where they were transformed into the ultimate form – that of an immortal akh.

The akh (star)

The akh was the fully resurrected and glorified form of the deceased in the next world. An akh was regarded as enduring and unchanging for all eternity and it was the goal of every Egyptian to become one. The word akh means an 'effective one' or 'powerful one.' The Egyptians believed the imperishable stars were akhs, the ancestors of those who had passed before them. Once a person had successfully become an akh they could guide their loved ones on Earth. It was believed that the akh could reach beyond the limits of the afterlife to have both positive and negative effects in the realm of the mortal world.

Below are typical Egyptian stars to be found on many tomb ceilings. This is a very unusual way to draw a star, this is because it represents the limbs and head of a human being i.e. two arms, two legs and the head.

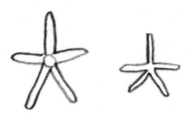

It always surprises me that the Egyptian belief in the transformation of humans into stars after death is brushed aside as a bizarre belief which cannot be explained. Yet this belief provides invaluable information – the Egyptians were not only showing themselves transposed as stars, but they were also revealing the location of their 'next world'. This was the hemispherical blackness of space which canopied the four corners of Earth. It was the 'next world' which all ancient cultures were obsessed with and which all aspired to be reborn in.

The meaning of akh as 'effective one' or 'powerful one' should be regarded as a descriptive name or title. This is because, although the name refers to the stars above, they were individual humans and each maintained their own distinct personalities and individual names. These were the traits and names given to them while they were on Earth. Similarly, although the deceased added the name of the god Osiris to their own (i.e. Ramesses-Osiris, Tutankhamun-Osiris), they still maintained their individuality.

There were basic reasons for the addition of the name Osiris. First, Osiris was a 'star attribute' and shrouded and protected the deceased as they made their way to heaven. The Egyptians were symbolically describing actual events by adding the name Osiris and they were also encapsulating the protective force of this god. Secondly, the inhabitants of above only came into view at night when they were in

'Osirian form' as stars. This was obviously seen as Osiris protecting the Egyptians – stars were reanimated Egyptians snugly wrapped up by Osiris as they slept.

I believe this belief was epitomised by the physical form of the akh which was usually portrayed as a mummiform figurine; this is clearly a direct symbolic representation of the Egyptians as they slept during the night. The coming into view of thousands of akhs (Osirians) during the night is also why Upper Egypt was often referred to as the 'Kingdom of Osiris'.

There is some evidence to suggest that the Egyptians believed that once you had attained the status of an akh, the tomb and the body had served its purpose (source; Hidden Egypt Discovery Channel, 2006). This seems logical because once eternal life had been attained there would be no need for either. However, this belief is not entirely clear. Would the Egyptians have tempted fate by disposing of their preserved body and tomb for eternity?

Through preservation of the body, they would at least maintain some kind of presence in this world. There are references to the spirit of the deceased rising anew each day as the Sun rose and this suggests the spirit of the mummified body came alive every morning. However, I believe the Egyptians were explaining how the inhabitants of Upper Egypt (the akhs) rose with their Earthly relatives as Re dawned in the East to illuminate the two lands of heaven and Earth.

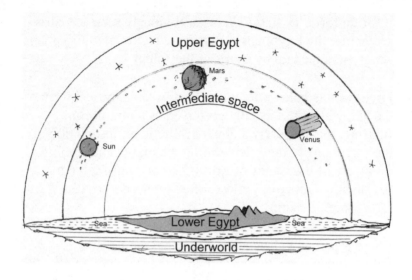

This is the world as seen through Egyptian eyes. The Egyptians believed that at birth, two of them were created _ an earthly form and a sky double or ka which dwelt in the intermediate space between heaven and Earth _ Upper and Lower Egypt. After they died, and by means of the ba bird transferring their personality, the earthly form would unite with its astral double to undertake a final and hazardous journey to a very real firmament above. Here a life of immortality was attained among the stars. This entire afterlife 'next world' belief was a direct result of planetary bodies traversing between our 'flat' Earth and the hemispherical dome of heaven.

THE HEAVENS DICTATE AND HUMANS FOLLOW

We have established the basic structure of the 'double concept'. We have the key to understanding how a world dominated by cosmic chaos formed the very foundation of the entire Egyptian concept of life, and more importantly death. It matters little how this concept was dressed up in the form of the many enigmatic tomb scenes. If we strip these scenes down to their most basic components, they are underpinned by the belief in the two lands of heaven and Earth and how individuals aspired to a life of eternity in the land above.

The 'double' concept and the monarchy

Although all Egyptians believed they possessed a real, physical 'double' above, the majority of the nation was unable to physically determine their double in the sky above. Size was the determining factor and the larger the planetary body, the easier it was to locate and observe the 'soul'. The ordinary man struggled to identify their 'soul' because they were associated with the smaller chunks of space debris such as asteroids and comets. During periods of celestial chaos, a continually changing and overcrowded sky made it extremely difficult to physically single out a particular piece of rock.

A slightly different scenario existed for those who were associated with larger bodies such as moons, satellites or large chunks of rock. They took on a variety of roles which depended on their actions and location in relation to the king, i.e. courtiers, dignitaries, viziers, concubines etc.

They stood a better chance of physically observing their astral counterparts even though cosmic chaos and the ever-changing sky caused identification problems.

One area where little or no confusion existed was with the largest bodies in the heavens, the red-orbed planets. There were few mistakes made when identifying these heavenly bodies. It was difficult to miss such large red orbs which dominated the heavens and earthly kings and queens easily singled out their divine astral counterparts. Yet, what happened if one or the other died, and what were the criteria for choosing the human royal family?

These above areas are not entirely clear and much research is still required to clarify matters, but for now it is important to remember that the heavens dictated events, divine order ruled, and where possible the mortals followed. It was never the other way round.

Who represented the astral monarchy? How were humans chosen to be at one with the sky kings?

The strongest and fittest humans took control of Egypt. Once established, they took over as the ruling royal family and reigned over Egypt with an iron fist, doing everything possible to maintain power and their royal bloodline. The pinnacle of this elite group, the king, had the right to be 'at one' with the strong and righteous king of the heavens, Mars (later Mercury and the Moon). All Egyptians believed in astral counterparts and an afterlife in a real Upper Egyptian 'duel world' and no dissention was permitted.

At what point were human monarchs declared king?

Ideally the birth of a human king coincided with the birth of an astral king and the two became bonded 'as one' from the very beginning. Unfortunately this happened rarely, if ever. So at what point were humans paired with astral counterparts? This is a grey area and not much is known about it. However, it may be possible to glean information from other areas to try to understand what occurred.

It is a fact that there were no rules for kingship. The Egyptians had no idea who would be king; they did not know who would be next in line for the throne. They believed 'divine order' and the gods dictated the entire process of kingship. The coronation and naming of the planets took precedence over the exaltation of mortal beings. In other words, there was no way a human king could take kingship without the presence of an astral 'double' because the gods would not allow it. Once a planet was 'born' to Earth, a human representative was chosen. That is why the naming of kings derived from the location and attributes of the planetary bodies and not from the behavioural traits of humans. In fact, humans played no part in this other than to record the attributes of planetary kings.

With the above in mind, the Egyptians probably had a 'king in waiting' who was not a newborn baby but a young male in readiness for kinship. This 'chosen one' would be prepared for Mars to move close to Earth before it shed its Osirian image and took on its familiar appearance of a red orb. Only when Mars became the 'Horus of the heavens' could it be named and simultaneously paired with a human counterpart. Although seemingly insignificant, I suggest this because there is a distinct lack of any references to royal babies in Egyptian history; it seems the infant stage was conveniently skipped in relation to kingship.

There were many references to young boys taking to the throne at a very early age, particularly in the New Kingdom. For example, Tutankhamun was only nine years old when he ascended the throne, yet there were no references to newborn god-kings. When planetary bodies became 'born' to Earth, the majority of them were perceived as red blooded young men and not newborn babies. The Egyptians would not have believed that a manifestation of the god Horus was a newly born baby sent down from heaven to reign over Egypt. The 'baby stage' probably occurred when astral bodies slowly transformed themselves from stars into distinctive red orbs. In the form of the true 'god of Earth', many immediately engaged in battling the forces of evil. This is another reason why they were regarded as young, red blooded warriors and not newborn battling babies.

What if there were no ruling planets?

Apart from Intermediate Periods, also known as dark ages, there was rarely a time when Egypt was not ruled by somebody including kings, queens, Theban princes and foreign rulers. The Egyptians latched onto the largest body or bodies as rulers of Egypt. In the absence of a true Horus of the heavens, they would have turned to lesser bodies as rulers of Egypt which may have included 'shepherd' moons or armies of rocky bodies. If they controlled the skies for long enough, they had to be appeased because the ancient skies dictated whether or not humans lived or died.

A good example of 'evil' lesser bodies ruling Egypt was the Hyksos. Records show that the Hyksos conquered and ruled Egypt sometime prior to the birth of the New Kingdom. Despite ruling Egypt for many decades, scholars are baffled by the Hyksos. They are mystified not only by their origins but also by how such an illusive people managed to form an army strong enough to defeat the mighty Egyptians. The Hyksos seemingly disappeared off the face of the Earth having being expelled, and this has left academics totally perplexed. It seems that the Hyksos existed in words only as there is no archaeological evidence to prove they ever existed.

Our only knowledge of the Hyksos comes from Egyptian hieroglyphs _ there were no specific Hyksos writings which told of their expulsion. Scholars struggle with the name Hyksos which was once translated as 'shepherd kings'. However, because scholars cannot envisage how shepherds were able to conquer a great nation such as Egypt, it is now translated as 'foreign kings'.

As we have already proposed, the Hyksos never existed on Earth as they were foreign celestial bodies. They were exactly as their name described _ 'shepherd kings'. They were large rogue moons that 'shepherded' debris in their wake. They also wreaked havoc above and below, hence their association with the evil god Seth. The names of the Hyksos kings were carved in cartouches. This was because the Egyptians, in the absence of Mars, Mercury and the moon, placated the dominant evil force above and the Egyptians once again made an association with the heavens.

In the absence of familiar kings, the Egyptians associated with whatever ruled the heavens at that time, whether evil or good, native or foreign. These bodies were worshiped and viewed as doubles of the people living on Earth. Humans joined with the doubles after death to take the final journey to the eternal and fixed land above.

It is unlikely that the Egyptians would have associated with foreign bodies on a whim. A foreign body would have existed for a number of years before the Egyptians accepted it as ordained by god. I believe up to ten years would have passed before foreign bodies were accepted as the just and righteous rulers and the 'doubles' of people on Earth. The Hyksos ruled for much longer than this, so it is easy to see why they commanded a mention in ancient history. With the firm belief that heaven was a dome-shaped canopy over the Earth, the Egyptians made associations and 'assimilated' with astral bodies.

What would happen if a human king died before his celestial counterpart?

Pharaonic Mars appeared as a red orb and a human king was chosen to be 'at one' with Mars and they reigned together for a few years. What happened if the human king died? Given the high mortality rate of ancient cultures (the average life expectancy was 35 years), this situation would have occurred many times. It was therefore unfeasible for an astral king to rule without a human counterpart because this would have severed any links to the afterlife. So, what was the procedure when a human king died before its respective planet?

We need to examine how royal families organised the line of succession to the throne. The eldest son of the monarch was heir to the throne followed by his sons and then his daughters. Next in line were any other sons of the monarch and their sons, followed by the monarch's daughters and their children (sons first, then daughters). Therefore when a king died, the eldest son took the throne followed by his sons etc. As kings and queens came and went, all heirs moved a step nearer to the throne. When a new king took to the throne, he immediately 'bonded' with the current reigning planetary king. He took over from his predecessor and joined with Mars to establish a vital link between heaven and earth. It was imperative to maintain this link because everything passed through the pharaoh.

The elite royal family did everything possible to maintain the royal bloodline and keep the power in the family. If no immediate family member was available to take the throne, a brother or distant cousin may be chosen followed by other distant relatives. If the bloodline died out, the all-powerful Egyptian priests (or those connected to the royal court) nominated a 'chosen one'. It was imperative that a replacement was found and 'paired' with the celestial king because one could not exist without the other. Divine order depended on this pairing and, by connecting with the above, a porthole to the gods and the afterlife was established.

Same birth names

Why did some kings maintain the same birth name? For example, there were at least eleven kings called Ramesses and nine of them ruled in succession. It is evident that each of these kings died while Mars still reigned. Mars was in close proximity to the Sun god Re and was therefore named Ramesses meaning 'fashioned by Re'. If a human king was paired with Mars but, for whatever reason, died within a few short years, the human incarnation of Mars had died. The next-in-line took over but, because Mars was still 'fashioned by Re', the new king retained the same birth name. However, by this time Mars had altered its attributes slightly and, in celebration of a new human king, the secondary name of Ramesses was changed slightly to give Ramesses I, II, III etc. This was Mars in the guise of Ramesses as he was separated into nine successive reigns as a result of the premature deaths of earthly 'doubles'.

There were a number of other kings who adopted the practice of keeping their predecessors birth name while ruling in succession. For example, Tuthmosis I, II & III (separated by only Hatshepsut), Amenhotep II, II and IV (separated only by Tuthmosis), Intef I, II and III and Mentuhotep I, II, and III etc. This rule was not set in stone, although the high mortality rates of the time played a part in this practice. However, the rule that the heavens dictated and the mortals followed still held true.

Genealogy: confusion reigns

The genealogy and chronology of Egypt's royal family is in turmoil as scholars are not certain who was related to who. The incomplete historical record was exacerbated by the fact that royal brothers and sisters, and even fathers and daughters, apparently inter-married. It is therefore difficult to work out how a particular pharaoh was related to his successor and many unidentified mummies add to the problem.

The example of Tutankhamun

Tutankhamun's parentage is uncertain. An inscription implies he was a king's son, but it is not clear which king this referred to. Most scholars think he was either the son of Amenhotep III (though probably not by his Great Royal Wife Tiye) or the son of Amenhotep III's son Akhenaten, born around 1342 BC. However, Professor James Allen argues that Tutankhamun was probably the son of the short-lived king Smenkhkare rather than Akhenaten. Allen argues that Akhenaten consciously chose a female co-regent named Neferneferuaten to succeed him rather than Tutankhamun. This would not have happened if Tutankhamun had been his son

(http://en.wikipedia.org/wiki/Tutankhamun).

Another example was that of the nine kings called Ramesses:

*'The exact relationships of the subsequent kings bearing the name Ramesses is at times **obscure**; certainly Ramesses IV, V, VI ad VIII **appear** to have been sons of Ramesses III (although, as noted, many of his sons died young), while Ramesses VII **seems** to have been a son of Ramesses VI.'*

(Clayton, 1994, p 166 – my bold emphasis)

I believe the genealogy problem existed partly because the royal bloodline did indeed die out. In effect, as changes occurred in the cosmos, the Egyptian families were sometimes left without a true bloodline representative. On these occasions, families forced the Egyptian priests to nominate non-family members to the role of king. This provides a simple and plausible explanation for the confusion surrounding the ancestry of the earthly royal family. Any confusion that exists could be ended by DNA testing. Unfortunately, DNA testing cannot be carried out on royal mummies. In an article at www.thetimes.co.uk, renowned Egyptian archaeologist Zahi Hawass (now Head of Egyptian Antiquities) stated regarding DNA testing: 'It is not always accurate and cannot be done with complete success when dealing with mummies. Until we know for sure that it is accurate, we will not use it in our research'.

This is perplexing because we could gain much knowledge by selective testing. Certain monarchs have been x-rayed and in the past mummies such as Tutankhamun were actually moved. It is likely that DNA testing will eventually be allowed, so it is puzzling that it is not permitted now. It may be possible that DNA cannot be extracted from a 4,000 year old mummy, but the situation is unclear.

If DNA testing is eventually allowed and successfully extracted, it will reveal much vital information. It will enable the identification of various kings and queens and their relatives. We will know if Ramesses IV through to VIII were the offspring of Ramesses III as records stated and we may also discover the true identity of Tutankhamun's father. DNA testing will also confirm whether the Egyptians adopted the practice of crowning non-royal family members when the true bloodline died out.

We have mentioned the Hyksos and how, in the absence of the main bodies, the Egyptian elite associated with lesser bodies such as rogue moons. If a body such as the Moon emerged among foreign bodies such as the Hyksos (which happened with the pharaoh Amose), the rulers of Egypt simply promoted themselves to join with these more familiar bodies, thereby associating themselves with the true Horus of the heavens.

The deceased human kings

What happened to the body of a king who died while Mars remained dominant above? Was he given full burial rights and embalmed and mummified amid various religious rituals even though Mars did not physically die? Could he look forward to an eternal life among the stars? It is likely that this situation occurred numerous times during 3,000 years of pharonic Egypt and it is therefore important to clarify what happened in such cases.

If a king died while Mars remained dominant, the deceased monarch was still treated as a royal one. They had served their term and had carried out their duty in maintaining divine order, albeit symbolically. It was the will of the gods that they should pass on to the next world, and this is how the Egyptians viewed matters. There were nine successive pharaohs called Ramesses and I believe they reigned as a result of the premature death of earthly doubles; many were chosen because the king died and a replacement had to be found. Yet, apart from Ramesses VIII, none were buried in the Valley of the Kings although they were all given traditional burials. Therefore it is logical to assume that every one of them attained an afterlife even though Ramesses/Mars was not physically observed being transported to the above by the god Osiris.

As Mars was not seen to physically die, this was a symbolic journey. In the early years of cosmic chaos, Mars set a precedent for the next world and the entire afterlife concept. All believed they would go on to attain a life of immortality. I have a number of theories regarding the after-death prospects of the Egyptian monarchy. I propose that if the king died during the day, he was perceived as spending an eternal life with the Sun god Re (there are many references to kings doing just that). If a king died at night, he was perceived as spending eternity among the stars. None of this is certain, but we do know that after death, the kings could take on any form of their choosing.

What if the planet died before its mortal representative?

Mars/Ramesses, along with its human form, reigned together in perfect harmony for a number of years before slowly moving away from Earth. Finally it died as it slowly transformed into the god Osiris. This was a temporary death as Mars/Ramesses was merely being transported to Upper Egypt, the duel world above. As this event occurred numerous times, what happened to the earthly Ramesses? What fate was in store for human kings when their ka died?

Where a planet died before its mortal representative, there would be a ritual sacrifice. The human form had to unite with its ka if it was to stand any chance of immortality. If a celestial king died by moving away from Earth, it was imperative for its human counterpart to unite with it. Ruling without an astral counterpart was sacrilege and was against the fundamental beliefs of divine order.

The doctrine of heaven had to be obeyed and if god-king planets died, human kings had to follow. The only way this could happen was through the death of the king. I believe human kings were ritually sacrificed when their respective bodies were physically observed transforming into the god Osiris. If we consider the God King Scenario and the practice of ritual sacrifice, this is the only logical and plausible explanation.

Although very much a grey area, Egyptologists do mention the possibility of ritual sacrifice of the kings:

'There is some speculation that the pharaohs of Egypt were ritually sacrificed at the end of their term, and that the Sed Festival, or jubilee, was originally the moment of truth for the pharaoh, who would celebrate his reign and then accept the bite of a poisonous asp.'

'While direct evidence for this practice is scanty now, it is interesting that Cleopatra chose this method to end her own life when she believed that it was futile for her to attempt to continue her rule of Egypt.'

'Did she know something we don't about the practice of ritual royal suicide in previous times?'

(http://www.touregypt.net/featurestories/isishiss.htm)

Renowned Egyptologist Bob Briar, in connection with the enigmatic Heb-Sed Festival, echoes these thoughts as follows:

'What happens if the pharaoh becomes old and feeble, what do you do? Well, there's a tradition, people talk about it, that in the early days, the pharaoh was killed, ritually…literally but ritually; as a ritual when he got too old so that a new king could take his place. We don't have a lot of evidence for that but we talk about it.'

(History of Ancient Egypt, Bob Briar, Lecture CDs)

'I am convinced that many kings over the 3,000 years of pharaonic Egypt were ritually sacrificed. This was not done because they were old and feeble but was carried out to enable them to unite with astral bodies in the heavens. Although dating from earlier times, there is physical evidence for this.'

(http://www.ancient-egypt.org/index.html)

'At the royal cemetery of Umm el-Qa'ab near Abydos, the tombs of the 1st Dynasty kings from Aha to Qa'a are accompanied by subsidiary burials. These burials are arranged in rows or blocks and either extend from the royal tomb, as with Aha, or surround it. The position of the subsidiary tombs compared to the royal tomb is believed to reflect the relationship of their occupants to the king during life.

Several tombs were found to contain skeletal remains. An analysis of the remains found in the subsidiary graves of Aha's tomb has shown that none of the individuals buried there were older than 25 years. This suggests that they were chosen to be buried along with the king.

The superstructure covering the tombs of Semerkhet and Qa'a also appears to cover the subsidiary burials. This indicates that the subsidiary burials occurred at the same time as the royal burial which means all subsidiary burials predate the royal burial or occurred at the same time. In the latter case, the tomb of Semerkhet provides the earliest known evidence of retainer sacrifice.

In view of the evidence, it is likely that, apart from Narmer, all kings of the 1st Dynasty chose members of their household and staff to be buried with them (Retainer sacrifice). It is, however, surprising that some of them held high office during their lives. The way they were put to death is not clear, as no trace of violence has been found on their skeletal remains.'

(http://www.ancient-egypt.org/index.html)

"Brenda Baker, a physical anthropologist from Arizona State University, examined all the skeletons from Aha's enclosure and found no signs of trauma. She stated: 'The method of their demise is still a mystery. My guess is that they were drugged.'"

(http://www7.nationalgeographic.com/ngm/0504/feature7/)

And from the same source we find the following quote:

'Beside his tomb more than 30 graves were laid out in three neat rows. As the ceremony climaxed, several lions were slain and placed in a separate burial pit. As Aha's body was lowered into a brick-lined burial chamber, a select group of loyal courtiers and servants also took poison and joined their king in the next world.'

'Archaeologists have been sifting through the dry sands of Abydos for more than a century. Now they have found compelling evidence that ancient Egyptians indeed engaged in human sacrifice, shedding new, and not always welcome, light on one of the ancient world's great civilizations.'
(ibid)

Retainer sacrifices are believed to have occurred when the king died and his followers took their own lives and followed the king to the next world. But what if the king, in order to unite with his soul, took his own life? Mars may have prompted this action by moving away from Earth. As the incarnation of Mars, the king's followers were represented by the numerous asteroids and comets orbiting the red planet. As Mars moved away from Earth, it died and took the royal court with him. Therefore the original warrior king was directly responsible for the early mass sacrificial events. We are still not clear how or why such a practice ever evolved if it was not ordained by the gods.

Scholars are not sure why retainer sacrifices died out. It may have been due to economics and a developing intelligence. In later times ushabtis were introduced – these were the small figurines which assisted the deceased in the next life. These 'helpers' may have partly negated the need to have the whole royal court take part in ritual suicide. If they had continued with a policy of ritual suicide as Egypt developed and its population expanded, it would have left a tremendous void with nobody to preside over Egypt's vast empire or worship the gods.

It is evident that the Egyptians were not unfamiliar with ritual sacrifice. It was most definitely practiced in earlier times and in all probability was a lot more widespread than we think. I believe the sacrificial death of royal figures continued right up until Egypt's demise sometime in the third century BC. Earthly kings committed suicide many times in order to join with their 'souls' as they departed Earth's skies.

A typical suicide in ancient Egypt involved taking poison because it left the body intact and a complete body was essential for resurrection in the next world. Is it possible to prove this through DNA? Unfortunately, DNA will not provide the cause of death. There has always been much speculation over the death of certain kings. For example,

Ramesses II had a severe abscess in his lower jaw and it has been claimed that he died from this. Whether he or other kings took a lethal dose of poison will never be known. We cannot rule out violent sacrificial deaths such as death by sword or something similar. Although there is little or no evidence for this with Egyptian royalty, there is speculation that some close aids of the royal family may have ended their days in this way.

There is much more that can be said about ritual sacrifices in ancient Egypt, and this subject will be covered in more detail in subsequent volumes. For now we must be satisfied with the fact that retainer sacrifices died out for whatever reason and there is insufficient evidence at present to establish exactly why this occurred.

As I draw 'An Ancient World in Chaos' to a close, do not think we have reached the end of our journey. This book has merely paved the way for us to unearth more historical and astronomical evidence concerning cosmic chaos and ancient Egyptian history. You may have found some of the facts contained in this book difficult to accept and this is to be expected. We all reside within our own comfort zone and anything that questions long-established beliefs makes us feel uncomfortable. But I urge you to keep an open mind and use your own reasoning. By doing so, you will be able to absorb a whole new world of endless possibilities. Science does not have the answers to all of life's mysteries, and certain scientific 'facts' are anything but! So continue with me as I strive to unravel further truths concerning our ancient forebears in the 'God King Scenario' series.

BIBLIOGRAPHY

Ackerman, J. (1999), *Firmament: Recent Catastrophic History of the Earth,* Angiras.

Ackerman, J. (1999), *Chaos: A New Solar System Paradigm,* Angiras.

Chapman, A. (2002), *Gods in the Sky: Astronomy from the Ancients to the Enlightenment,* Channel 4 Books, London.

Clayton, P. (1994), *Chronicle of the Pharaohs,* Thames & Hudson Ltd, London

Davies,W. (1987) *Egyptian Hieroglyphs (Reading the Past),* British Museum Press, London.

Excerpts from a hymn dedicated to Hathor at the Temple of Horus and Edfu.

Faulkner, R. (1989), *The Ancient Egyptian Book of the Dead,* British Museum Press, London.

Faulkner, R. (1994), *Egyptian Book of the Dead: Book of Going Forth by Day*, Chronicle Books, California.

Gardiner, A. (1957) *Egyptian Grammar,* Oxford University Press, Oxford.

Henry, J. (2001), *Breasted Ancient Records of Egypt: Eighteenth Dynasty v. 2,* University of Illinois Press, Illinois, US.

Naville, E. (1913) *Eleventh Dynasty Temple at Deir El Bahari: Pt. 3*, Egypt Exploration Society, Egypt.

Partridge, R. (2002), *Fighting Pharaohs: Weapons and Warfare in Ancient Egypt,* Peartree Publishing, London.

Poortman, J. (1978), *Vehicles of Consciousness: The concept of hylic pluralism (Ochema)* Theosophical Publishing House, London.

Robins, G. (2000), *The Art of Ancient Egypt*, British Museum Press, London.

Shaw, I., Nicholson, P. (2002), *The British Museum Dictionary of Ancient Egypt,* British Museum Press, London.

Velikovsky, I. (1950), *Worlds in Collision,* Gollancz, London.

WEBSITES

http://www.astrobio.net/cgi-bin/xls.cgi?sid=1329&ext=.xls

http://www.touregypt.net/featurestories/re.htm

http://saturn.jpl.nasa.gov/multimedia/images/image-details.cfm?imageID=2347

INDEX

Akerman, 42
Akhenaten, 48, 154, 187, 188, 224, 250, 251, 252, 253, 255, 256, 257, 258, 259, 271, 273, 284, 16, 52
Akhenaten., 15, 257, 258, 269, 52
Amarna period, 69, 85, 86, 87, 91, 101, 196, 197, 255
Amarna Period, 48
Amen, 7, 175, 231, 249, 36
Amon, 7
Amun, 7, 8, 9, 11, 13, 14, 15, 16, 17, 18, 22, 23, 24, 50, 63, 72, 73, 83, 116, 171, 176, 185, 186, 187, 190, 191, 194, 196, 197, 222, 224, 231, 248, 249, 250, 251, 252, 254, 260, 263, 265, 272, 275, 276, 283, 36
An Ancient World in Chaos, xi, 1
ancient culture prior to 300 BC, 24
Anqet, 6
anthropomorphic deities, 2
Anubis, 10, 171, 25, 26, 27, 28, 29, 30
aphelion of Venus, 37
aphelion to its inferior conjunctions, 37
Assyrian army, 30
asteroid, 58, 102, 103
astronomers, 23, 44, 103
atef crown, 10, 17
Aten, 48, 62, 69, 70, 75, 85, 86, 91, 99, 101, 142, 162, 250, 251, 252, 253, 255, 256, 258
axis mundi, 39
Baal was a rider of clouds, 6
Bible, 31
birth of pharonic Egypt, 111
bizarre world \dominated by hundreds of fictitious gods, 25
bizarre world of the ancient Egyptians, 3
blinding, yellow Sun, 92
Bronze Age I (BA I), 36
bubbling caldron of molten lava, 98

bubbling caldron of molten lava, 98
Cairo Museum, 18, 64, 178
Cassini division, 129
catastrophic explosions, 95
catastrophists, 27, 42, 47, 49, 55, 56, 158, 177
celestial bodies, 11, 31, 48, 103, 124, 125, 127, 131, 135, 180, 228, 229, 253, 48
Christ, 66
CIAS, 35, 67
Cleopatra, 46, 62, 146, 154, 158, 170, 188, 224, 277, 56
Coast to Coast AM,, 94
concentric landmasses, 39
constellation Orion, 23
cosmic chaos, 1, 10, 16, 27, 33, 34, 35, 43, 44, 46, 56, 57, 59, 60, 61, 64, 65, 66, 68, 96, 98, 99, 101, 103, 108, 110, 111, 117, 148, 149, 154, 158, 162, 166, 167, 169, 174, 185, 192, 199, 201, 232, 234, 238, 240, 241, 243, 246, 259, 263, 266, 269, 270, 293, 306

Cosmic hoover, 95
Cosmologists, 100, 108, 159
creator god Anu, his sons Enlil and Enki, 25
crook and the flail, 2
Dark Age in the 6th century AD, 21
daughter of Re, 13, 123, 132
Dog Star, Sirius, 23
duck glyph, 83, 91
Earth as meteorites, 105
Earth in Upheaval, 28
Earth and its flora and fauna were wiped out, 99
Earth. Mars dominated the heavens 97
Egypt, vi, 1, 2, 4, 5, 7, 8, 11, 19, 26, 33, 34, 46, 48, 57, 61, 64, 65, 67, 68, 69, 70, 72, 75, 76, 79, 82, 84, 85, 87, 89, 90, 92, 101, 106, 110, 111, 112, 114, 116, 119, 121, 123, 125, 132, 133, 138, 144, 145, 149, 150, 152, 154, 157, 158, 164, 167, 170, 171, 173, 175, 176, 179, 180, 181, 182, 185, 186, 187, 189, 190, 191,

193, 195, 196, 197,
199, 200, 201, 202,
204, 205, 206, 208,
209, 210, 213, 214,
216, 219, 220, 221,
222, 224, 226, 228,
232, 235, 236, 240,
244, 245, 247, 248,
249, 252, 253, 256,
258, 259, 262, 264,
270, 271, 274, 275,
277, 278, 279, 280,
282, 283, 285, 286,
287, 288, 289, 290,
291, 292, 293, 294,
295, 297, 299, 300,
301, 302, 304, 305, 306
Egyptian civilisation
totally collapsed, 20
Egyptians, 1, 2, 3, 4, 5, 6,
7, 10, 11, 13, 16, 18,
19, 20, 21, 22, 23, 25,
26, 27, 33, 34, 47, 48,
53, 59, 61, 62, 63, 64,
65, 66, 69, 70, 71, 72,
73, 74, 75, 76, 79, 80,
84, 85, 86, 87, 88, 90,
91, 92, 93, 105, 110,
113, 114, 115, 116,
118, 122, 127, 128,
135, 140, 142, 143,
148, 153, 154, 155,
162, 166, 167, 168,
169, 170, 176, 177,
178, 180, 184, 185,
186, 189, 191, 192,
195, 196, 197, 199,
200, 202, 204, 205,
206, 208, 209, 210,
211, 213, 216, 220,
225, 226, 233, 234,
238, 240, 241, 247,
250, 252, 253, 254,
255, 256, 258, 261,
262, 264, 265, 267,
268, 271, 275, 276,
277, 278, 280, 282,
283, 286, 287, 288,
289, 290, 291, 292,
293, 295, 296, 297,
298, 299, 300, 302,
303, 304, 306
Egyptologists, 3, 8, 14,
16, 20, 23, 56, 115,
134, 175, 193, 197,
214, 217, 233, 234,
237, 239, 241, 243,
245, 257, 261, 263,
264, 274, 279, 283,
291, 292, 300, 306
El Amarna, 101
electromagnetic force,
156
energy dissipation, 40
enormous ocean tide, 40
enormous volcanic
impact-crater, 94
entire GKS, 93

erratic bodies, 104
explain the workings of the cosmos, 3, 11, 12, 13, 26, 27, 189
Fertile Crescent., 41
fig tree excreted 'milk', 131
Firmament', 35, 38, 42
five-pointed stars, 91
flat top crown with two long plumes, 7
flat-topped yellow crown, 88
flooding, 40, 41, 202, 281
form of light, 135, 139
four 'kalpas', 39
fragmented and dispersed, 104
galactic interloper smashed into Jupiter, 93
Gay Robins, 88
Geb, 6
gigantic stars, 60, 61, 144, 146, 19
Giver of Life, Queen of the Gods, 134
glaring light, 91, 253, 255
God King Scenario, ii, xi, 1, 61, 19, 27, 32, 55
god of evil and chaos, 10
god of the afterlife, 9, 23, 20, 21
Goddess of Love and War, 134
Goddess of Magic, 134
Goddess of Marriage and Protection, 134
gold flesh, 90
gravitational powers, 102
great battles, 62, 115
Great Enchantress, 134
Great Red Spot, 36, 51, 52, 55, 58, 94
Great Temple of Ramesses II at Abu Simbel, 17
GRS, 51, 52, 94
Hapi, 6
Hathor, vi, 5, 9, 10, 11, 12, 13, 14, 17, 22, 23, 49, 61, 63, 72, 73, 83, 93, 106, 117, 118, 119, 120, 121, 122, 123, 124, 125, 126, 127, 128, 130, 131, 132, 133, 134, 135, 136, 137, 138, 139, 140, 171, 176, 179, 187, 191, 224, 251, 254, 260, 305
Hathor hairdo, 126
Hathor Sekhmet, 121
Hathor's milk., 130
Hathor's musical instrument, 126

Hatshepsut, 13, 36, 51, 62, 128, 131, 146, 154, 158, 170, 171, 172, 173, 180, 181, 182, 183, 185, 188, 198, 224, 243, 244, 245, 246, 247, 248, 249
hawk-headed human wearing a sun-disk headdress, 5
Heaven, vi, 12, 25, 65, 134, 137, 12
heretic' pharaoh Akhenaten, 15, 85, 101, 256, 269
Heryshef, 6
hieroglyphics, 1, 70, 71, 72, 76, 77, 82, 84
Hindu myths, 35, 38, 49
historians believe that Ramesses II had over, 69
historians believe that Ramesses II had over 200 children, 69
Horakhty, 17, 179, 186, 276
Horizon of the Aten, 48
Horus, the hawk-headed god, 10
immortality, 2, 71, 206, 211, 213, 3, 55
impact crater, 52, 95
inner orbit, 42

Intermediate Periods, 20, 47
Ishtar, 25, 30, 50, 154
Isis goddess of countless names, 134
Isis, 13, 23, 61, 88, 93, 117, 133, 135, 140, 174, 179, 19, 27
John Ackerman, 35
Jupiter, 6, 19, 23, 24, 29, 31, 32, 36, 42, 43, 50, 51, 52, 53, 54, 55, 58, 93, 94, 95, 96, 97, 98, 101, 103, 104, 105, 107, 141, 148, 153, 161, 175, 235
Jupiter a planet of gigantic proportions, 23
Kadesh and Megiddo, 47
Karnak, 7, 15, 116, 194, 222, 248, 260
Kek and Kauket, 6
khepesh, 7
Khnemu, 6
Kia, 15
King Narmer, 46
lack of yellow suns, 92
lava fountain, 38
lava tubes, 39
long lived of world powers, 1
low density 'planet', 42
luminous beings, 3

lush, blue-green planet, 98
ma'at, 18, 19, 20, 63, 73, 106, 149, 187, 196, 227, 242, 244, 246, 260, 275, 10, 11
Mafdet, 6
malachite, 119, 120
Mars, 5, 10, 17, 19, 24, 30, 31, 32, 35, 36, 37, 38, 39, 40, 41, 43, 44, 46, 48, 49, 51, 54, 55, 57, 59, 60, 61, 63, 64, 66, 68, 69, 70, 73, 77, 79, 80, 86, 93, 95, 97, 98, 99, 100, 102, 103, 104, 105, 108, 121, 124, 131, 133, 137, 139, 140, 142, 143, 144, 149, 150, 151, 152, 155, 156, 157, 158, 160, 161, 162, 164, 166, 167, 169, 170, 172, 173, 175, 177, 178, 180, 182, 184, 186, 191, 196, 197, 200, 201, 214, 218, 220, 221, 224, 227, 229, 230, 231, 232, 233, 234, 235, 241, 242, 243, 247, 249, 250, 251, 252, 253, 254, 255, 256, 258, 259, 262, 263, 266, 268, 269, 270, 273, 284, 298
Mars and the Earth, 37
Mars approximately half the size of Earth, 99
Mars great oceans and atmosphere were sucked, 99
Martian landscape, 55
Martian surface, 100
Mediterranean and Red seas, 41
Mercury, 6, 9, 24, 30, 36, 41, 43, 44, 46, 47, 48, 49, 51, 53, 55, 57, 58, 59, 60, 61, 62, 63, 64, 65, 66, 68, 69, 70, 73, 75, 77, 79, 80, 86, 96, 99, 101, 102, 104, 107, 108, 113, 124, 133, 137, 139, 142, 144, 149, 150, 151, 155, 157, 158, 159, 161, 163, 164, 168, 169, 170, 173, 177, 180, 185, 186, 191, 196, 197, 200, 214, 218, 220, 221, 224, 227, 229, 234, 241, 250, 251, 253, 254, 255, 258, 262, 265, 266, 272
Mercury from Mars, 69
Mercury joined Mars and Venus, 60, 169

Mercury, the red planet, 69
millennia, 1, 44, 46, 59, 75, 80, 98, 148, 150, 161, 191, 200, 220, 221, 225, 235, 278
Min, 6
modern day Iraq, 25
Moon, 58, 94, 104, 130, 148, 161, 163, 164, 169, 213, 221, 225, 229, 235, 5, 6
mother of the sky god Horus, 9
Mount Everest, 100
mummified, 1, 10, 189, 192, 196, 206, 207, 209, 211, 296, 297, 18, 24, 25, 31, 34, 39, 40, 42, 54
Mycenaean citadels, 30
myriad of gods, 1, 2, 3, 15, 33, 195, 246
mysterious of form, 8, 9
Napoleon of ancient Egypt, 7, 47, 164, 188, 223, 224
NASA Voyager, 36
Near Earth Asteroids, 40
Nefertem, 6
Nephthys, 10
New Kingdom, vi, 7, 9, 15, 68, 75, 83, 108, 112, 133, 139, 153, 154, 155, 169, 170, 173, 180, 181, 184, 185, 190, 215, 237, 273, 275, 276, 47, 48
Nile, 1, 6, 18, 63, 114, 192, 200, 202, 204, 211, 213, 224, 232, 244, 245, 277, 280, 281, 282, 287, 288, 289, 290, 291, 292, 294, 300, 301, 302, 308
northern India, 40
Nun, 6, 18
Nun and Naunet, 6
Nut, 6
Oceanus Borealis, 38
Olympus Mons, 54, 100, 267
Orient and Occident, 28
Osiris, 5, 9, 10, 11, 14, 17, 22, 23, 27, 30, 39, 42, 50, 63, 72, 73, 79, 88, 125, 127, 137, 140, 174, 187, 194, 228, 238, 251, 295, 297, 304
Our Moon, 6, 58, 94, 104, 105, 130, 132, 164, 225, 235
Pandora and Prometheus, 129
perennial cycle is so predictable, 4
periods when skies blackened and blotted

out the Sun, crops failed leading to starvation, death and disease, 20
pharaoh Amenhotep, 13, 14, 128, 249
pharaohs, 2, 7, 8, 10, 13, 14, 15, 16, 18, 19, 21, 22, 38, 47, 54, 62, 63, 67, 70, 71, 80, 82, 83, 85, 102, 106, 111, 125, 130, 145, 146, 148, 152, 157, 161, 166, 172, 178, 184, 187, 189, 194, 195, 196, 197, 198, 199, 200, 201, 202, 206, 208, 210, 212, 213, 214, 215, 217, 220, 221, 222, 223, 224, 226, 227, 231, 239, 243, 260, 264, 266, 268, 273, 284, 285, 286, 301, 305
physics, 43, 299
planetary chaos, 6, 8, 17, 27, 32, 35, 43, 44, 45, 46, 48, 49, 50, 51, 56, 57, 70, 73, 74, 79, 80, 93, 99, 100, 106, 118, 141, 158, 160, 199, 273, 293, 297
planetary ring systems, 103

Planetary scientists, 55, 238
polytheistic culture evolved, 3
patron god of the dead, funerals, the house, and women and companion of Isis, 10
primary deities, 22
priori-Mars, 37, 38, 39, 40, 41, 42
Priori-Mars, 36, 39
Prometheus, 129, 130
proto-Venus, 37, 40
Ptah, 17, 22, 186, 187, 224, 260
purpose for the cosmos, 3
pyramids, 1, 71, 63
Queen or 'king's great wife', 62
Ramesses, 7, 8, 10, 14, 17, 18, 22, 42, 47, 52, 55, 62, 69, 70, 72, 79, 82, 143, 149, 154, 186, 187, 188, 191, 193, 194, 195, 196, 197, 199, 201, 203, 204, 207, 215, 217, 218, 224, 247, 260, 261, 266, 267, 268, 269, 270, 274, 284, 301
Ramesses II., 7, 26, 69, 193, 195, 215
Ramesses Osiris, 10, 22

Ramesses the Great, 7, 8, 14, 47, 62, 143, 149, 186, 188, 191, 193, 194, 260, 266, 269
Ramesses the Great, Tuthmosis III, 7
Re, 1, 5, 7, 8, 9, 11, 12, 13, 14, 17, 22, 24, 43, 47, 49, 50, 55, 61, 73, 79, 80, 81, 82, 83, 84, 85, 86, 91, 92, 93, 97, 108, 110, 112, 113, 119, 123, 124, 132, 133, 135, 140, 145, 146, 147, 149, 151, 163, 167, 171, 175, 176, 179, 191, 223, 230, 231, 232, 234, 239, 241, 242, 244, 245, 246, 249, 251, 254, 255, 256, 260, 262, 264, 266, 267, 268, 272, 275, 276, 277, 280, 288, 293, 298, 304, 305, 306
receptacles of the supernatural, 2
red disk, 47, 82, 83, 84, 86, 87, 88, 92, 110, 111, 112, 123, 125, 136, 137, 141, 143, 144, 146, 150, 153, 154, 162, 163, 167, 225, 241, 243, 253

red flesh, 90, 171
Red Planet., 37
Red Sea, 29
red Sun is a diminished Sun, 91
Restoration Stele, 13
Rig Veda, 35, 38, 49
Rig Veda and Hindu myths,, 38
rogue moons, 68, 201, 48, 53
rogue planets, 32, 49
Romulus, 42
rotating flat disk, 96
Ruler of the Riverbanks, 6
sa-re, 13, 80, 83, 91, 93, 111, 223, 225, 231, 264, 266
Satet, 6
Saturn, 24, 36, 43, 50, 96, 103, 105, 107, 111, 120, 129, 130
Saturn outshines all visible stars except Sirius and Canopus, 24
Saturn like a gigantic spinning top, 104
Saturn's equator, 104
scorching Sun, 116
secondary source of debris, 97
Seth, 10, 18, 21, 22, 30, 48, 62, 63, 73, 93, 106,

120, 121, 137, 150, 163, 199, 204, 220, 228, 259, 261, 262, 265, 273
Seti after Seth, 62
Seti I, 14, 88, 16, 18, 30
sexual relations possible between gods and mortals, 16
Shoemaker-Levy 9, 95
Shu, 6
solar disk, 5, 23, 82, 136, 138, 146, 63
solar system, 22, 23, 24, 27, 30, 31, 34, 35, 36, 41, 42, 51, 54, 55, 56, 58, 79, 90, 92, 93, 95, 96, 97, 100, 101, 102, 107, 108, 109, 116, 117, 153, 158, 161, 200, 225, 269
Solar System, vi, 49, 56
space debris, 32, 47, 55, 58, 62, 63, 66, 77, 79, 92, 93, 95, 97, 98, 102, 104, 106, 107, 117, 121, 149, 150, 151, 155, 158, 159, 160, 161, 166, 168, 169, 173, 198, 199, 200, 201, 202, 210, 218, 220, 221, 224, 227, 228, 234, 235, 236, 238, 255, 267, 270
space rubble, 95, 102, 108, 155
Sphinx at Giza, 1
spinning planets, 103
sub-surface rock, 38
Sumerian pantheon of gods, 25
Sumerians, 25, 17
Sun, vi, 71, 87, 89, 96, 123, 148, 169, 243, 249, 265, 283, 305
Sun and Moon, 6
Sun god Re, 305
Tefnut, 6, 61, 114
temples, 1, 11, 15, 34, 46, 77, 122, 193, 194, 196, 215, 247, 253, 283
the goddess of fertility, women, and childbirth, 14
the incarnation of the 'good and just' god Horus, 18
the kings as the son of the goddess Isis, 14
the red Sun, 85, 88, 113, 133, 137, 140, 141, 146, 229, 230, 247, 250, 255, 272, 290, 300
the Sun as a red disk, 88, 92, 110
The Valles Marineris, 55
Thoth, 5, 11, 24, 94, 148, 162, 163, 164, 168,

182, 214, 226, 231, 236, 237, 238, 265, 276, 30, 31
three Dark Ages, 20
Tigris and Euphrates rivers, 25
Titan,, 129
tombs, 46, 64, 71, 77, 82, 168, 207, 209, 222, 253, 271, 283, 295, 297, 299, 2, 12, 15, 32, 34, 57, 63
Transhimalayas., 40
trauma for the Earth, 40
Tutankhamun, 1, 10, 13, 15, 22, 42, 52, 62, 86, 116, 167, 168, 187, 217, 218, 222, 224, 252, 254, 255, 284, 296
Tuthmosis III, 8, 14, 47, 62, 128, 145, 164, 169, 170, 173, 181, 182, 183, 188, 198, 202, 205, 208, 213, 214, 215, 216, 223, 224, 238, 260, 276, 284
uniform degree, 39
Upper Egypt, 10, 13, 22, 28, 42, 55, 276, 277, 278, 279, 280, 282, 283, 287, 293, 295, 298, 299, 300, 302, 303, 304, 305

Uranus and Neptune, 36, 96, 103
V/A, 35, 36, 42, 94, 175
V/A Scenario, 35, 94
vacuumed up by the warrior god-kings, 92
Valles Marineris, 41, 43, 55, 59, 101, 157, 250, 267
vaporized an enormous mass of material, 36
Vedic period, 37, 40, 41
Velikovsky, 27, 28, 29, 31, 32, 34, 35, 36, 42, 43, 46, 49, 53, 56, 57, 67, 98, 174, 199, 271
Velikovsky/Angiras scenario, 35
Velikovsky's 'Worlds in Collision.', 49
Velikovsky's research, 35, 57
Venus, 24, 29, 30, 31, 32, 35, 36, 37, 39, 40, 41, 42, 43, 46, 47, 48, 49, 50, 51, 52, 53, 54, 55, 57, 58, 59, 60, 61, 62, 64, 65, 66, 68, 69, 73, 77, 79, 86, 93, 94, 95, 96, 97, 98, 100, 101, 102, 104, 107, 108, 113, 121, 124, 128, 131, 134, 137, 139, 141, 142, 144, 149,

150, 152, 153, 154, 155, 156, 158, 159, 160, 161, 167, 168, 169, 170, 173, 174, 177, 180, 182, 184, 185, 186, 191, 198, 200, 221, 224, 229, 233, 234, 235, 238, 241, 245, 246, 247, 248, 250, 251, 252, 258, 259, 262, 263, 269, 270, 271, 273, 274, 298

volcanic impact-crater, 94